THE PATRIOTIC ANTHOLOGY

THE
PATRIOTIC
ANTHOLOGY

INTRODUCED BY
CARL VAN DOREN

THE LITERARY GUILD OF AMERICA, INC.
New York, N. Y.

PRINTED AT THE *Country Life Press*, GARDEN CITY, N. Y., U. S. A.

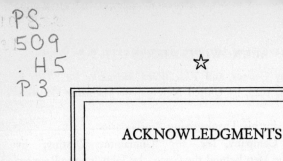

ACKNOWLEDGMENTS

THE COMPILERS AND THE PUBLISHERS have made every effort to trace the ownership of all copyrighted poems. In the event of any question arising as to the use of any poem the compilers, while expressing regret for any error they have unconsciously made, will be pleased to make the necessary correction in future editions of this book.

Thanks are due to the following authors, publishers, publications and agents for permission to use the selections indicated:

D. Appleton-Century Company—for "Song of Marion's Men," "Our Country's Call," "Abraham Lincoln," and "Oh, Mother of a Mighty Race, by William Cullen Bryant.

William Rose Benét—for his poem "The Oregon Trail," from *Man Possessed,* Doubleday, Doran & Company, Inc., publishers.

Martha T. Bennett—for "The Flag Goes By," by Henry Holcomb Bennett.

The Bobbs Merrill Company—for "One Country," from *Comes with a Song,* by Frank L. Stanton, copyright, 1898, 1925.

Brandt & Brandt—for "Invocation," "Lincoln's Soliloquy Before Manassas," and "The Significance of John Brown," from *John Brown's Body,* copyright 1927, 1928, by Stephen Vincent Benét.

The Clarenden Press, Oxford, England—for "To the United States of America," from *October and Other Poems,* by Robert Bridges.

Grace Stone Coates—for her poem "Prairie Birth," from *Mead and Mangel-wurzel,* Caxton Printers, Ltd., publishers.

v

Katharine Janeway Conger, and *This Week Magazine* for "This Is America," copyright, 1940, by United Newspapers Magazine Corporation.

Wilbur L. Cross—for his Thanksgiving Proclamation.

Dodd, Mead & Company, Inc.—for "Unmanifest Destiny," by Richard Hovey; "The Men Behind the Guns," by John Jerome Rooney; "The Founders of Ohio" and "Johnny Appleseed," by William Henry Venable.

Doubleday, Doran & Company, Inc.—for "Pioneers! O Pioneers!" "When Lilacs Last in the Dooryard Bloom'd," "O Captain! My Captain!" "I Hear America Singing," "For You, O Democracy," and "Preface," from *Leaves of Grass*, by Walt Whitman.

E. P. Dutton & Company, Inc.—for "America the Beautiful," from *The Retinue and Other Poems*, by Katharine Lee Bates; "The Blue Hen's Chickens," "Daniel Boone," "The Call to the Colors," "The Snarlers," and "New York," by Arthur Guiterman; "Yanks," by James W. Foley.

Farrar & Rinehart, Inc.—for "Lincoln," from *Selected Poems*, by John Gould Fletcher, copyright, 1938.

Harcourt, Brace & Company, Inc.—for "Reveille," from *These Times*, by Louis Untermeyer.

Mrs. J. Borden Harriman—for "What America Expects of Its Youth."

Sam H. Harris—for "German-Americans," from *The American Way*, by George S. Kaufman and Moss Hart.

Daniel Henderson—for "The Road to France," from *Life's Minstrel*, E. P. Dutton & Co., publishers, and for "Hard Rows to Hoe."

Henry Holt & Company, Inc.—for "Victory Bells," from *Wilderness Songs*, by Grace Hazard Conkling; "Shenandoah," from *The Cornhuskers*, by Carl Sandburg.

Houghton Mifflin Company—for "Fredericksburg," by Thomas Bailey Aldrich; "The River Fight" and "The Bay Fight," by Henry Howard Brownell; "Out Where the West Begins," by Arthur Chapman; "Boston Hymn," "Ode," "Our Intellectual Declaration of Independence," "Concord Hymn," "Comment at Lincoln's Funeral," by Ralph Waldo Emerson; "Land That We Love," by Richard Watson Gilder; "How Are You, Sanitary?" "The Reveille," "John Burns of Gettysburg," by Bret Harte; "Jim Bludso," by John Hay; "A Ballad of the Boston Tea-Party," "Old Ironsides," "Brother Jonathan's Lament for Sister Caroline," by Oliver Wendell Holmes; "Battle-Hymn of the Republic" and "Our Country," by Julia Ward Howe; "Civil War," by Lucy Larcom; "Paul Revere's Ride," "The Revenge of Rain-in-the-Face," "The Cumberland," "The Building of a Ship," by Henry Wadsworth Longfellow; "Jonathan to John," "Abraham Lincoln," "Ode Recited at Harvard Commemoration, July 21, 1865," "On a Certain Condescension in Foreigners," and "Freedom," by James Russell Lowell; "An Ode in Time of Hesitation" and "On a Soldier Fallen in the Philippines," by William Vaughn Moody; "Dirge," by Thomas William Parsons; "How Cyrus Laid the Cable," by John Godfrey Saxe; "The Political Life of America," by Carl Schurz; "The March to the Sea," by William Tecumseh Sherman; "Kearney at Seven Pines," "How Old Brown Took Harper's Ferry," "Peter Stuyvesant's New Year's Call," and "Hymn of the West," by Edmund Clarence Stedman; "Scott and the Veteran," by Bayard Taylor; "The Kansas Emigrants," "Barbara Frietchie," "Laus Deo," "Centennial Hymn," "The Bartholdi Statue," by John Greenleaf Whittier; "The Old Sergeant," by Willson Forceythe.

P. J. Kenedy & Sons—for "The Sword of Robert Lee" and "The Conquered Banner," from *Father Ryan's Poems,* by Abram J. Ryan.

Mrs. Aline Kilmer—for "Rogue Bouquet," from *Poems, Essays and Letters,* by Joyce Kilmer, copyright 1914, 1917, 1918, by Doubleday, Doran & Company, Inc.

Elias Lieberman—for "I Am an American," from *Paved Streets,* copyright by Elias Lieberman.

J. B. Lippincott Company—for "Dirge for a Soldier" and "The Black Regiment," by George Henry Boker; "The Flag of the Constellation" and "Sheridan's Ride," by Thomas Buchanan Read.

Little Brown & Company—for "The American Dream," from *The Epic of America,* by James Truslow Adams; "Letter to His Wife," by John Adams; "The Declaration of 1776" and "Soliloquy in the White House," by John Quincy Adams; "America," by Arlo Bates, from *Torch-Bearers;* "The Better Way," from *A Few More Verses,* by Susan Coolidge; "Coolidge's Father Administers the Presidential Oath," from *Calvin Coolidge,* by Claude M. Fuess; "The Yankee Privateer," by Arthur Hale; extract from *The Man Without a Country,* by Edward Everett Hale.

Longmans, Green & Company, Inc.—for "The Defense of Liberty," from *Give Me Liberty,* by Rose Wilder Lane.

Lothrop, Lee & Shepard Company—for "The Coming American," by Sam Walter Foss.

The Macmillan Company—for "The Stone Crop," from *Collected Poems,* by Robert P. Tristram Coffin; "Abraham Lincoln Walks at Midnight" and "On the Building of Springfield," from *Collected Poems,* by Vachel Lindsay; "The Klondike," from *Collected Poems,* by Edwin Arlington Robinson; and "America, the Land We Love," from *The Melting Pot,* by Israel Zangwill.

Virgil Markham—for "Lincoln, the Man of the People" and "The Need of the Hour," from *Collected Poems,* by Edwin Markham, Doubleday, Doran & Company, Inc., publishers.

Edgar Lee Masters—for his poem, "Anne Rutledge."

John Steven McGroarty—for his poem "Blow, Bugles, Blow."

Professor H. G. Merriam—for "Eliza Spaulding" and "Henry Spaulding," from *Tsceminicum: Snake River People,* by Donald Burnie (Robert D. Leeper); and "Oregon Trail: 1851," by James Marshall, from *The Frontier.*

Miss Juanita Miller—for "Columbus," "Crossing the Plains" and "The Defence of the Alamo," by Joaquin Miller.

The New York *Times*—for "Flag Day 1940."

The Pilot Publishing Company—for "Gettysburg" and "The Flag," from *Ballads of Blue Water and Other Poems,* by James Jeffrey Roche.

G. P. Putnam's Sons—for "Lee to the Rear" and "Music in Camp," by John R. Thompson, from *American War Ballads and Lyrics,* edited by George Cary Eggleston.

Burton Rascoe, and *Newsweek*—for "Self-Evident Truths," from "We the People."

Fleming H. Revell Company—for "Battle Song of the Oregon" and "Blood Is Thicker Than Water," from *Ballads of Valor and Victory,* by Clinton Scollard and Wallace Rice.

Grantland Rice—for "The First Division Marches" and "Songs Above the Dust."

Jessie B. Rittenhouse, Literary Executor—for "Ad Patriam," by Clinton Scollard.

Kenneth Allen Robinson—for "American Laughter."

Estate of Theodore Roosevelt—for "The Winning of the West," from *The Winning of the West,* by Theodore Roosevelt, G. P. Putnam's Sons, publishers; and "High of Heart," from *The Foes of Our*

Own Household, by Theodore Roosevelt, copyright, 1917, by Double-day, Doran & Company, Inc.

Ryerson Press, Toronto—for "In Flanders Field," from *In Flanders Field,* by John McCrae.

Robert Haven Schauffler—for "Scum o' the Earth" and "Washington," from *Scum o' the Earth and Other Poems,* Dodd, Mead & Company, publishers.

Charles Scribner's Sons—for "The Full-Fledged American," from *Escape from America,* by Struthers Burt; "God, Give Us Men!" by Josiah Gilbert Holland; "Lexington," from *Poems,* by Sidney Lanier; "The Master," by Edwin Arlington Robinson; "The American Character," from *Character and Opinion in the United States,* by George Santayana; "I Have a Rendezvous with Death," by Alan Seeger; "America for Me" and "Mare Liberum," by Henry Van Dyke.

Frederick A. Stokes Company—for "The Last Reservation," from *Treasury of American Verse,* by Walter Learned.

A. P. Watt & Son—for "My America," from *Pilgrim's Way,* by John Buchan, published in the United States by Houghton Mifflin, Boston; in England by Hodder & Stoughton, Ltd., London.

Yale University Press—for "In the Green Mountain Country," by Clarence Day.

Particular thanks are due Barbara Moses Olds, whose indefatigable research made this book possible.

CONTENTS

CONTENTS

THE REVOLUTION

POETRY

PROSE

CONTENTS xiii

PROSE

THE CIVIL WAR
POETRY

PROSE

LINCOLN

POETRY

PROSE

CONTENTS   xix

1865–1900

POETRY

BASIC AMERICAN IDEALS

POETRY

xxii   CONTENTS

Like other collections of patriotic poetry and prose, this anthology will be found to have many things in it that are already familiar to many readers. No other kind of patriotic anthology could be a good one. For patriots instinctively cherish common memories and hopes, expressed in words that have come to seem inseparable from them. Patriotism aims at uniting people in a few essential thoughts and feelings. Personally they may think and feel as differently as they happen to. They need to do this for the sake of the individual happiness which is the basis of their general strength. But unless they agree on the main points of national history and policy, attitude and faith, their nation will sooner or later fall apart.

Some people insist that all patriots must at all times hold identical opinions. Without bothering to argue about so shortsighted an idea, look at the record in this volume. At the time of the American Revolution perhaps a third of the Americans honestly believed that independence would be bad for America and that it ought to remain a part of the British Empire. The conflict between these loyalists and the patriots was even more bitter than that between the patriots and the British. The thousands of loyalists who after the war took refuge in Canada hated the United States with an intense and natural resentment. But that, like the American animosity toward England, has largely disappeared. Americans, Canadians and British have learned to live without quarreling antagonisms, each respecting and honoring the others' patriotic sentiments. There has even grown up among them, during the past three or four years, what may be called an international patriotism binding the democratic states together in a defensive unity against the totalitarian dictators.

So with the Civil War which Southerners prefer to call the War between the States. There were sincerity and heroism on both sides and poets to praise and commemorate each cause. This volume represents North and South as a matter of course. To leave out either would be to falsify the record and also to impoverish it. It is perfectly possible for a modern American to venerate Lee as well as Lincoln, Lincoln as well as Lee. They were lofty men who were divided by the temporary passions of their day but afterward united in the hearts of their countrymen. The whole nation, however it may regret the damage done by that dark struggle, may treasure its proofs of stamina and valor and rejoice that a union enforced by arms has become a union supported by intersectional friendship.

Patriotism is a fellow feeling that consolidates a nation. The same man may at the same time feel devotion to his country and affection for his neighborhood or town or state. American patriotism is built on such double but not contradictory loyalties. The first Americans were attached to their particular colonies and ordinarily suspected or disliked the others. The Revolution, obliging them to act more or less together, led them to think together and in the process influenced them to feel together. Since most of them in all the states immensely valued Washington, he was not only the first national hero but also the first symbol to which the national emotion attached itself. The local patriotisms persisted, but they were regarded as only local and not opposed to national patriotism. Except for the secession movement, which was in a sense an effort to return to the older sectional patriotisms, the history of the United States has seen a steady widening of the national feeling, which has come to embrace the continent. Even

Americans who have never been outside their own states have a sympathetic knowledge of the others. And the countless Americans who have driven thousands of miles across the country are likely to bring home with them an exultant pride in the nation at large that does not interfere with their pleasant comfort in their own localities.

If American patriotism sometimes seems grandiose in its language, this is partly because it has a continent for the object of its affection instead of a compact territory wedged in among rival neighbors or an island aloof in the sea. It may not be as close knit as some patriotisms, but neither is it so narrow and intolerant. And in spite of the bitterness which much of the earlier patriotic poetry and prose exhibits—the white settlers toward the Indians, the Americans toward the British, the North and South toward each other—American patriotism has for more than half a century been concerned with the hope of human fellowship more often than with the recollection and perpetuation of ancient enmities. There is a saying that the English have aimed primarily at liberty, the French at equality, and the Americans at fraternity. And it is certain that American patriotic literature more than any other celebrates the desire of all sorts of Americans to be friendly and easy together, without distinction of class or race. Whitman, greatest of all American patriotic poets, is for the entire world the classic poet of comradeship. Whatever divisions there may be in actual American life are there against the will, or without the knowledge, of most Americans, who rank fraternity among the precious virtues and graces of mankind.

Different nations have different kinds of patriotism because they have different histories. Some of them after long adversity fix all their patriotic emotions on the national past, recalling its rare triumphs, lamenting its more numerous defeats. Others have been so used to jealousies and wars with traditional foes that their patriotism seems to have in it less love for their own countries than hatred for others. The United States, most fortunate of nations, can remember its past without lamenting or despairing. Circumstances have almost conspired to show favor to America.

The first Americans came from crowded countries to a new country where there was room for everybody. Nationals who had been regularly at war in Europe or elsewhere found they did not have to be in America. Peace could flourish and former enemies fraternize in the common interests of their new nation. Nothing in American life was more striking than the rapid change which came over immigrants within a generation. Though they might affectionately remember their parent lands, they lost their violent partisanships. The past became relatively unimportant to them because they could be united in the common expectation of a future in which all might have something like a just share.

No doubt the situation has altered within the past quarter century, and the American future is less bright and dependable than it long appeared. But it is still the brightest and most nearly dependable future on the earth. This should not be allowed to encourage arrogance in American patriotism. There has been enough of that. Americans should be, rather, a little humble, grateful for their happy fortune and freshly resolved to deserve it by holding on to the best elements in the national life while letting the worst fade out of it. Europe and Asia are full of warning examples which it will be fatal for Americans to disregard.

At present they do not seem likely to disregard them. Whatever differences of opinion there may be in America on this or that point of procedure, there is a profound national unity. Americans mean to cherish what they have achieved and to continue in all the liberty, equality and fraternity which the times will possibly permit. There may be some necessary restrictions in the freedom of the individual to consider his own ends without taking into account what is due to other individuals. The theory of equality may have to be re-examined, not to make men unequal but to make more of them justly accessible to equality. But as to fraternity there must be no falling off either in the principle or in the practice. The future of the human world can be happy only if men are everywhere united in a common brotherhood of resistance to tyrants.

Meanwhile here is a panorama of American patriotism chosen

to illustrate high moments in American history, high thoughts, high emotions, high hopes. No one need claim that all Americans have always lived at such a pitch. Men relax between crises, and the customary life goes on with its failures and ignominies and follies and evils. But such moments, thoughts, emotions and hopes as these have been preserved in the American memory, to be remembered on occasions, borne in mind by later patriots and accepted by Americans as the record they most like to cherish and most hope to see repeated in the years to come. Men do not live merely day by day, self-centered and isolated. They live also in the guiding shadow of the past in which they have been associated, in the beckoning light of the future toward which they must advance together. And patriotism, while often at fault, is at its best their simplest and most natural bond of union.

CARL VAN DOREN

THE DISCOVERY AND EARLY
HISTORY OF AMERICA

COLUMBUS

August 3—October 12, 1492

BEHIND him lay the gray Azores,
  Behind the Gates of Hercules;
Before him not the ghost of shores,
  Before him only shoreless seas.
The good mate said: "Now must we pray,
  For lo! the very stars are gone.
Brave Admiral, speak, what shall I say?"
  "Why, say 'Sail on! sail on! and on!'"

"My men grow mutinous day by day;
  My men grow ghastly wan and weak."
The stout mate thought of home; a spray
  Of salt wave washed his swarthy cheek.
"What shall I say, brave Admiral, say,
  If we sight naught but seas at dawn?"
"Why, you shall say at break of day,
  'Sail on! sail on! sail on! and on!'"

They sailed and sailed, as winds might blow,
  Until at last the blanched mate said:
"Why, now not even God would know
  Should I and all my men fall dead.
These very winds forget their way,
  For God from these dread seas is gone.
Now speak, brave Admiral, speak and say"—
  He said: "Sail on! sail on! and on!"

They sailed. They sailed. Then spake the mate:
  "This mad sea shows his teeth to-night.
He curls his lip, he lies in wait,
  With lifted teeth, as if to bite!
Brave Admiral, say but one good word:
  What shall we do when hope is gone?"
The words leapt like a leaping sword:
  "Sail on! sail on! sail on! and on!"

Then, pale and worn, he kept his deck,
  And peered through darkness. Ah, that night
Of all dark nights! And then a speck—
  A light! a light! a light! a light!
It grew, a starlit flag unfurled!
  It grew to be Time's burst of dawn.
He gained a world; he gave that world
  Its grandest lesson: "On! sail on!"

JOAQUIN MILLER

TO THE VIRGINIAN VOYAGE

You brave heroic minds,
Worthy your country's name,
  That honor still pursue,
  Go and subdue,
Whilst loitering hinds
Lurk here at home, with shame.

Britons, you stay too long:
Quickly aboard bestow you,
  And with a merry gale
  Swell your stretch'd sail,
With vows as strong
As the winds that blow you.

Your course securely steer,
West and by south forth keep!
  Rocks, lee-shores, nor shoals,
  When Eolus scowls,
You need not fear,
So absolute the deep.

And cheerfully at sea,
Success you still entice,
  To get the pearl and gold,
  And ours to hold
Virginia,
Earth's only paradise.

Where nature hath in store
Fowl, venison, and fish,
  And the fruitful'st soil,
  Without your toil,
Three harvests more,
All greater than your wish.

And the ambitious vine
Crowns with his purple mass
  The cedar reaching high
  To kiss the sky,
The cypress, pine,
And useful sassafras.

To whom the Golden Age
Still nature's laws doth give,
  No other cares attend,
  But them to defend
From winter's rage,
That long there doth not live.

When as the luscious smell
Of that delicious land,
  Above the seas that flows,
  The clear wind throws,
Your hearts to swell
Approaching the dear strand;

In kenning of the shore
(Thanks to God first given)
  O you the happiest men,
  Be frolic then!
Let cannons roar,
Frighting the wide heaven;

And in regions far
Such heroes bring ye forth
  As those from whom we came,
  And plant our name
Under that star
Not known unto our North;

And as there plenty grows
Of laurel everywhere,—
  Apollo's sacred tree,—
  You it may see,
A poet's brows
To crown, that may sing there.

Thy *Voyages* attend
Industrious Hackluit,
  Whose reading shall inflame
  Men to seek fame,
And much commend
To after-times thy wit.

                   MICHAEL DRAYTON

THE LANDING OF THE PILGRIM FATHERS
IN NEW ENGLAND

THE BREAKING WAVES dashed high
  On a stern and rock-bound coast,
And the woods against a stormy sky
  Their giant branches tossed;

And the heavy night hung dark
  The hills and waters o'er,
When a band of exiles moored their bark
  On the wild New England shore.

Not as the conqueror comes,
  They, the true-hearted, came;
Not with the roll of the stirring drums,
  And the trumpet that sings of fame:

Not as the flying come,
  In silence and in fear;
They shook the depths of the desert gloom
  With their hymns of lofty cheer.

Amidst the storm they sang,
  And the stars heard, and the sea;
And the sounding aisles of the dim woods rang
  To the anthem of the free.

The ocean eagle soared
  From his nest by the white wave's foam,
And the rocking pines of the forest roared,—
  This was their welcome home.

There were men with hoary hair
  Amidst that pilgrim-band:
Why had they come to wither there,
  Away from their childhood's land?

There was woman's fearless eye,
  Lit by her deep love's truth;
There was manhood's brow serenely high,
  And the fiery heart of youth.

What sought they thus afar?
  Bright jewels of the mine?
The wealth of seas, the spoils of war?—
  They sought a faith's pure shrine!

Ay, call it holy ground,
  The soil where first they trod;
They have left unstained what there they found,—
  Freedom to worship God.
                          FELICIA D. HEMANS

PETER STUYVESANT'S NEW YEAR'S CALL

WHERE nowadays the Battery lies,
  New York had just begun,
A new-born babe, to rub its eyes,
  In Sixteen Sixty-One.
They christened it Nieuw Amsterdam,
  Those burghers grave and stately,
And so, with schnapps and smoke and psalm,
  Lived out their lives sedately.

Two windmills topped their wooden wall,
    On Stadthuys gazing down,
On fort, and cabbage-plots, and all
    The quaintly gabled town;
These flapped their wings and shifted backs,
    As ancient scrolls determine,
To scare the savage Hackensacks,
    Paumanks, and other vermin.

At night the loyal settlers lay
    Betwixt their feather-beds;
In hose and breeches walked by day,
    And smoked, and wagged their heads.
No changeful fashions came from France,
    The freulen to bewilder,
And cost the burgher's purse, perchance,
    Its every other guilder.

In petticoats of linsey-red,
    And jackets neatly kept,
The vrouws their knitting-needles sped
    And deftly spun and swept.
Few modern-school flirtations there
    Set wheels of scandal trundling,
But youths and maidens did their share
    Of staid, old-fashioned bundling.

—The New Year opened clear and cold;
    The snow, a Flemish ell
In depth, lay over Beeckman's Wold
    And Wolfert's frozen well.
Each burgher shook his kitchen-doors,
    Drew on his Holland leather,
Then stamped through drifts to do the chores,
    Beshrewing all such weather.

But—after herring, ham, and kraut—
    To all the gathered town
The Dominie preached the morning out,
    In Calvinistic gown;
While tough old Peter Stuyvesant
    Sat pewed in foremost station,—
The potent, sage, and valiant
    Third Governor of the nation.

Prayer over, at his mansion hall,
    With cake and courtly smile,
He met the people, one and all,
    In gubernatorial style;
Yet missed, though now the day was old,
    An ancient fellow-feaster,—
Heer Govert Loockermans, that bold
    Brewer and burgomeester;

Who, in his farmhouse, close without
    The picket's eastern end,
Sat growling at the twinge of gout
    That kept him from his friend.
But Peter strapped his wooden peg,
    When tea and cake were ended
(Meanwhile the sound remaining leg
    Its high jack-boot defended),

A woolsey cloak about him threw,
    And swore, by wind and limb,
Since Govert kept from Peter's view,
    Peter would visit him;
Then sallied forth, through snow and blast,
    While many a humbler greeter
Stood wondering whereaway so fast
    Strode bluff Hardkoppig Pieter.

Past quay and cowpath, through a lane
   Of vats and mounded tans,
He puffed along, with might and main,
   To Govert Loockermans;
Once there, his right of entry took,
   And hailed his ancient crony:
"Myn Gód! in dese Manhattoes, Loock,
   Ve gets more snow as money!"

To which, and after whiffs profound,
   With doubtful wink and nod,
There came at last responsive sound:
   "Yah, Peter; yah, Myn Gód!"
Then goedevrouw Marie sat her guest
   Beneath the chimney-gable,
And courtesied, bustling at her best
   To spread the New Year's table.

She brought the pure and genial schnapps,
   That years before had come—
In the "Nieuw Nederlandts," perhaps—
   To cheer the settlers' home;
The long-stemmed pipes; the fragrant roll
   Of pressed and crispy Spanish;
Then placed the earthen mugs and bowl,
   Nor long delayed to vanish.

Thereat, with cheery nod and wink,
   And honors of the day,
The trader mixed the Governor's drink
   As evening sped away.
That ancient room! I see it now:
   The carven nutwood dresser;
The drawers, that many a burgher's vrouw
   Begrudged their rich possessor;

The brace of high-backed leathern chairs.
  Brass-nailed at every seam;
Six others, ranged in equal pairs;
  The bacon hung abeam;
The chimney-front, with porcelain shelft;
  The hearty wooden fire;
The picture, on the steaming delft,
  Of David and Goliah.

I see the two old Dutchmen sit
  Like Magog and his mate,
And hear them, when their pipes are lit,
  Discuss affairs of state:
The clique that would their sway demean;
  The pestilent importation
Of wooden nutmegs, from the lean
  And losel Yankee nation.

But when the subtle juniper
  Assumed its sure command,
They drank the buxom loves that were,—
  They drank the Motherland;
They drank the famous Swedish wars,
  Stout Peter's special glory,
While Govert proudly showed the scars
  Of Indian contests gory.

Erelong, the berry's power awoke
  Some music in their brains,
And, trumpet-like, through rolling smoke,
  Rang long-forgotten strains,—
Old Flemish snatches, full of blood,
  Of phantom ships and battle;
And Peter, with his leg of wood,
  Made floor and casement rattle.

Then round and round the dresser pranced,
  The chairs began to wheel,
And on the board the punch-bowl danced
  A netherlandish reel;
Till midnight o'er the farmhouse spread
  Her New Year's skirts of sable,
And inch by inch, each puzzled head
  Dropt down upon the table.

But still to Peter, as he dreamed,
  The table spread and turned;
The chimney-log blazed high, and seemed
  To circle as it burned;
The town into the vision grew
  From ending to beginning;
Fort, wall, and windmill met his view,
  All widening and spinning.

The cowpaths, leading to the docks,
  Grew broader, whirling past,
And checkered into shining blocks,—
  A city fair and vast;
Stores, churches, mansions, overspread
  The metamorphosed island,
While not a beaver showed his head
  From Swamp to Kalchook highland.

Eftsoons the picture passed away;
  Hours after, Peter woke
To see a spectral streak of day
  Gleam in through fading smoke;
Still slept old Govert, snoring on
  In most melodious numbers;
No dreams of Eighteen Sixty-One
  Commingled with his slumbers.

But Peter, from the farmhouse door,
  Gazed doubtfully around,
Rejoiced to find himself once more
  On sure and solid ground.
The sky was somewhat dark ahead,
  Wind east, the morning lowery;
And on he pushed, a two-miles' tread,
  To breakfast at his Bouwery.
                EDMUND CLARENCE STEDMAN

FORT DUQUESNE

A HISTORICAL CENTENNIAL BALLAD

I

COME, fill the beaker, while we chaunt a pean of old days:
By Mars! no men shall live again more worthy of our praise,
Than they who stormed at Louisburg and Frontenac amain,
And shook the English standard out o'er the ruins of Duquesne.

For glorious were the days they came, the soldiers strong and true,
And glorious were the days, they came for Pennsylvania, too;
When marched the troopers sternly on through forest's autumn
    brown,
And where St. George's cross was raised, the oriflame went down.

Virginia sent her chivalry and Maryland her brave,
And Pennsylvania to the cause her noblest yeomen gave:
Oh, and proud were they who wore the garb of Indian hunters
    then,
For every sturdy youth was worth a score of common men!

They came from Carolina's pines, from fruitful Delaware—
The staunchest and the stoutest of the chivalrous were there;
And calm and tall above them all, i' the red November sun,
Like Saul above his brethren, rode Colonel Washington.

O'er leagues of wild and waste they passed, they forded stream
    and fen,
Where danger lurked in every glade, and death in every glen;
They heard the Indian ranger's cry, the Frenchman's far-off hail,
From purple distance echoed back through the hollows of the vale.

And ever and anon they came, along their dangerous way,
Where, ghastly, 'mid the yellow leaves, their slaughtered com-
    rades lay;
The tartans of Grant's Highlanders were sodden yet and red,
As routed in the rash assault, they perished as they fled.

—Ah! many a lass ayont the Tweed shall rue the fatal fray,
And high Virginian dames shall mourn the ruin of that day,
When gallant lad and cavalier i' the wilderness were slain,
'Twixt laurelled Loyalhanna and the outposts of Duquesne.

And there before them was the field of massacre and blood,
Of panic, rout and shameful flight, in that disastrous wood
Where Halket fell and Braddock died, with many a noble one
Whose. white bones glistened through the leaves i' the pale No-
    vember sun.

Then spoke the men of Braddock's Field, and hung their heads in
    shame,
For England's tarnished honor and for England's sullied fame;
"And, by St. George!" the soldiers swore, "we'll wipe away the
    stain
Before to-morrow's sunset, at the trenches of Duquesne."

II

'Twas night along the autumn hills, the sun's November gleam
Had left its crimson on the leaves, its tinge upon the stream;
And Hermit Silence kept his watch 'mid ancient rocks and trees,
And placed his finger on the lip of babbling brook and breeze.

The bivouac's set by Turtle Creek; and while the soldiers sleep,
The swarthy chiefs around the fires an anxious council keep;
Some spoke of murmurs in the camp, scarce whispered to the air,
But tokens of discouragement, the presage of despair.

Some a retreat advised; 'twas late; the winter drawing on;
The forage and provision, too,—so Ormsby said,—were gone.
Men could not feed on air and fight; whatever Pitt might say;
In praise or censure, still, they thought, 't were wiser to delay.

Then up spoke iron-headed Forbes, and through his feeble frame
There ran the lightning of a will that put them all to shame!
"I'll hear no more," he roundly swore; "we'll storm the fort amain!
I'll sleep in hell to-morrow night, or sleep in Fort Duquesne!"

So said: and each to sleep addressed his wearied limbs and mind,
And all was hushed i' the forest, save the sobbing of the wind,
And the tramp, tramp, tramp of the sentinel, who started oft in
    fright
At the shadows wrought 'mid the giant trees by the fitful camp-
    fire light.

Good Lord! what sudden glare is that that reddens all the sky,
As though hell's legions rode the air and tossed their torches high!
Up, men! the alarm drum beats to arms! and the solid ground
    seems riven
By the shock of warring thunderbolts in the lurid depth of heaven!

O there was clattering of steel, and mustering in array,
And shouts and wild huzzas of men, impatient of delay,
As came the scouts swift-footed in—"They fly! the foe! they fly!
They've fired the powder magazine and blown it to the sky!"

III

Now morning o'er the frosty hills in autumn splendor came,
And touched the rolling mists with gold, and flecked the clouds
    with flame;
And through the brown woods on the hills—those altars of the
    world—
The blue smoke from the settler's hut and Indian's wigwam curled.

Yet never, here, had morning dawned on such a glorious din
Of twanging trump, and rattling drum, and clanging culverin,
And glittering arms and sabre gleams and serried ranks of men,
Who marched with banners high advanced along the river glen.

Oh, and royally they bore themselves who knew that o'er the seas
Would speed the glorious tidings from the loyal colonies,
Of the fall of French dominion with the fall of Fort Duquesne,
And the triumph of the English arms from Erie to Champlain.

Before high noon they halted; and while they stood at rest,
They saw, unfolded gloriously, the "Gateway of the West,"
There flashed the Alleghany, like a scimetar of gold,
And king-like in its majesty, Monongahela rolled.

Beyond, the River Beautiful swept down the woody vales,
Where Commerce, ere a century passed, should spread her thou-
    sand sails;
Between the hazy hills they saw Contrecoeur's armed batteaux,
And the flying, flashing, feathery oars of the Ottawa's canoes.

Then, on from rank to rank of men, a shout of triumph ran,
And while the cannon thundered, the leader of the van,

The tall Virginian, mounted on the walls that smouldered yet,
And shook the English standard out, and named the place Fort
    Pitt.

Again with wild huzzas the hills and river valleys ring,
And they swing their loyal caps in air, and shout—"Long live the
    King!
Long life unto, King George!" they cry, "and glorious be the reign
That adds to English statesmen Pitt, to English arms Duquesne!"

                                        FLORUS B. PLIMPTON

PRIVILEGES AND PREROGATIVES GRANTED
TO COLUMBUS

April 30, 1492

FERDINAND and ELIZABETH, . . .

For as much of you, *Christopher Columbus,* are going by our
command, with some of our vessels and men, to discover and subdue some Islands and Continent in the ocean, and it.is hoped that
by God's assistance, some of the said Islands and Continent in the
ocean will be discovered and conquered by your means and conduct, therefore it is but just and reasonable, that since you expose
yourself to such danger to serve us, you should be rewarded for it.
And we being willing to honour and favour you for the reasons
aforesaid; Our will is, That you, *Christopher Columbus,* after
discovering and conquering the said Islands and Continent in the
said ocean, or any of them, shall be our Admiral of the said
Islands and Continent you shall so discover and conquer;
and that you be our Admiral, Vice-Roy, and Governour in
them, and that for the future, you may call and stile yourself,
D. *Christopher Columbus,* and that your sons and successors
in the said employment, may call themselves Dons, Admirals,
Vice-Roys, and Governours of them; and that you may exercise the office of Admiral, with the charge of Vice-Roy and

Governour of the said Islands and Continent, which you and your
Lieutenants shall conquer, and freely decide all causes, civil and
criminal, appertaining to the said employment of Admiral, Vice-
Roy, and Governour, as you shall think fit in justice, and as the
Admirals of our kingdoms use to do; and that you have power to
punish offenders; and you and your Lieutenants exercise the
employments of Admiral, Vice-Roy, and Governour, in all things
belonging to the said offices, or any of them; and that you enjoy
the perquisites and salaries belonging to the said employments,
and to each of them, in the same manner as the High Admiral of
our kingdoms does. And by this our letter, or a copy of it signed
by a *Public Notary:* We command Prince *John,* our most dearly
beloved Son, the Infants, Dukes, Prelates, Marquesses, Great
Masters and Military Orders, Priors, Commendaries, our Counsel-
lors, Judges, and other Officers of Justice whatsoever, belonging to
our Household, Courts, and Chancery, and Constables of Castles,
Strong Houses, and others, and all Corporations, Bayliffs, Governours, Judges, Commanders, Sea Officers; and the Aldermen,
Common Council, Officers, and Good People of all Cities, Lands,
and Places in our Kingdoms and Dominions, and in those you
shall conquer and subdue, and the captains, masters, mates, and
other officers and sailors, our natural subjects now being, or that
shall be for the time to come, and any of them, that when you
shall have discovered the said Islands and Continent in the ocean;
and you, or any that shall have your commission, shall have taken
the usual oath in such cases, that they for the future, look upon
you as long as you live, and after you, your son and heir, and so
from one heir to another forever, as our Admiral on our said
Ocean, and as Vice-Roy and Governour of the said Islands and
Continent, by you, *Christopher Columbus,* discovered and conquered; and that they treat you and your Lieutenants, by you appointed, for executing the employments of Admiral, Vice-Roy,
and Governour, as such in all respects, and give you all the
perquisites and other things belonging and appertaining to the
said officers; and allow, and cause to be allowed you, all the
honours, graces, concessions, prehaminences, prerogatives, im-

munities, and other things, or any of them which are due to you, by virtue of your commands of Admiral, Vice-Roy, and Governour, and to be observed completely, so that nothing be diminished; and that they make no objection to this, or any part of it, nor suffer it to be made; forasmuch as we from this time forward, by this our letter, bestow on you the employments of Admiral, Vice-Roy, and perpetual Governour forever; and we put you into possession of the said offices, and of every of them, and full power to use and exercise them, and to receive the perquisites and salaries belonging to them, or any of them, as was said above. Concerning all which things, if it be requisite, and you shall desire it, We command our Chancellour, Notaries, and other Officers, to pass, seal, and deliver to you, our Letter of Privilege, in such form and legal manner, as you shall require or stand in need of. And that none of them presume to do any thing to the contrary, upon pain of our displeasure, and fortfeiture of 30 ducats for each offence. And we command him, who shall show them this our Letter, that he summon them to appear before us at our Court, where we shall then be, within fifteen days after such summons, under the said penalty. Under which same, we also command any Public Notary whatsoever, that he give to him that shows it him, a certificate under his seal, that we may know how our command is obeyed.

GIVEN at *Granada,* on the 30th of April, in the year of our Lord, 1492.—

I, THE KING, I, THE QUEEN

THE MAYFLOWER COMPACT

November 11, 1620

THE SEPARATISTS living in Leyden, Holland, desired for various reasons to transplant their colony to America. In 1619 they secured from the Virginia Company a patent for a private plantation. The

Pilgrims, reinforced by some seventy persons from London, sailed from Plymouth in September, 1620, and arrived off Cape Cod in November. Some of the London recruits were an "undesirable lot" and, Bradford tells us, boasted that they were not under the jurisdiction of the Virginia Company and "would use their owne libertie". In order to establish some form of government, therefore, the Pilgrim leaders drew up the famous Mayflower Compact. The Compact was not intended as a constitution, but was an extension of the customary church covenant to civil circumstances. Inasmuch as the Plymouth settlers were never able to secure a charter, the Mayflower compact remained the only form of constitution of the colony. See, W. Bradford, *History of the Plymouth Plantation*, various eds.; A. Young, *Chronicles of the Pilgrim Fathers, 1602–25;* E. Arber, ed. *Story of the Pilgrim Fathers, 1606–23;* J. Fiske, *Beginnings of New England;* J. G. Palfrey, *History of New England*, Vol. 1; J. A. Doyle, *The English Colonies in America*, Vol. II, pt. I; E. Eggleston, *The Beginners of a Nation;* J. T. Adams, *The Founding of New England;* C. M. Andrews, *The Fathers of New England;* C. M. Andrews, *The Colonial Period of American History*, Vol. I, ch. xiii; L. G. Tyler, *England in America*, ch. ix; H. L. Osgood, *American Colonies in the Seventeenth Century*, Vol. I; J. A. Goodwin, *The Pilgrim Republic;* A. Lord, "The Mayflower Compact," *Proceedings* of the Am. Antiquarian Soc., 1921; A. C. McLaughlin, *Foundations of American Constitutionalism*, ch. i; V. L. Parrington, *The Colonial Mind*, p. 16ff.

IN The Name of God, Amen. We, whose names are underwritten, the Loyal Subjects of our dread Sovereign Lord King *James,* by the Grace of God, of *Great Britain, France,* and *Ireland,* King, *Defender of the Faith,* &c. Having undertaken for the Glory of God, and Advancement of the Christian Faith, and the Honour of our King and Country, a Voyage to plant the first colony in the northern Parts of Virginia; Do by these Presents, solemnly and mutually in the Presence of God and one another, covenant and combine ourselves together into a civil Body Politick, for our better Ordering and Preservation, and Furtherance of the Ends aforesaid; And by Virtue hereof do enact, constitute, and frame, such just and equal Laws, Ordinances, Acts, Constitutions, and Offices, from time to time, as shall be thought most meet and convenient for the general Good of the Colony; unto which we promise all due Submission and Obedience. In WITNESS whereof we have hereunto subscribed our names at *Cape Cod* the eleventh of *November,* in the Reign of our Sovereign Lord King *James* of *England, France,* and *Ireland,* the eighteenth and of *Scotland,* the fifty-fourth. *Anno Domini,* 1620

Mr. John Carver	Mr. Stephen Hopkins
Mr. William Bradford	Digery Priest
Mr. Edward Winslow	Thomas Williams
Mr. William Brewster	Gilbert Winslow
Isaac Allerton	Edmund Margesson
Miles Standish	Peter Brown
John Alden	Richard Bitteridge
John Turner	George Soule
Francis Eaton	Edward Tilly
James Chilton	John Tilly
John Craxton	Francis Cooke
John Billington	Thomas Rogers
Joses Fletcher	Thomas Tinker
John Goodman	John Ridgate
Mr. Samuel Fuller	Edward Fuller
Mr. Christopher Martin	Richard Clark
Mr. William Mullins	Richard Gardiner
Mr. William White	Mr. John Allerton
Mr. Richard Warren	Thomas English
John Howland	Edward Doten
	Edward Liester

THE VOYAGE OF THE MAYFLOWER

By

WILLIAM BRADFORD

Septr. 6. These troubls being blowne over, and now all being
compacte togeather in one shipe, they put to sea againe with a
prosperus winde, which continued diverce days togeather, which
was some incouragmente unto them; yet according to the usual
maner many were afflicted with sea-sicknes. And I may not omite
hear a spetiall worke of Gods providence. Ther was a proud &
very profane yonge man, one of the sea-men, of a lustie, able body,
which made him the more hauty; he would allway be contemning
the poore people in their sicknes, & cursing them dayly with
gree(v)ous execrations, and did not let to tell them, that he
hoped to help to cast halfe of them over board before they came
to their jurneys end, and to make mery with what they had;
and if he were by any gently reproved, he would curse and swear
most bitterly. But it plased God before they came halfe seas over,
to smite this yong man with a greeveous disease, of which he
dyed in a desperate maner, and so was him selfe the first that was
throwne overbord. Thus his curses light on his owne head; and it
was an astonishmente to all his fellows, for they noted it to be the
just hand of God upon him.

After they had injoyed faire winds and weather for a season,
they were incountred many times with crosse winds, and mete
with many feirce stormes, with which the shipe was shroudly
shaken, and her upper works made very leakie; and one of the
maine beames in the midd ships was bowed & craked, which put
them in some fear that the shipe could not be able to performe
the vioage. So some of the cheefe of the company, perceiveing
the mariners to feare the suffisiencie of the shipe, as appeared by
their mutterings, they entred into serious consulltation with the
mr. & other officers of the ship, to consider in time of the danger;
and rather to returne then to cast them selves into a desperate &

inevitable perill. And truly ther was great distraction & differance of opinion amongst the mariners them selves; faine would they doe what could be done for their wages sake, (being now halfe the seas over,) and on the other hand they were loath to hazard their lives too desperatly. But in examening of all opinions, the mr. & others affirmed they knew the ship to be stronge & firme under water; and for the buckling of the maine became, ther was a great iron scrue the passengers brought out of Holland, which would raise the beame into his place; the which being done, the carpenter & mr. affirmed that with a post put under it, set firme in the lower deck, & otherways bounde, he would make it sufficiente. And as for the decks & uper workes they would calke them as well as they could, and though with the workeing of the ship they would not longe keepe stanch, yet ther would otherwise be no great danger, if they did not overpress her with sails. So they commited them selves to the will of God, & resolved to proseede. In sundrie of these stormes the winds were so feirce, & the seas so high, as they could not beare a knote of saile, but were forced to hull, for diverce days togither. And in one of them as they thus lay at hull, in a mighty storme, a lustie yonge man (called John Howland) coming upon some occasion above the grattings, was, with a seele of the shipe throwne into sea; but it pleased God that he caught hould of the top-saile halliards, which hunge over board, & rane out at length; yet he held his hould (though he was sundrie fadomes under water) till he was hald up by the same rope to the brime of the water, and then with a boat hooke & other means got into the shipe againe, & his life saved; and though he was something ill with it, yet he lived many years after, and became a profitable member both in church & commone wealthe. In all this viage their died but one of the passengers, which was William Butten, a youth, servant to Samuell Fuller, when they drew near the coast. But to omite other things, (that I may be breefe,) after longe beating at sea they fell with that land which is called Cape Cod; the which being made & certainly knowne to be it, they were not a litle joyfull. After some deliberation had amongst them selves & with the mr. of the ship, they tacked aboute and resolved to stande for the southward (the wind & weather being faire) to finde some place aboute Hudsons river for their habitation. But after they had sailed that course aboute halfe the day, they fell amongst deangerous shoulds and roring breakers, and they were so farr intangled ther with as they conceived them selves in great danger; & the wind shrinking upon them withall, they resolved to bear up againe for the Cape, and thought them sleves hapy to gett out of those dangers before night overtooke them, as by Gods providence they did. And the next day they gott into the Cape-harbor wher they ridd in saftie. A word or too by the way of this cape; it was thus first named by Capten Gosnole & his company, Anno 1602, and after by Capten Smith was caled Cape James; but it retains the former name amongst seamen. Also that pointe which first shewed those dangerous shoulds unto them, they called Pointe Care, & Tuckers Terrour; but the French & Dutch to this day call it Malabarr, by reason of those perilous shoulds, and the losses they have suffered their.

JOHN WINTHROP TO HIS WIFE

Charleton *in* New England, *July* 16, 1630

My Dear Wife,

Blessed be the Lord, our good God and merciful Father, that yet hath preserved me in life and health to salute thee, and to comfort thy long longing heart with the joyful news of my welfare, and the welfare of thy beloved children.

We had a long and troublesome passage, but the Lord made it safe and easy to us; and though we have met with many and great troubles, (as this bearer can certify thee,) yet he hath pleased to uphold us, and to give us hope of a happy issue.

I am so overpressed with business, as I have no time for these or other mine own private occasions. I only write now, that thou mayest know, that yet I live and am mindful of thee in all my affairs. The larger discourse of all things thou shalt receive from my brother Downing, which I must send by some of the last ships. We have met with many sad and discomfortable things, as thou shalt hear after; and the Lord's hand hath been heavy upon myself in some very near to me. My son Henry! my son Henry! ah, poor child! Yet it grieves me much more for my dear daughter. The Lord strengthen and comfort her heart, to bear this cross patiently. I know thou wilt not be wanting to her in this distress. Yet, for all these things, (I praise my God,) I am not discouraged; nor do I see cause to repent or despair of those good days here, which will make amends for all.

I shall expect thee next summer, (if the Lord please,) and by that time I hope to be provided for thy comfortable entertainment. My most sweet wife, be not disheartened; trust in the Lord, and thou shalt see his faithfulness. Commend me heartily to all our kind friends at Castleins, Groton Hall, Mr. Leigh and his wife, my neighbour Cole, and all the rest of my neighbours and their wives, both rich and poor. Remember me to them at Assington Hall, and Codenham Hall, Mr. Brand, Mr. Alston, Mr. Mott, and their wives, goodman Pond, Charles Neale, &c. The good Lord be with thee and bless thee and all our children and servants. Commend my love to them all. I kiss and embrace thee, my dear wife, and all my children, and leave thee in his arms, who is able to preserve you all, and to fulfil our joy in our happy meeting in his good time. Amen.

Thy faithful husband,

Jo. Winthrop

I shall write to my son John by London.
To my very loving Wife, Mrs. Winthrop, *the elder, at Groton in Suffolk, near Sudbury.*
From New England.

THE REVOLUTION

PAUL REVERE'S RIDE

LISTEN, MY CHILDREN, and you shall hear
Of the midnight ride of Paul Revere,
On the eighteenth of April, in Seventy-five;
Hardly a man is now alive
Who remembers that famous day and year.

He said to his friend, "If the British march
By land or sea from the town tonight,
Hang a lantern aloft in the belfry arch
Of the North Church tower as a signal light,—
One, if by land, and two, if by sea;
And I on the opposite shore will be,
Ready to ride and spread the alarm
Through every Middlesex village and farm,
For the country folk to be up and to arm."

Then he said, "Good night!" and with muffled oar
Silently rowed to the Charlestown shore,
Just as the moon rose over the bay,
Where swinging wide at her moorings lay
The Somerset, British man-of-war;
A phantom ship, with each mast and spar
Across the moon like a prison bar,
And a huge black hulk, that was magnified
By its own reflection in the tide.

Meanwhile, his friend, through alley and street,
Wanders and watches with eager ears,
Till in the silence around him he hears

The muster of men at the barrack door,
The sound of arms, and the tramp of feet,
And the measured tread of the grenadiers,
Marching down to their boats on the shore.

Then he climbed the tower of the Old North Church,
By the wooden stairs, with stealthy tread,
To the belfry-chamber overhead,
And startled the pigeons from their perch
On the somber rafters, that round him made
Masses and moving shapes of shade,—
By the trembling ladder, steep and tall,
To the highest window in the wall,
Where he paused to listen and look down
A moment on the roofs of the town,
And the moonlight flowing over all.

Beneath, in the churchyard, lay the dead,
In their night-encampment on the hill,
Wrapped in silence so deep and still
That he could hear, like a sentinel's tread,
The watchful night-wind, as it went
Creeping along from tent to tent,
And seeming to whisper, "All is well!"
A moment only he feels the spell
Of the place and the hour, and the secret dread
Of the lonely belfry and the dead;
For suddenly all his thoughts are bent
On a shadowy something far away,
Where the river widens to meet the bay,—
A line of black that bends and floats
On the rising tide, like a bridge of boats.

Meanwhile, impatient to mount and ride,
Booted and spurred, with a heavy stride
On the opposite shore walked Paul Revere.

Now he patted his horse's side,
Now gazed at the landscape far and near,
Then, impetuous, stamped the earth,
And turned and tightened his saddle-girth;
But mostly he watched with eager search
The belfry-tower of the Old North Church,
As it rose above the graves on the hill,
Lonely and spectral and somber and still.
And lo! as he looks, on the belfry's height
A glimmer, and then a gleam of light!
He springs to the saddle, the bridle he turns,
But lingers and gazes, till full on his sight
A second lamp in the belfry burns!

A hurry of hoofs in a village street,
A shape in the moonlight, a bulk in the dark,
And beneath, from the pebbles, in passing, a spark
Struck out by a steed flying fearless and fleet;
That was all! And yet, through the gloom and the light,
The fate of a nation was riding that night;
And the spark struck out by that steed in his flight,
Kindled the land into flame with its heat.

He has left the village and mounted the steep,
And beneath him, tranquil and broad and deep,
Is the Mystic, meeting the ocean tides;
And under the alders, that skirt its edge,
Now soft on the sand, now loud on the ledge,
Is heard the tramp of his steed as he rides.

It was twelve by the village clock
When he crossed the bridge into Medford town.
He heard the crowing of the cock,
And the barking of the farmer's dog,
And felt the damp of the river fog,
That rises after the sun goes down.

It was one by the village clock,
When he galloped into Lexington.
He saw the gilded weathercock
Swim in the moonlight as he passed,
And the meeting-house windows, blank and bare,
Gaze at him with a spectral glare,
As if they already stood aghast
At the bloody work they would look upon.

It was two by the village clock,
When he came to the bridge in Concord town.
He heard the bleating of the flock,
And the twitter of birds among the trees,
And felt the breath of the morning breeze
Blowing over the meadows brown.
And one was safe and asleep in his bed
Who at the bridge would be first to fall,
Who that day would be lying dead,
Pierced by a British musket-ball.

You know the rest. In the books you have read,
How the British Regulars fired and fled,—
How the farmers gave them ball for ball,
From behind each fence and farmyard wall,
Chasing the redcoats down the lane,
Then crossing the fields to emerge again
Under the trees at the turn of the road,
And only pausing to fire and load.
So through the night rode Paul Revere;
And so through the night went his cry of alarm
To every Middlesex village and farm,—
A cry of defiance, and not of fear,
A voice in the darkness, a knock at the door,
And a word that shall echo forevermore!
For, borne on the night-wind of the Past,
Through all our history, to the last,

In the hour of darkness and peril and need,
The people will waken and listen to hear
The hurrying hoofbeats of that steed,
And the midnight message of Paul Revere.

HENRY WADSWORTH LONGFELLOW

A BALLAD OF THE BOSTON TEA-PARTY

December 16, 1773

No! never such a draught was poured
    Since Hebe served with nectar
The bright Olympians and their Lord,
    Her over-kind protector,—
Since Father Noah squeezed the grape
    And took to such behaving
As would have shamed our grandsire ape
    Before the days of shaving,—
No! ne'er was mingled such a draught
    In palace, hall, or arbor,
As freemen brewed and tyrants quaffed
    That night in Boston Harbor!
It kept King George so long awake
    His brain at last got addled,
It made the nerves of Britain shake,
    With sevenscore millions saddled;
Before that bitter cup was drained
    Amid the roar of cannon,
The Western war-cloud's crimson stained
    The Thames, the Clyde, the Shannon;
Full many a six-foot grenadier
    The flattened grass had measured,
And many a mother many a year
    Her tearful memories treasured;

Fast spread the tempest's darkening pall,
   The mighty realms were troubled,
The storm broke loose, but first of all
   The Boston teapot bubbled!

An evening party,—only that,
   No formal invitation,
No gold-laced coat, no stiff cravat,
   No feast in contemplation,
No silk-robed dames, no fiddling band,
   No flowers, no songs, no dancing,—
A tribe of red men, axe in hand,—
   Behold the guests advancing!
How fast the stragglers join the throng,
   From stall and workshop gathered!
The lively barber skips along
   And leaves a chin half-lathered;
The smith has flung his hammer down,—
   The horseshoe still is glowing;
The truant tapster at the Crown
   Has left a beer-cask flowing;
The cooper's boys have dropped the adze,
   And trot behind their master;
Up run the tarry ship-yard lads,—
   The crowd is hurrying faster,—
Out from the Millpond's purlieus gush
   The streams of white-faced millers,
And down their slippery alleys rush
   The lusty young Fort-Hillers;
The ropewalk lends its 'prentice crew,—
   The tories seize the omen:
"Ay, boys, you'll soon have work to do
   For England's rebel foemen,
'King Hancock,' Adams, and their gang,
   That fire the mob with treason,—

When these we shoot and those we hang
  The town will come to reason."

Oh—on to where the tea-ships ride!
  And now their ranks are forming,—
A rush, and up the Dartmouth's side
  The Mohawk band is swarming!
See the fierce natives! What a glimpse
  Of paint and fur and feather,
As all at once the full-grown imps
  Light on the deck together!
A scarf the pigtail's secret keeps,
  A blanket hides the breeches,—
And out the cursèd cargo leaps,
  And overboard it pitches!

O woman, at the evening board
  So gracious, sweet, and purring,
So happy while the tea is poured,
  So blest while spoons are stirring,
What martyr can compare with thee,
  The mother, wife, or daughter,
That night, instead of best Bohea,
  Condemned to milk and water!

Ah, little dreams the quiet dame
  Who plies with rock and spindle
The patient flax, how great a flame
  Yon little spark shall kindle!
The lurid morning shall reveal
  A fire no king can smother
Where British flint and Boston steel
  Have clashed against each other!
Old charters shrivel in its track,
  His Worship's bench has crumbled,
It climbs and clasps the union-jack,
  Its blazoned pomp is humbled,

The flags go down on land and sea
  Like corn before the reapers;
So burned the fire that brewed the tea
  That Boston served her keepers!

The waves that wrought a century's wreck
  Have rolled o'er whig and tory;
The Mohawks on the Dartmouth's deck
  Still live in song and story;
The waters in the rebel bay
  Have kept the tea-leaf savor;
Our old North-Enders in their spray
  Still taste a Hyson flavor;
And Freedom's teacup still o'erflows
  With ever fresh libations,
To cheat of slumber all her foes
  And cheer the wakening nations!
                        OLIVER WENDELL HOLMES

CONCORD HYMN

Sung at the Completion of the Concord Monument,
April 19, 1836.

By THE RUDE BRIDGE that arched the flood,
  Their flag to April's breeze unfurled,
Here once the embattled farmers stood,
  And fired the shot heard round the world.

The foe long since in silence slept;
  Alike the conqueror silent sleeps;
And Time the ruined bridge has swept
  Down the dark stream which seaward creeps.

On this green bank, by this soft stream,
  We set today a votive stone;
That memory may their deed redeem,
  When, like our sires, our sons are gone.

Spirit, that made those heroes dare
To die, and leave their children free
Bid Time and Nature gently spare
The shaft we raise to them and thee.
RALPH WALDO EMERSON

THE MARYLAND BATTALION

SPRUCE MACARONIS, and pretty to see,
Tidy and dapper and gallant were we;
Blooded fine gentlemen, proper and tall,
Bold in a fox-hunt and gay at a ball;
Prancing soldados, so martial and bluff,
Billets for bullets, in scarlet and buff—
But our cockades were clasped with a mother's low prayer.
And the sweethearts that braided the sword-knots were fair.

There was grummer of drums humming hoarse in the hills,
And the bugles sang fanfaron down by the mills,
By Flatbush the bagpipes were droning amain,
And keen cracked the rifles in Martense's lane;
For the Hessians were flecking the hedges with red,
And the Grenadiers' tramp marked the roll of the dead.

Three to one, flank and rear, flashed the files of St. George,
The fierce gleam of their steel as the glow of a forge.
The brutal boom-boom of their swart cannoneers
Was sweet music compared with the taunt of their cheers—
For the brunt of their onset, our crippled array,
And the light of God's leading gone out in the fray!

Oh, the rout on the left and the tug on the right!
The mad plunge of the charge and the wreck of the flight!

When the cohorts of Grant held stout Stirling at strain,
And the mongrels of Hesse went tearing the slain;
When at Freeke's Mill the flumes and the sluices ran red,
And the dead choked the dyke and the marsh choked the dead!

"Oh, Stirling, good Stirling! How long must we wait?
Shall the shout of your trumpet unleash us too late?
Have you never a dash for brave Mordecai Gist,
With his heart in his throat, and his blade in his fist?
Are we good for no more than to prance in a ball,
When the drums beat the charge and the clarions call?"

Tralára! Tralára! Now praise we the Lord,
For the clang of His call and the flash of His sword!
Tralára! Tralára! Now forward to die;
For the banner, hurrah! and for sweethearts, good-by!
"Four hundred wild lads!" Maybe so. I'll be bound
'T will be easy to count us, face up, on the ground.
If we hold the road open, though Death take the toll,
We'll be missed on parade when the States call the roll—
When the flags meet in peace and the guns are at rest,
And fair Freedom is singing Sweet Home in the West.

                              John Williamson Palmer

WARREN'S ADDRESS TO THE
AMERICAN SOLDIERS

Stand! the ground's your own, my braves!
Will ye give it up to slaves?
Will ye look for greener graves?
      Hope ye mercy still?
What's the mercy despots feel?
Hear it in that battle-peal!
Read it on yon bristling steel!
      Ask it,—ye who will.

Fear ye foes who kill for hire?
Will ye to your homes retire?
Look behind you! they're a-fire!
    And, before you, see
Who have done it!—From the vale
On they come!—And will ye quail?—
Leaden rain and iron hail
    Let their welcome be!

In the God of battles trust!
Die we may,—and die we must;
But, oh, where can dust to dust
    Be consigned so well,
As where Heaven its dews shall shed
On the martyred patriot's bed,
And the rocks shall raise their head,
    Of his deeds to tell!
                    JOHN PIERPONT

MOLLY MAGUIRE AT MONMOUTH

ON THE bloody field of Monmouth
    Flashed the guns of Greene and Wayne,
Fiercely roared the tide of battle,
    Thick the sward was heaped with slain.
Foremost, facing death and danger,
    Hessian, horse, and grenadier,
In the vanguard, fiercely fighting,
    Stood an Irish Cannonier.

Loudly roared his iron cannon,
    Mingling ever in the strife,
And beside him, firm and daring,
    Stood his faithful Irish wife.

Of her bold contempt of danger
   Greene and Lee's Brigades could tell,
Every one knew "Captain Molly,"
   And the army loved her well.

Surged the roar of battle round them,
   Swiftly flew the iron hail,
Forward dashed a thousand bayonets,
   That lone battery to assail.
From the foeman's foremost columns
   Swept a furious fusillade,
Mowing down the massed battalions
   In the ranks of Greene's Brigade.

Fast and faster worked the gunner,
   Soiled with powder, blood, and dust,
English bayonets shone before him,
   Shot and shell around him burst;
Still he fought with reckless daring,
   Stood and manned her long and well,
Till at last the gallant fellow
   Dead—beside his cannon fell.

With a bitter cry of sorrow,
   And a dark and angry frown,
Looked that band of gallant patriots
   At their gunner stricken down.
"Fall back, comrades, it is folly
   Thus to strive against the foe."
"No! not so," cried Irish Molly;
   "We can strike another blow."

*   *   *   *   *   *   *

Quickly leaped she to the cannon,
   In her fallen husband's place,
Sponged and rammed it fast and steady,
   Fired it in the foeman's face.

Flashed another ringing volley,
  Roared another from the gun;
"Boys, hurrah!" cried gallant Molly,
  "For the flag of Washington."

Greene's Brigade, though shorn and shattered,
  Slain and bleeding half their men,
When they heard that Irish slogan,
  Turned and charged the foe again.
Knox and Wayne and Morgan rally,
  To the front they forward wheel,
And before their rushing onset
  Clinton's English columns reel.

Still the cannon's voice in anger
  Rolled and rattled o'er the plain,
Till there lay in swarms around it
  Mangled heaps of Hessian slain.
"Forward! charge them with the bayonet!"
  'Twas the voice of Washington,
And there burst a fiery greeting
  From the Irish woman's gun.

Monckton falls; against his columns
  Leap the troops of Wayne and Lee,
And before their reeking bayonets
  Clinton's red battalions flee.
Morgan's rifles, fiercely flashing,
  Thin the foe's retreating ranks,
And behind them onward dashing
  Ogden hovers on their flanks.

Fast they fly, these boasting Britons,
  Who in all their glory came,
With their brutal Hessian hirelings
  To wipe out our country's name.

Proudly floats the starry banner,
  Monmouth's glorious field is won,
And in triumph Irish Molly
  Stands beside her smoking gun.

WILLIAM COLLINS

LEXINGTON

April 19, 1775

O'ER Cambridge set the yeoman's mark:
Climb, patriot, through the April dark.
O lanthorn! kindle fast thy light,
Thou budding star in the April night,
For never a star more news hath told,
Or later flame in heaven shall hold.
Ay, lanthorn on the North Church tower,
When that thy church hath had her hour,
Still from the top of Reverence high
Shalt thou illume Fame's ampler sky;
For, statured large o'er town and tree,
Time's tallest Figure stands by thee,
And, dim as now thy wick may shine,
The Future lights his lamp at thine.

Now haste thee while the way is clear,
      Paul Revere!
Haste, Dawes! but haste thou not, O Sun!
      To Lexington.

Then Devens looked and saw the light:
He got him forth into the night,
And watched alone on the river-shore,
And marked the British ferrying o'er.

John Parker! rub thine eyes and yawn,
But one o'clock and yet 't is Dawn!
Quick, rub thine eyes and draw thy hose:
The Morning comes ere darkness goes.
Have forth and call the yeomen out,
For somewhere, somewhere close about
Full soon a Thing must come to be
Thine honest eyes shall stare to see—
Full soon before thy patriot eyes
Freedom from out of a Wound shall rise.

Then haste ye, Prescott and Revere!
Bring all the men of Lincoln here;
Let Chelmsford, Littleton, Carlisle,
Let Acton, Bedford, hither file—
Oh hither file, and plainly see
Out of a wound leap Liberty.
Say, Woodman April! all in green,
Say, Robin April! hast thou seen
In all thy travel round the earth
Ever a morn of calmer birth?
But Morning's eye alone serene
Can gaze across yon village-green
To where the trooping British run
      Through Lexington.

Good men in fustian, stand ye still;
The men in red come o'er the hill.
Lay down your arms, damned Rebels! cry
The men in red full haughtily.
But never a grounding gun is heard;
The men in fustian stand unstirred;
Dead calm, save maybe a wise bluebird
Puts in his little heavenly word.
O men in red! if ye but knew
The half as much as bluebirds do,

Now in this little tender calm
Each hand would out, and every palm
With patriot palm strike brotherhood's stroke
Or ere these lines of battle broke.

O men in red! if ye but knew
The least of the all that bluebirds do,
Now in this little godly calm
Yon voice might sing the Future's Psalm—
The Psalm of Love with the brotherly eyes
Who pardons and is very wise—
Yon voice that shouts, high-hoarse with ire,
      Fire!
The red-coats fire, the homespuns fall:
The homespuns' anxious voices call,
Brother, art hurt? and *Where hit, John?*
And, *Wipe this blood,* and, *Men, come on,*
And, *Neighbor, do but lift my head,*
And, *Who is wounded? Who is dead?*
Seven are killed. My God! my God!
Seven lie dead on the village sod.
Two Harringtons, Parker, Hadley, Brown,
Monroe and Porter,—these are down.
Nay, look! Stout Harrington not yet dead!
He crooks his elbow, lifts his head.
He lies at the step of his own house-door;
He crawls and makes a path of gore.
The wife from the window hath seen, and rushed;
He hath reached the step, but the blood hath gushed;
He hath crawled to the step of his own house-door,
But his head hath dropped: he will crawl no more.
Clasp, Wife, and kiss, and lift the head:
Harrington lies at his doorstep dead.

But, O ye Six that round him lay
And bloodied up that April day!

As Harrington fell, ye likewise fell—
At the door of the House wherein ye dwell;
As Harrington came, ye likewise came
And died at the door of your House of Fame.

SIDNEY LANIER

THE SWAMP FOX

WE FOLLOW where the Swamp Fox guides,
   His friends and merry men are we;
And when the troop of Tarleton rides,
   We burrow in the cypress-tree.
The turfy hammock is our bed,
   Our home is in the red deer's den,
Our roof, the tree-top overhead,
   For we are wild and hunted men.

We fly by day and shun its light,
   But, prompt to strike the sudden blow,
We mount and start with early night,
   And through the forest track our foe.
And soon he hears our chargers leap,
   The flashing sabre blinds his eyes,
And ere he drives away his sleep,
   And rushes from his camp, he dies.

Free bridle-bit, good gallant steed,
   That will not ask a kind caress
To swim the Santee at our need,
   When on his heels the foemen press,—
The true heart and the ready hand,
   The spirit stubborn to be free,
The twisted bore, the smiting brand,—
   And we are Marion's men, you see.

Now light the fire and cook the meal,
 The last perhaps that we shall taste;
I hear the Swamp Fox round us steal,
 And that's a sign we move in haste.
He whistles to the scouts, and hark!
 You hear his order calm and low.
Come, wave your torch across the dark,
 And let us see the boys that go.

We may not see their forms again,
 God help 'em, should they find the strife!
For they are strong and fearless men,
 And make no coward terms for life;
They'll fight as long as Marion bids,
 And when he speaks the word to shy,
Then, not till then, they turn their steeds,
 Through thickening shade and swamp to fly.

Now stir the fire and lie at ease,—
 The scouts are gone, and on the brush
I see the Colonel bend his knee,
 To take his slumbers too. But hush!
He's praying, comrades; 't is not strange;
 The man that's fighting day by day
May well, when night comes, take a change,
 And down upon his knees to pray.

Break up that hoe-cake, boys, and hand
 The sly and silent jug that's there;
I love not it should idly stand
 When Marion's men have need of cheer.
'T is seldom that our luck affords
 A stuff like this we just have quaffed,
And dry potatoes on our boards
 May always call for such a draught.

Now pile the brush and roll the log;
   Hard pillow, but a soldier's head
That's half the time in brake and bog
   Must never think of softer bed.
The owl is hooting to the night,
   The cooter crawling o'er the bank,
And in that pond the flashing light
Tells where the alligator sank.

What! 't is the signal! start so soon,
   And through the Santee swamp so deep,
Without the aid of friendly moon,
   And we, Heaven help us! half asleep!
But courage, comrades! Marion leads.
   The Swamp Fox takes us out to-night;
So clear your swords and spur your steeds,
   There's goodly chance, I think, of fight.

We follow where the Swamp Fox guides,
   We leave the swamp and cypress-tree,
Our spurs are in our coursers' sides,
   And ready for the strife are we.
The Tory camp is now in sight,
   And there he cowers within his den;
He hears our shouts, he dreads the fight,
   He fears, and flies from Marion's men.
                 WILLIAM GILMORE SIMMS

CARMEN BELLICOSUM

IN THEIR ragged regimentals,
Stood the old Continentals,
  Yielding not,
While the grenadiers were lunging,
And like hail fell the plunging
  Cannon-shot;
    When the files
    Of the isles,
From the smoky night-encampment, bore the banner of the rampant
      Unicorn;
And grummer, grummer, grummer, rolled the roll of the drummer,
      Through the morn!

Then with eyes to the front all,
And with guns horizontal,
  Stood our sires;
And the balls whistled deadly,
And in streams flashing redly
  Blazed the fires;
    As the roar
    On the shore,
Swept the strong battle-breakers o'er the green-sodded acres
      Of the plain;
And louder, louder, louder, cracked the black gunpowder,
      Cracking amain!

Now like smiths at their forges
Worked the red St. George's
  Cannoneers;
And the villainous saltpetre

Rung a fierce, discordant metre
  Round their ears:
    As the swift
    Storm-drift
With hot sweeping anger, came the horse-guards' clangor
    On our flanks.
Then higher, higher, higher, burned the old-fashioned fire
    Through the ranks!

  Then the bare-headed colonel
  Galloped through the white infernal
    Powder-cloud;
  And his broadsword was swinging,
  And his brazen throat was ringing
    Trumpet-loud.
    Then the blue
    Bullets flew,
And the trooper-jackets redden at the touch of the leaden
    Rifle-breath;
And rounder, rounder, rounder, roared the iron six-pounder,
    Hurling death!

GUY HUMPHREYS McMASTER

THE BATTLE OF THE KEGS

GALLANTS attend, and hear a friend
  Trill forth harmonious ditty;
Strange things I'll tell which late befel
  In Philadelphia city.

'T was early day, as Poets say,
  Just when the sun was rising,
A soldier stood on a log of wood,
  And saw a slight surprising.

As in a maze he stood to gaze
  (The truth can't be deny'd, Sir),
He spy'd a score of kegs, or more,
  Come floating down the tide, Sir.

A sailor, too, in jerkin blue,
  This strange appearance viewing,
First damn'd his eyes, in great surprise,
  Then said "Some mischief's brewing:

"These kegs now hold, the rebels bold,
  Packed up like pickl'd herring;
And they're come down t' attack the town
  In this new way of ferry'ng."

The soldier flew, the sailor too,
  And, scar'd almost to death, Sir,
Wore out their shoes to spread the news,
  And ran 'til out of breath, Sir.

Now up and down, throughout the town
  Most frantic scenes were acted;
And some ran here, and others there,
  Like men almost distracted.

Some fire cry'd, which some deny'd,
  But said the earth had quaked;
And girls and boys, with hideous noise,
  Ran thro' the streets half naked.

Sir William he, snug as a flea,
  Lay all this time a snoring;
Nor dream'd of harm as he lay warm
  In bed with Mrs. Loring.

Now in a fright, he starts upright,
    Awaked by such a clatter;
He rubs both eyes, and boldly cries,
    "For God's sake, what's the matter?"

At his bedside he then espy'd,
    Sir Erskine at command, Sir;
Upon one foot he had one boot,
    And t' other in his hand, Sir.

"Arise, arise," Sir Erskine cries,
    "The rebels—more's the pity—
Without a boat, are all afloat,
    And rang'd before the city.

"The motley crew, in vessels new,
    With Satan for their guide, Sir,
Pack'd up in bags, and wooden kegs,
    Come driving down the tide, Sir.

"Therefore prepare for bloody war;
    These kegs must all be routed;
Or surely we dispis'd shall be,
    And British valor doubted."

The royal band now ready stand,
    All ranged in dread array, Sir,
On every slip, on every ship,
    For to begin the fray, Sir.

The cannons roar from shore to shore;
    The small-arms loud did rattle;
Since wars began I'm sure no man
    E'er saw so strange a battle.

The *rebel* dales, the *rebel* vales,
   With *rebel* trees surrounded,
The distant woods, the hills and floods,
   With *rebel* echoes sounded.

The fish below swam to and fro,
   Attack'd from every quarter;
Why, sure (thought they), the De'il's to pay
   'Mong folks above the water.

The kegs, 't is said, though strongly made
   Of *rebel* staves and hoops, Sir,
Could not oppose their pow'rful foes,
   The conq'ering British troops, Sir.

From morn to night these men of might
   Display'd amazing courage;
And when the sun was fairly down,
   Retired to sup their porridge.

A hundred men, with each a pen,
   Or more, upon my word, Sir,
It is most true, would be too few,
   Their valor to record, Sir.

Such feats did they perform that day
   Against these wicked kegs, Sir,
That years to come, *if they get home,*
   They'll make their boasts and brags, Sir.
               FRANCIS HOPKINSON

WASHINGTON

OFF with the ruffle!
Away with the wig!
No more shall they muffle
The soul of our big
Father of men.
Stockings of silk,—
All of that ilk—
Strip them away
Swift as we may!
Joyously then
Burn the false reams
Of the Reverend Weems,—
Myth of the hatchet,—
Others to match it.
Now see a man
Young for his age,
With a hearty laugh,
Lips that could quaff,
Lips that could rage,
An eye for the stage,
Or a fishing-rod,
A close-run race,
Or a charming face.
No statue, he!
Look, and we see
No carefully shod
Gray demi-god
Carved by smug preachers
And treacherous teachers.
Down with the wig
And the mask of the prig!
Do what they can

To smooth and conceal it,
They're forced to reveal it—
He was a *man!*

His was the kind
Of young man's mind
That never said "die"
As the ice crunched by
And shattered his raft
In the frontier stream.
He but sputtered and laughed
And clove with his friend
By the moon's pale gleam
To the grim swim's end.
None other bore
On that bloody shore
By dread Duquesne
A heart so cool,
A head so high,
(Though fever-sore
And spent with pain)
As Braddock's "fool."

Pray, what kind
But a sportsman's mind
Could so often rebound
At no matter what cost
From shock and disaster
And swiftly re-master
More than was lost,
To the heartening sound
Of the fife's cheery round?
Or was it some nice
Powdered prig in a wig
Poled the Delaware's ice

To the jubilant foe
To bring him that shocking
Torn Christmas stocking
That ruddied the snow?

And, when as Chief
Men labeled him "thief,"
"Ingrate," "traitor,"
"Would-be king,"
"People-hater,"—
Everything
That could cause him grief,—
How the serpent's tooth
Devoured his youth!
Mark how he aged,
Agonized, raged,
Swore—for relief—
He had rather be pent
Safe in the womb
Of the wordless tomb
Than be President.
(When burst such a groan
From a statue of stone?)
Yet helmward abided
That sportsman's hand
Until it had guided
The vessel to land.

Here, then, he stands,
The true Washington,
Sire of the lands
Of the North and the South.
Love he commands
As no second one
Under our sun.

Mind not the mouth
So prim and so stern;
An old age heroic
But made it *seem* stoic.
Mark the kind eyes
That glimmer and burn
So wistful and wise
So brimmed with concern,
The brotherly hands
That beckon and yearn.

Ah, no less brotherly hands
Had welded these western lands;
Eyes of no cooler light
Had held these states, by the might
Of their loving, passionate will,
In the cording of common bands.
Full well know we whence came
Those spirits of thunder and flame
That met at Chancellorsville!
Aye, and we know full well
Whence, after that four years' hell,
Came the soul of a later day
When sad Mississippi mothers
And girls with slain sweethearts and brothers
Bore lilies and roses to lay
On the mounds both of Blue and of Gray.

No! 't was no statuesque sire
That left us in Lincoln his son—
A great-heart with malice toward none,
A great-hand with sinews of fire;—
That left us a Roosevelt at need,
When Mammon had blunted the breed,
To rake our souls out of the mire.

Off with the ruffle!
Away with the wig!
No more shall they muffle
The soul of our big
Father of men.
Though they do what they can
To smooth and conceal it,
Manfully, then,
Let us reveal it:—
He was a man!

ROBERT HAVEN SCHAUFFLER

TO THE MEMORY OF THE BRAVE AMERICANS UNDER GENERAL GREENE, IN SOUTH CAROLINA, WHO FELL IN THE ACTION OF SEPTEMBER 8, 1781

AT EUTAW SPRINGS the valiant died;
  Their limbs with dust are covered o'er—
Weep on, ye springs, your tearful tide;
  How many heroes are no more!

If in this wreck of ruin, they
  Can yet be thought to claim a tear,
O smite your gentle breast, and say
  The friends of freedom slumber here!

Thou, who shalt trace this bloody plain,
  If goodness rules thy generous breast,
Sigh for the wasted rural reign;
  Sigh for the shepherds, sunk to rest!

Stranger, their humble graves adorn;
  You too may fall, and ask a tear;
'Tis not the beauty of the morn
  That proves the evening shall be clear.—

They saw their injured country's woe;
  The flaming town, the wasted field;
Then rushed to meet the insulting foe;
  They took the spear—but left the shield.

Led by thy conquering genius, Greene,
  The Britons they compelled to fly;
None distant viewed the fatal plain,
  None grieved, in such a cause to die—

But, like the Parthian, famed of old,
  Who, flying, still their arrows threw,
These routed Britons, full as bold,
  Retreated, and retreating slew.

Now rest in peace, our patriot band;
  Though far from nature's limits thrown,
We trust they find a happier land,
  A brighter sunshine of their own.

                    PHILIP FRENEAU

TICONDEROGA

THE cold, gray light of the dawning
  On old Carillon falls,
And dim in the mist of the morning
  Stand the grim old fortress walls.
No sound disturbs the stillness
  Save the cataract's mellow roar,
Silent as death is the fortress,
  Silent the misty shore.

But up from the wakening waters
  Comes the cool, fresh morning breeze,

Lifting the banner of Britain,
  And whispering to the trees
Of the swift gliding boats on the waters
  That are nearing the fog-shrouded land,
With the old Green Mountain Lion,
  And his daring patriot band.

But the sentinel at the postern
  Heard not the whisper low;
He is dreaming of the banks of the Shannon
  As he walks on his beat to and fro,
Of the starry eyes in Green Erin
  That were dim when he marched away,
And a tear down his bronzed cheek courses,
  'T is the first for many a day.

A sound breaks the misty stillness,
  And quickly he glances around;
Through the mist, forms like towering giants
  Seem rising out of the ground;
A challenge, the firelock flashes,
  A sword cleaves the quivering air,
And the sentry lies dead by the postern,
  Blood staining his bright yellow hair.

Then, with a shout that awakens
  All the echoes of hillside and glen,
Through the low, frowning gate of the fortress,
  Sword in hand, rush the Green Mountain men.
The scarce wakened troops of the garrison
  Yield up their trust pale with fear;
And down comes the bright British banner,
And out rings a Green Mountain cheer.

Flushed with pride, the whole eastern heavens
　　With crimson and gold are ablaze;
And up springs the sun in his splendor
　　And flings down his arrowy rays,
Bathing in sunlight the fortress,
　　Turning to gold the grim walls,
While louder and clearer and higher
　　Rings the song of the waterfalls.

Since the taking of Ticonderoga
　　A century has rolled away;
But with pride the nation remembers
　　That glorious morning in May.
And the cataract's silvery music
　　Forever the story tells,
Of the capture of old Carillon,
　　The chime of the silver bells.

V. B. WILSON

THE YANKEE PRIVATEER

COME listen and I'll tell you
　　How first I went to sea,
To fight against the British
　　And earn our liberty.
We shipped with Cap'n Whipple
　　Who never knew a fear,
The Captain of the Providence,
　　The Yankee Privateer.

We sailed and we sailed
　　And made good cheer,
There were many pretty men
　　On the Yankee Privateer.

The British Lord High Admiral
  He wished old Whipple harm,
He wrote that he would hang him
  At the end of his yard arm.
"My Lord," wrote Cap'n Whipple back,
  "It seems to me it's clear
That if you want to hang him,
  You must catch your Privateer."

We sailed and we sailed
  And made good cheer,
For not a British frigate
  Could come near the Privateer.

We sailed to the south'ard,
  And nothing did we meet,
Till we found three British frigates
  And their West Indian fleet.
Old Whipple shut our ports
  As we crawled up near,
And he sent us all below
  On the Yankee Privateer.

So slowly he sailed
  We dropped to the rear,
And not a soul suspected
  The Yankee Privateer.

At night we put the lights out
  And forward we ran
And silently we boarded
  The biggest merchantman.
We knocked down the watch,—
  And the lubbers shook for fear,
She's a prize without a shot
  To the Yankee Privateer.

We sent the prize north
  While we lay near
And all day we slept
  On the bold Privateer.

For ten nights we followed,
  And ere the moon rose,
Each night a prize we'd taken
  Beneath the Lion's nose.
When the British looked to see
  Why their ships should disappear,
They found they had in convoy
  A Yankee Privateer.

But we sailed and sailed
  And made good cheer!
Not a coward was on board
  Of the Yankee Privateer.

The biggest British frigate
  Bore round to give us chase,
But though he was the fleeter
  Old Whipple wouldn't race,
Till he'd raked her fore and aft,
  For the lubbers couldn't steer,
Then he showed them the heels
  Of the Yankee Privateer.

Then we sailed and we sailed
  And we made good cheer,
For not a British frigate
  Could come near the Privateer.

Then northward we sailed
  To the town we all know,

And there lay our prizes
　　All anchored in a row;
And welcome were we
　　To our friends so dear,
And we shared a million dollars
　　On the bold Privateer.

We'd sailed and we'd sailed
　　And we made good cheer,
We had all full pockets
　　On the bold Privateer.

Then we each manned a ship
　　And our sails we unfurled,
And we bore the Stars and Stripes
　　O'er the oceans of the world.
From the proud flag of Britain
　　We swept the seas clear,
And we earned our independence
　　On the Yankee Privateer.

Then landsmen and sailors,
　　One more cheer!
Here is three times three
　　For the Yankee Privateer!
　　　　　　　　　ARTHUR HALE

YANKEE DOODLE

ONCE on a time old Johnny Bull flew in a raging fury,
And swore that Jonathan should have no trials, sir, by Jury;
Then down he sate in burly state and blustered like a grandee,
And in derision made a tune called "Yankee doodle dandy."

That no ellections should be held across the briny waters;
"And now," said he, "I'll tax the tea of all his sons and daughters.
  Yankee doodle these are facts,—Yankee doodle dandy;
  My son of wax your tea I'll tax, you Yankee doodle dandy."

John sent the tea from o'er the sea with heavy duties rated,
But whether hyson or bohea I never heard it stated.
Then Jonathan to pout began,—he laid a strong embargo,—
"I'll drink no tea, by Jove!" so he threw overboard the cargo.
Then Johnny sent a regiment, big words and looks to bandy,
Whose martial band, when near the land, played "Yankee doodle
    Dandy."
  Yankee doodle, keep it up, Yankee doodle dandy,
  I'll poison with a tax your cup; you—"Yankee doodle dandy."

A long war then they had, in which John was at last defeated,
And "Yankee Doodle" was the march to which his troops retreated.
'Cute Jonathan, to see them fly, could not restrain his laughter,
"That tune," said he, "suits to a T, I'll sing it ever after."
Old Johnny's face, to his disgrace, was flushed with beer and
    brandy.
E'en when he swore to sing no more this "Yankee doodle Dandy."
  Yankee doodle, ho, ha, he, Yankee doodle dandy;
  We kept the tune but not the tea—Yankee doodle dandy.

I've told you now the origin of this most lively ditty,
Which Johnny Bull dislikes as "dull and stupid"—what a pity!
With "Hail Columbia" it is sung, in chorus full and hearty,
On land and main we breathe the strain John made for his tea-
    party.
No matter how we rhyme the words, the music speaks them handy,
And where's the fair can't sing the air of "Yankee doodle Dandy"?
  Yankee doodle, firm and true, Yankee doodle dandy,
  Yankee doodle, doodle, doo, Yankee doodle dandy.

ORIGINAL YANKEE WORDS

FATHER and I went down to camp,
  Along with Cap'n Goodin',
And there we saw the men and boys
  As thick as hasty puddin'.

Yankee Doodle, keep it up,
  Yankee Doodle dandy,
Mind the music and the step,
  And with the girls be handy.

And there we saw a thousand men
  As rich as squire David,
And what they wasted every day
  I wish it could be saved.
    Yankee Doodle, keep it up, *etc.*

The 'lasses they eat every day
  Would keep a house a winter;
They have so much, that I'll be bound
  They eat it when they've mind ter.
    Yankee Doodle, keep it up, *etc.*

And there I see a swamping gun
  Large as a log of maple,
Upon a deuced little cart,
  A load for father's cattle.
    Yankee Doodle, keep it up, *etc.*

And every time they shoot it off
  It takes a horn of powder,
And makes a noise like father's gun,
  Only a nation louder.
    Yankee Doodle, keep it up, *etc.*

I went as nigh to one myself
  As 'Siah's inderpinning;
And father went as nigh again,
  I thought the deuce was in him.
    Yankee Doodle, keep it up, *etc*.

Cousin Simon grew so bold,
  I thought he would have cocked it;
It scared me so I shrinked it off
  And hung by father's pocket.
    Yankee Doodle, keep it up, *etc*.

And Cap'n Davis had a gun,
  He kind of clapt his hand on't,
And stuck a crooked stabbing iron
  Upon the little end on't.
    Yankee Doodle, keep it up, *etc*.

And there I see a pumpkin shell
  As big as mother's bason,
And every time they touched it off
  They scampered like the nation.
    Yankee Doodle, keep it up, *etc*.

I see a little barrel, too,
  The heads were made of leather;
They knocked on it with little clubs
  And called the folks together.
    Yankee Doodle, keep it up, *etc*.

And there was Cap'n Washington,
  And gentle folks about him;
They say he's grown so 'tarnal proud
  He will not ride without 'em.
    Yankee Doodle, keep it up, *etc*.

He got him on his meeting clothes
  Upon a slapping stallion;
He sat the world along in rows,
  In hundreds and in millions.
    Yankee Doodle, keep it up, *etc.*

The flaming ribbons in his hat,
  They looked so tearing fine, ah,
I wanted dreadfully to get
  To give to my Jemima.
    Yankee Doodle, keep it up, *etc.*

I see another snarl of men
  A digging graves they told me,
So 'tarnal long, so 'tarnal deep,
  They 'tended they should hold me.
    Yankee Doodle, keep it up, *etc.*

It scared me so, I hooked it off,
  Nor stopped, as I remember,
Nor turned about till I got home,
  Locked up in mother's chamber.
    Yankee Doodle, keep it up, *etc.*
      Gen. George P. Morris

LA FAYETTE

Born, nurtured, wedded, prized, within the pale
  Of peers and princes, high in camp—at court—
  He hears, in joyous youth, a wild report,
Swelling the murmurs of the Western gale,
Of a young people struggling to be free!
  Straight quitting all, across the wave he flies,
  Aids with his sword, wealth, blood, the high emprize!

And shares the glories of its victory.
   Then comes for fifty years a high romance
Of toils, reverses, sufferings, in the cause
   Of man and justice, liberty and France,
Crowned, at the last, with hope and wide applause.
Champion of Freedom! Well thy race was run!
All time shall hail thee, *Europe's noblest Son!*

DOLLY MADISON

PEACE HYMN FOR ENGLAND AND AMERICA

   Two empires by the sea,
   Two nations great and free,
      One anthem raise.
   One race of ancient fame,
   One tongue, one faith, we claim:
   One God, whose glorious name
      We love and praise.

   What deeds our fathers wrought,
   What battles we have fought,
      Let fame record.
   Now, vengeful passion cease,
   Come, victories of peace;
   Nor hate nor pride's caprice
      Unsheathe the sword.

   Though deep the sea, and wide,
   'Twixt realm and realm, its tide
      Binds strand and strand.
   So be the gulf between
   Gray coasts and islands green
   With bonds of peace serene
      And friendship spanned.

Now, may the God above
Guard the dear land we love,
    Both east and west.
Let love more fervent glow
As peaceful ages go,
And strength yet stronger grow,
    Blessing and blest.

GEORGE HUNTINGTON

WASHINGTON

WHERE may the wearied eye repose
    When gazing on the Great;
Where neither guilty glory glows,
    Nor despicable state?
Yes—one—the first—the last—the best
The Cincinnatus of the West
    Whom envy dared not hate,
Bequeath the name of Washington
To make men blush there was but one!

LORD BYRON

From RESOLUTIONS OF THE STAMP ACT CONGRESS

October 19, 1765

THE members of this Congress, sincerely devoted with the warmest sentiments of affection and duty to His Majesty's person and Government, inviolably attached to the present happy establishment of the Protestant succession, and with minds deeply impressed by a sense of the present and impending misfortunes of the British colonies on this continent; having considered as maturely as time will permit the circumstances of the said colonies, esteem it our indispensable duty to make the following declarations of our humble opinion respecting the most essential rights and liberties of the colonists, and of the grievances under which they labour, by reason of several late Acts of Parliament.

I. That His Majesty's subjects in these colonies owe the same allegiance to the Crown of Great Britain that is owing from his subjects born within the realm, and all due subordination to that august body the Parliament of Great Britain.

II. That His Majesty's liege subjects in these colonies are intitled to all the inherent rights and liberties of his natural born subjects within the kingdom of Great Britain.

III. That it is inseparably essential to the freedom of a people, and the undoubted right of Englishmen, that no taxes be imposed on them but with their own consent, given personally or by their representatives.

From DEFENSE OF THE
COLONIES' STAND ON TAXATION

By
EDMUND BURKE

AGAIN, and again, revert to your old principles,—seek peace and ensue it,—leave America, if she has taxable matter in her, to tax herself. I am not here going into the distinctions of rights, nor attempting to mark their boundaries. I do not enter into these metaphysical distinctions; I hate the very sound of them. Leave the Americans as they anciently stood, and these distinctions, born of our unhappy contest, will die along with it. They and we, and their and our ancestors, have been happy under that system. Let the memory of all actions in contradiction to that good old mode, on both sides, be extinguished forever. Be content to bind America by laws of trade: you have always done it. Let this be your reason for binding their trade. Do not burden them by taxes: you were not used to do so from the beginning. Let this be your reason for not taxing. These are the arguments of states and kingdoms. Leave the rest to the schools; for there only they may be discussed with safety. But if, intemperately, unwisely, fatally, you sophisticate and poison the very source of government, by urging subtle deductions, and consequences odious to those you govern, from the unlimited and illimitable nature of supreme sovereignty, you will teach them by these means to call that sovereignty itself in question. When you drive him hard, the boar will surely turn upon the hunters. If that sovereignty and their freedom cannot be reconciled, which will they take? They will cast your sovereignty in your face.

THESE ARE THE TIMES THAT TRY MEN'S SOULS

By
THOMAS PAINE

THESE are the times that try men's souls. The summer soldier and the sunshine patriot will, in this crisis, shrink from the service of their country; but he that stands it *now,* deserves the love and thanks of man and woman. Tyranny, like hell, is not easily conquered; yet we have this consolation with us, that the harder the conflict, the more glorious the triumph. What we obtain too cheap, we esteem too lightly: it is dearness only that gives everything its value. Heaven knows how to put a proper price upon its goods; and it would be strange indeed, if so celestial an article as FREEDOM should not be highly rated. Britain, with an army to enforce her tyranny, has declared that she has a right (*not only to* TAX) but "to BIND *us in* ALL CASES WHATSOEVER," and if being *bound in that manner,* is not slavery, then is there not such a thing as slavery upon earth. Even the expression is impious; for so unlimited a power can belong only to God.

Whether the independence of the continent was declared too soon, or delayed too long, I will not now enter into as an argument; my own simple opinion is, that had it been eight months earlier, it would have been much better. We did not make a proper use of last winter, neither could we, while we were in a dependent state. However, the fault, if it were one, was all our own; we have none to blame but ourselves. But no great deal is lost yet. All that Howe has been doing for this month past, is rather a ravage than a conquest, which the spirit of the Jerseys, a year ago, would have quickly repulsed, and which time and a little resolution will soon recover.

I have as little superstition in me as any man living, but my secret opinion has ever been, and still is, that God Almighty will not give up a people to military destruction, or leave them unsupportedly to perish, who have so earnestly and so repeatedly sought to avoid the calamities of war, by every decent method which wisdom could invent. Neither have I so much of the infidel in me, as to suppose that He has relinquished the government of the world, and given us up to the care of devils; and as I do not, I cannot see on what grounds the king of Britain can look up to heaven for help against us: a common murderer, a highwayman, or a housebreaker, has as good a pretence as he.

*   *   *   *   *   *   *

"The times that tried men's souls" are over—and the greatest and completest revolution the world ever knew, gloriously and happily accomplished.

But to pass from the extremes of danger to safety—from the tumult of war to the tranquillity of peace, though sweet in contemplation, requires a gradual composure of the senses to receive it. Even calmness has the power of stunning, when it opens too instantly upon us. The long and raging hurricane that should cease in a moment, would leave us in a state rather of wonder than enjoyment; and some moments of recollection must pass, before we could be capable of tasting the felicity of repose. There are but few instances, in which the mind is fitted for sudden transitions: it takes in its pleasures by reflection and comparison and those must have time to act, before the relish for new scenes is complete.

In the present case—the mighty magnitude of the object—the various uncertainties of fate it has undergone—the numerous and complicated dangers we have suffered or escaped—the eminence we now stand on, and the vast prospect before us, must all conspire to impress us with contemplation.

To see it in our power to make a world happy—to teach mankind the art of being so—to exhibit, on the theater of the universe a character hitherto unknown—and to have, as it were, a new creation intrusted to our hands, are honours that command reflection, and can neither be too highly estimated, nor too gratefully received.

In this pause then of recollection—while the storm is ceasing, and the long agitated mind vibrating to a rest, let us look back on the scenes we have passed, and learn from experience what is yet to be done.

Never, I say, had a country so many openings to happiness as this. Her setting out in life, like the rising of a fair morning, was unclouded and promising. Her cause was good. Her principles just and liberal. Her temper serene and firm. Her conduct regulated by the nicest steps, and everything about her wore the mark of honor. It is not every country (perhaps there is not another in the world) that can boast so fair an origin. Even the first settlement of America corresponds with the character of the revolution. Rome, once the proud mistress of the universe, was originally a band of ruffians. Plunder and rapine made her rich, and her oppression of millions made her great. But America need never be ashamed to tell her birth, nor relate the stages by which she rose to empire.

THE ADDRESS OF THANKS TO THE KING

By
WILLIAM PITT

THIS, my Lords, is a perilous and tremendous moment. It is no time for adulation. The smoothness of flattery cannot save us, in this awful and rugged crisis. It is now necessary to instruct the Throne, in the language of TRUTH. We must, if possible, dispel the delusion and darkness which envelop it; and display in its full danger and genuine colours, the ruin which is brought to our doors. Can Ministers still presume to expect support in their infatuation? Can Parliament be so dead to its dignity and duty as to be thus deluded into the loss of the one, and the violation of the other;—as to give an unlimited support to measures which have heaped disgrace and misfortune upon us; measures which have reduced this late flourishing empire to ruin and contempt? *But yesterday, and England might have stood against the world: now none so poor to do her reverence!* France, my Lords, has insulted you. She has encouraged and sustained America; and, whether America be wrong or right, the dignity of this country ought to spurn at the officious insult of French interference. Can even *our* Ministers sustain a more humiliating disgrace? Do they dare to resent it? Do they presume even to hint a vindication of their honour, and the dignity of the State, by requiring the dismissal of the plenipotentiaries of America? The People, whom they affected to call contemptible rebels, but whose growing power has at last obtained the name of enemies,—the People with whom they have engaged this country in war, and against whom they now command our implicit support in every measure of desperate hostility,—this People, despised as rebels, or acknowledged as enemies, are abetted against you, supplied with every military store, their interests consulted, and their Ambassadors entertained, by your inveterate enemy,—and our Ministers dare not interpose with dignity or effect!

My Lords, this ruinous and ignominious situation, where we cannot act with success nor suffer with honour, calls upon us to remonstrate in the strongest and loudest language of truth, to rescue the ear of Majesty from the delusions which surround it. You cannot, I venture to say it, you CANNOT conquer America. What is your present situation there? We do not know the worst; but we know that in three campaigns we have done nothing and suffered much. You may swell every expense, and strain every effort, still more extravagantly; accumulate every assistance you can beg or borrow; traffic and barter with every pitiful German Prince, that sells and sends his subjects to the shambles of a foreign country: your efforts are forever vain and impotent,—doubly so from this mercenary aid on which you rely; for it irritates to an incurable resentment the minds of your enemies, to overrun them with the sordid sons of rapine and of plunder, devoting them and their possessions to the rapacity of hireling cruelty! If I were an American, as I am an Englishman, while a foreign troop was landed in my country, I never would lay down my arms!—never! never! never!

THE FIRST STEP TO RECONCILIATION WITH AMERICA

WILLIAM PITT (EARL OF CHATHAM)

I. REMOVAL OF TROOPS FROM BOSTON.

AMERICA, my Lords, *cannot* be reconciled to this country,—she *ought* not to be reconciled,—till the troops of Britain are withdrawn. How can America trust you, with the bayonet at her breast? How can she suppose that you mean less than bondage or death? I therefore move that an address be presented to his

Majesty, advising that immediate orders be despatched to General Gage, for removing his Majesty's forces from the town of Boston. The way must be immediately opened for reconciliation. It will soon be too late. An hour, now lost in allaying ferments in America, may produce years of calamity. Never will I desert, for a moment, the conduct of this weighty business. Unless nailed to my bed by the extremity of sickness, I will pursue it to the end. I will knock at the door of this sleeping and confounded Ministry, and will, if it be possible, rouse them to a sense of their danger.

I contend not for *indulgence,* but for *justice,* to America. What is our right to persist in such cruel and vindictive acts against a loyal, respectable people! They say you have no right to tax them without their consent. They say truly. Representation and taxation must go together. They are inseparable. I therefore urge and conjure your Lordships immediately to adopt this conciliating measure. If illegal violences have been, as is said, committed in America, prepare the way,—open the door of possibility,—for acknowledgment and satisfaction. But proceed not to such coercion—such proscription. Cease your indiscriminate inflictions. Amerce not thirty thousand. Oppress not three millions; irritate them not to unappeasable rancour, for the fault of forty or fifty. Such severity of injustice must forever render incurable the wounds you have inflicted. What though you march from town to town, from province to province? What though you enforce a temporary and local submission? How shall you secure the obedience of the country you leave behind you in your progress? How grasp the dominion of eighteen hundred miles of continent, populous in numbers, strong in valour, liberty, and the means of resistance?

The spirit which now resists your taxation, in America, is the same which formerly opposed loans, benevolences, and ship-money, in England; the same spirit which called all England on its legs, and, by the Bill of Rights, vindicated the English Constitution;—the same spirit which established the great fundamental essential maxim of your liberties, THAT NO SUBJECT OF ENGLAND SHALL BE TAXED BUT BY HIS OWN CONSENT. This glorious Whig spirit animates three millions in America, who prefer poverty with liberty, to gilded chains and sordid affluence; and who will die in defence of their rights as men, as free men. What shall oppose this spirit, aided by the congenial flame glowing in the breast of every Whig in England? " 'Tis liberty to liberty engaged," that they will defend themselves, their families, and their country. In this great cause they are immovably allied; it is the alliance of God and nature,—immutable, eternal,—fixed as the firmament of Heaven.

IRONICAL ADVICE TO GREAT BRITAIN

By

BENJAMIN FRANKLIN

(From "Rules by which a Great Empire may be reduced to a small one." Published in the *Gentleman's Magazine,* London, 1773.)

AN ANCIENT SAGE BOASTED, that, tho' he could not fiddle, he knew how to make a *great city* of a *little one.* The science that I, a modern simpleton, am about to communicate, is the very reverse.

I address myself to all ministres who have the management of extensive dominions, which from their very greatness are become troublesome to govern, because the multiplicity of their affiars leaves no time for *fiddling.*

I. In the first place, gentlemen, you are to consider, that a great empire, like a great cake, is most easily diminished at the edges. Turn your attention, therefore, first to your *remotest* provinces; that, as you get rid of them, the next may follow in order.

II. That the possibility of this separation may always exist, take special care the provinces are never incorporated with the mother country; that they do not enjoy the same common rights, the same privileges in commerce; and that they are governed by *severer laws,* all of *your enacting,* without allowing them any share in the choice of the legislators. By carefully making and preserving such distinctions, you will (to keep to my simile of the cake) act like a wise ginger-bread-baker, who, to facilitate a division, cuts his dough half through in those places where, when baked, he would have it *broken to pieces*.

III. Those remote provinces have perhaps been acquired, purchased, or conquered, at the *sole expence* of the settlers, or their ancestors, without the aid of the mother country. If this should happen to increase her *strength,* by their growing numbers, ready to join in her wars; her *commerce,* by their growing demand for her manufactures; or her *naval power,* by greater employment for her ships and seamen, they may probably suppose some merit in this, and that it entitles them to some favour; you are therefore to *forget it all, or resent it,* as if they had done you injury. If they happen to be zealous whigs, friends of liberty, nurtured in revolution principles, *remember all that* to their prejudice, and resolve to punish it; for such principles, after a revolution is thoroughly established, are of *no more use;* they are even *odious* and *abominable*.

THE COLONIES TO THE MOTHER COUNTRY

By
RICHARD HENRY LEE

SOLDIERS who have sheathed their swords in the bowels of their American brethren, will not draw them with more reluctance against you. When too late, you may lament the loss of that freedom which we exhort you, while still in your power, to preserve.

On the other hand, should you prove unsuccessful; should that connection which we most ardently wish to maintain, be dissolved; should your ministers exhaust your treasures, and waste the blood of your countrymen in vain attempts on our liberty, do they not deliver you, weak and defenceless, to your natural enemies?

Since, then, your liberty must be the price of your victories, your ruin of your defeat—what blind fatality can urge you to a pursuit destructive of all that Britons hold dear?

If you have no regard to the connection which has for ages subsisted between us; if you have forgot the wounds we have received fighting by your side for the extension of the empire; if our commerce is not an object below your consideration; if justice and humanity have lost their influence on your hearts, still motives are not wanting to excite your indignation at the measures now pursued. Your wealth, your honor, your liberty are at stake.

Notwithstanding the distress to which we are reduced, we sometimes forget our own afflictions, to anticipate and sympathize in yours. We grieve that rash and inconsiderate counsels should precipitate the destruction of an empire, which has been the envy and admiration of ages; and call God to witness! that we would part with our property, endanger our lives, and sacrifice everything but liberty, to redeem you from ruin.

A cloud hangs over your heads and ours: ere this reaches you, it may probably burst upon us; let us, then (before the remembrance of former kindness is obliterated) once more repeat those appelations which are ever grateful in our ears; let us entreat Heaven to avert our ruin, and the destruction that threatens our friends, brethren, and countrymen on the other side of the Atlantic.

GEORGE WASHINGTON

ANSWER TO CONGRESS ON HIS APPOINTMENT AS COMMANDER-IN-CHIEF

In Congress, 16 June, 1775

MR. PRESIDENT,

Though I am truly sensible of the high honor done me, in this appointment, yet I feel great distress, from a consciousness that my abilities and military experience may not be equal to the extensive and important trust. However, as the Congress desire it, I will enter upon the momentous duty, and exert every power I possess in their service, and for the support of the glorious cause. I beg they will accept my cordial thanks for this distinguished testimony of their approbation.

But, lest some unlucky event should happen, unfavorable to my reputation, I beg it may be remembered by every gentleman in the room, that I, this day, declare with the utmost sincerity, I do not think myself equal to the command I am honored with.

As to pay, Sir, I beg leave to assure the Congress, that, as no pecuniary consideration could have tempted me to accept this arduous employment, at the expense of my domestic ease and happiness, I do not wish to make any profit from it. I will keep an exact account of my expenses. Those, I doubt not, they will discharge; and that is all I desire.

To Mrs. Martha Washington

Philadelphia, 18 June, 1775

My Dearest,

I am now set down to write to you on a subject, which fills me with inexpressible concern, and this concern is greatly aggravated and increased, when I reflect upon the uneasiness I know it will give you. It has been determined in Congress, that the whole army raised for the defence of the American cause shall be put under my care, and that it is necessary for me to proceed immediately to Boston to take upon me the command of it.

You may believe me, my dear Patsy, when I assure you, in the most solemn manner, that, so far from seeking this appointment, I have used every endeavour in my power to avoid it, not only from my unwillingness to part with you and the family, but from a consciousness of its being a trust too great for my capacity, and that I should enjoy more real happiness in one month with you at home, than I have the most distant prospect of finding abroad, if my stay were to be seven times seven years. But as it has been a kind of destiny, that has thrown me upon this service, I shall hope that my undertaking it is designed to answer some good purpose. You might, and I suppose did perceive, from the tenor of my letters, that I was apprehensive I could not avoid this appointment, as I did not pretend to intimate when I should return. That was the case. It was utterly out of my power to refuse this appointment, without exposing my character to such censures, as would have reflected dishonor upon myself, and given pain to my friends. This, I am sure, could not, and ought not, to be pleasing to you, and must have lessened me considerably in my own esteem. I shall rely, therefore, confidently on that Providence, which has heretofore preserved and been bountiful to me, not doubting but that I shall return safe to you in the fall. I shall feel no pain from the toil or the danger of the campaign; my unhappiness will flow from the uneasiness I know you will feel from being left alone. I therefore beg, that you will summon your whole fortitude, and pass your time as agreeably as possible. Nothing will give me so much sincere satisfaction as to hear this, and to hear it from your own pen. My earnest and ardent desire is, that you would pursue any plan that is most likely to produce content, and a tolerable degree of tranquillity; as it must add greatly to my uneasy feelings to hear, that you are dissatisfied or complaining at what I really could not avoid.

As life is always uncertain, and common prudence dictates to every man the necessity of settling his temporal concerns, while it is in his power, and while the mind is calm and undisturbed, I have, since I came to this place (for I had not time to do it before I left home) got Colonel Pendleton to draft a will for me, by the directions I gave him, which will I now enclose. The provision made for you in case of my death will, I hope, be agreeable.

I shall add nothing more, as I have several letters to write, but to desire that you will remember me to your friends, and to assure you that I am, with the most unfeigned regard, my dear Patsy, your affectionate, &c.

AN APPEAL TO ARMS

By

PATRICK HENRY

MR. PRESIDENT, this is no time for ceremony. The question before the house is one of awful moment to this country. For my own part, I consider it as nothing less than a question of freedom or slavery.

And in proportion to the magnitude of the subject ought to be the freedom of the debate.

It is only in this way that we can hope to arrive at truth, and fulfil the great responsibility which we hold to God and our country.

Should I keep back my opinions at this time, through fear of giving offence, I should consider myself as guilty of treason towards my country, and of an act of disloyalty towards the majesty of Heaven, which I revere above all earthly kings.

Mr. President, it is natural to man to indulge in the illusions of Hope. We are apt to shut our eyes against a painful truth—and listen to the song of that siren, till she transforms us into beasts.

Is this the part of wise men engaged in a great and arduous struggle for liberty? Are we disposed to be of the numbers of those, who having eyes, see not, and having ears, hear not, the things which so nearly concern their temporal salvation? For my part, whatever anguish of spirit it may cost, I am willing to know the whole truth;—to know the worst and to provide for it!

I have but one lamp by which my feet are guided; and that is the lamp of experience. I know of no way of judging of the future but by the past. And judging by the past, I wish to know what there has been in the conduct of the British ministry, for the last ten years, to justify those hopes with which gentlemen have been pleased to solace themselves and the House? Is it that insidious smile with which our petition has been lately received? Trust it not, Sir; it will prove a snare to your feet!

Suffer not yourselves to be betrayed by a kiss!

Ask yourselves how this gracious reception of our petition comports with those warlike preparations which cover our waters, and darken our land.

Are fleets and armies necessary to a work of love and reconciliation? Have we shown ourselves so unwilling to be reconciled, that force must be called in to win back our love? Let us not deceive ourselves, Sir.

These are the implements of war and subjugation—the last arguments to which Kings resort.

I ask, Sir, what means this martial array, if its purpose be not to force us to submission?

Can gentlemen assign any other possible motive for it? Has Great Britain any enemy in this quarter of the world, to call for all this accumulation of navies and armies? No, Sir, she has none. They are meant for us; they can be meant for no other. They are sent over to bind and rivet upon us those chains which the British ministry have been so long forging.

And what have we to oppose to them? Shall we try argument? Sir, we have been trying that for the last ten years. Have we anything new to offer upon the subject? Nothing. We have held the subject in every light of which it is capable; but it has been all in vain. Shall we resort to entreaty and humble supplication? What terms shall we find, which have not been already exhausted? Let us not, I beseech you, Sir, deceive ourselves longer.

Sir, we have done everything that could be done, to avert the storm that is now coming on. We have petitioned—we have remonstrated—we have supplicated—we have prostrated ourselves before the Throne, and have implored its interposition to arrest the tyrannical hands of the Ministry and Parliament.

Our petitions have been slighted; our remonstrances have produced additional violence and insult; our supplications have been disregarded; and we have been spurned with contempt, from the foot of the Throne.

In vain, after these things, may we indulge the fond hope of peace and reconciliation.

There is no longer any room for hope.

If we wish to be free,—if we mean to preserve inviolable those inestimable privileges for which we have been so long contending, —if we mean not basely to abandon the noble struggle in which we have been so long engaged, and which we have pledged ourselves never to abandon until the glorious object of our contest shall be obtained,—we must fight; I repeat it, Sir, we must fight! An appeal to arms, and to the God of Hosts, is all that is left us!

GIVE ME LIBERTY, OR GIVE ME DEATH

By
Patrick Henry

They tell us, Sir, that we are weak,—unable to cope with so formidable an adversary. But when shall we be stronger? Will it be the next week, or the next year? Will it be when we are totally disarmed, and when a British guard shall be stationed in every house? Shall we gather strength by irresolution and inaction? Shall we acquire the means of effectual resistance by lying supinely on our backs, and hugging the delusive phantom of hope, until our enemies shall have bound us hand and foot? Sir, we are not weak, if we make a proper use of those means which the God of nature hath placed in our power.

Three millions of People, armed in the holy cause of liberty, and in such a country as that which we possess, are invincible by any force which our enemy can send against us. Besides, Sir, we shall not fight our battles alone. There is a just God who presides over the destinies of Nations, and who will raise up friends to fight our battles for us. The battle, Sir, is not to the strong alone, it is to the vigilant, the active, the brave. Besides, Sir, we have no election. If we were base enough to desire it, it is now too late to retire from the contest. There is no retreat but in submission and slavery! Our chains are forged! Their clanking may be heard on the plains of Boston! THE WAR IS INEVITABLE; AND LET IT COME! I REPEAT IT, SIR, LET IT COME!

It is in vain, Sir, to extenuate the matter. Gentlemen may cry, peace, peace!—but there is no peace. The war is actually begun! The next gale that sweeps from the North will bring to our ears the clash of resounding arms! Our brethren are already in the field! Why stand we here idle? What is it that Gentlemen wish? What would they have? Is life so dear, or peace so sweet, as to be purchased at the price of chains and slavery? Forbid it, Almighty God! I know not what course others may take, but as for me, GIVE ME LIBERTY, or GIVE ME DEATH!

THE DECLARATION OF INDEPENDENCE

By

THOMAS JEFFERSON

A Declaration by the Representatives of the United States of America in Congress assembled, July 4, 1776.

WHEN, in the course of human events, it becomes necessary for one people to dissolve the political bands which have connected them with another, and to assume, among the powers of the earth, the separate and equal station to which the laws of nature and of nature's God entitle them, a decent respect to the opinions of mankind requires that they should declare the causes which impel them to the separation.

We hold these truths to be self-evident, that all men are created equal; that they are endowed by their Creator with certain un-alienable rights; that among these, are life, liberty, and the pursuit of happiness. That, to secure these rights, governments are in-stituted among men, deriving their just powers from the consent of the governed; that, whenever any form of government becomes destructive of these ends, it is the right of the people to alter or to abolish it, and to institute a new government, laying its foundation on such principles, and organising its powers in such form, as to them shall seem most likely to effect their safety and happiness. Prudence, indeed, will dictate that governments long established, should not be changed for light and transient causes; and, accordingly, all experience hath shown, that mankind are more disposed to suffer, while evils are sufferable, than to right themselves by abolishing the forms to which they are accustomed. But, when a long train of abuses and usurpations, pursuing invariably the same object, evinces a design to reduce them under absolute despotism, it is their right, it is their duty, to throw off such government, and to provide new guards for their future security. Such has been the patient sufferance of these colonies, and such is now the necessity which constrains them to alter their former systems of government. The history of the present King of Great Britain is a history of repeated injuries and usurpations, all having, in direct object, the establishment of an absolute tyranny over these States. To prove this, let facts be submitted to a candid world:—

He has refused his assent to laws the most wholesome and necessary for the public good.

He has forbidden his governors to pass laws of immediate and pressing importance, unless suspended in their operation till his assent should be obtained; and, when so suspended, he has utterly neglected to attend to them.

He has refused to pass other laws for the accommodation of large districts of people, unless those people would relinquish the right of representation in the legislature; a right inestimable to them, and formidable to tyrants only.

He has called together legislative bodies at places unusual, uncomfortable, and distant from the depository of their public records, for the sole purpose of fatiguing them into compliance with his measures.

He has dissolved representative houses repeatedly, for opposing, with manly firmness, his invasions on the rights of the people.

He has refused, for a long time after such dissolutions, to cause others to be elected; whereby the legislative powers, incapable of annihilation, have returned to the people at large for their exercise; the state remaining, in the mean time, exposed to all the danger of invasion from without, and convulsions within.

He has endeavoured to prevent the population of these States; for that purpose, obstructing the laws for naturalisation of foreigners, refusing to pass others to encourage their migration hither, and raising the conditions of new appropriations of lands.

He has obstructed the administration of justice, by refusing his assent to laws for establishing judiciary powers.

He has made judges dependent on his will alone, for the tenure of their offices, and the amount and payment of their salaries.

He has erected a multitude of new offices, and sent hither swarms of officers to harass our people, and eat out their substance.

He has kept among us, in time of peace, standing armies, without the consent of our legislatures.

He has affected to render the military independent of, and superior to, the civil power.

He has combined, with others, to subject us to a jurisdiction foreign to our Constitution, and unacknowledged by our laws; giving his assent to their acts of pretended legislation:

For quartering large bodies of armed troops among us:

For protecting them by a mock trial, from punishment, for any murders which they should commit on the inhabitants of these States:

For cutting off our trade with all parts of the world:

For imposing taxes on us without our consent:

For depriving us, in many cases, of the benefit of trial by jury:

For transporting us beyond seas to be tried for pretended offences.

For abolishing the free system of English laws in a neighbouring province, establishing therein an arbitrary government, and enlarging its boundaries, so as to render it at once an example and fit instrument for introducing the same absolute rule into these colonies:

For taking away our charters, abolishing our most valuable laws, and altering, fundamentally, the powers of our governments:

For suspending our own legislatures, and declaring themselves invested with power to legislate for us in all cases whatsoever.

He has abdicated government here, by declaring us out of his protection, and waging war against us.

He has plundered our seas, ravaged our coasts, burnt our towns, and destroyed the lives of our people.

He is, at this time, transporting large armies of foreign mercenaries to complete the works of death, desolation, and tyranny, already begun, with circumstances of cruelty and perfidy scarcely paralleled in the most barbarous ages, and totally unworthy the head of a civilised nation.

He has constrained our fellow-citizens, taken captive on the high seas, to bear arms against their country, to become the executioners of their friends and brethren, or to fall themselves by their hands.

He has excited domestic insurrections amongst us, and has endeavoured to bring on the inhabitants of our frontiers, the merciless Indian savages, whose known rule of warfare is an undistinguished destruction of all ages, sexes, and conditions.

In every stage of these oppressions, we have petitioned for redress, in the most humble terms; our repeated petitions have been answered only by repeated injury. A prince, whose character is thus marked by every act which may defile a tyrant, is unfit to be the ruler of a free people.

Nor have we been wanting in attention to our British brethren. We have warned them, from time to time, of attempts made by their legislature to extend an unwarrantable jurisdiction over us. We have reminded them of the circumstances of our emigration and settlement here. We have appealed to their native justice and magnanimity, and we have conjured them, by the ties of our common kindred, to disavow these usurpations, which would inevitably interrupt our connections and correspondence. They, too, have been deaf to the voice of justice and consanguinity. We must, therefore, acquiesce in the necessity which denounces our separation, and hold them, as we hold the rest of mankind, enemies in war, in peace, friends.

We, therefore, the representatives of the United States of America, in general Congress assembled, appealing to the Supreme Judge of the world for the rectitude of our intentions, do, in the name, and by the authority of the good people of these colonies, solemnly publish and declare, that these united colonies are, and of right ought to be, free and independent states; that they are absolved from all allegiance to the British Crown, and that all political connection between them and the state of Great Britain is, and ought to be, totally dissolved; and that, as free and independent states, they have full power to levy war, conclude peace, contract alliances, establish commerce, and to do all other acts and things which independent states may of right do. And, for the support of this declaration, with a firm reliance on the protection of Divine Providence, we mutually pledge to each other our lives, our fortunes, and our sacred honour.

THE DECLARATION OF 1776

By
JOHN QUINCY ADAMS

THE Declaration of Independence! The interest which, in that paper, has survived the occasion upon which it was issued,—the interest which is of every age and every clime,—the interest which quickens with the lapse of years, spreads as it grows old, and brightens as it recedes,—is in the principles which it proclaims. It was the first solemn declaration by a Nation of the only legitimate foundation of civil Government. It was the corner-stone of a new fabric, destined to cover the surface of the globe. It demolished at a stroke the lawfulness of all Governments founded upon conquest. It swept away the accumulated rubbish of centuries of servitude. It announced, in practical form, to the world, the transcendent truth of the inalienable sovereignty of the People. It proved that the social compact was no figment of the imagination, but a real, solid, and sacred bond of the social union. From the day of this Declaration, the people of North America were no longer the fragment of a distant empire, imploring justice and mercy from an inexorable master in another hemisphere. They were no longer children appealing in vain to the sympathies of a heartless mother; no longer subjects leaning upon the shattered columns of royal promises, and invoking the faith of parchment to secure their rights. They were a nation, asserting as a right, and maintaining by war, its own existence. A nation was born in a day.

> *"How many ages hence*
> *Shall this, their lofty scene, be acted o'er*
> *In States unborn and accents yet unknown."*

It will be acted o'er, fellow-citizens, but it can never be repeated.

It stands, and must forever stand, alone; a beacon on the summit of the mountain, to which all the inhabitants of the earth may turn their eyes for a genial and saving light, till time shall be lost in eternity, and this globe itself dissolve, nor leave a wreck behind. It stands forever, a light of admonition to the rulers of men, a light of salvation and redemption to the oppressed. So long as this planet shall be inhabited by human beings, so long as man shall be of a social nature; so long as Government shall be necessary to the great moral purposes of society, and so long as it shall be abused to the purposes of oppression,—so long shall this Declaration hold out to the sovereign and to the subject, the extent and the boundaries of their respective rights and duties, founded in the laws of Nature and of Nature's God.

JOHN ADAMS

To His Wife, on the Birth of the New Nation

YESTERDAY, the greatest question was decided, which ever was debated in America, and a greater, perhaps, never was nor will be decided among men. A resolution was passed without one dissenting colony, "that these United Colonies are, and of right ought to be, free and independent States, and as such they have, and of right ought to have, full power to make war, conclude peace, establish commerce, and to do all other acts and things which other States may rightfully do." You will see in a few days a Declaration setting forth the causes which have impelled us to this mighty revolution, and the reasons which will justify it in the sight of God and man. A plan of confederation will be taken up in a few days.

You will think me transported with enthusiasm, but I am not. I am well aware of the toil, and blood, and treasure, that it will cost us to maintain this declaration, and support and defend these States. Yet, through all the gloom, I can see the rays of ravishing light and glory. I can see that the end is more than worth all the means, and that posterity will triumph in that day's transaction, even although we should rue it, which I trust in God we shall not.

PHILADELPHIA, *3 July, 1776.*

A LETTER

From Abigail Adams to Her Husband, John Adams

Sunday, 18th of June, 1775.

DEAREST FRIEND:—

The day, perhaps the decisive day, is come, on which the fate of America depends. My bursting heart must find vent at my pen. I have just heard that our friend, Dr. Warren, is no more, but fell gloriously fighting for his country; saying, "better to die honorably in the field, than ignominiously hang upon the gallows." Great is our loss. He has distinguished himself in every engagement, by his courage and fortitude, by animating the soldiers, and leading them on by his example. A particular account of these dreadful, but I hope glorious, days, will be transmitted you, no doubt, in the exactest manner.

"The call is not to the swift, nor the battle to the strong; but the God of Israel is he that giveth strength and power unto his people. Trust in him at all times, ye people, pour out your hearts before him; God is a refuge for us." Charlestown is laid in ashes. The battle began upon our entrenchments, upon Bunker Hill, Saturday morning about three o'clock, and has not ceased yet, and it is now three o'clock Sabbath afternoon.

It is expected they will come out over the Neck to-night, and a dreadful battle must ensue. Almighty God, cover the heads of our countrymen, and be a shield to our dear friends! How many have fallen, we know not. The constant roaring of the cannon is so distressing, that we cannot eat, drink, or sleep. May we be supported and sustained in the dreadful conflict! I shall tarry here until it is thought unsafe by my friends, and then I have secured myself a retreat at your brother's, who has kindly offered me part of his house. I cannot compose myself to write any further at present. I will add more as I hear further.

From DANIEL WEBSTER'S REPLY TO HAYNE

January 26, 1830

I HAVE not allowed myself, sir, to look beyond the Union, to see what might lie hidden in the dark recess behind. I have not coolly weighed the chances of preserving liberty when the bonds that unite us together shall be broken asunder. I have not accustomed myself to hang over the precipice of disunion, to see whether, with my short sight, I can fathom the depth of the abyss below; nor

could I regard him as a safe counselor, in the affairs of this government, whose thoughts should be mainly bent on considering,
not how the Union should be best preserved, but how tolerable
might be the condition of the people when it shall be broken up
and destroyed. While the Union lasts, we have high, exciting,
gratifying prospects spread out before us, for us and our children. Beyond that, I seek not to penetrate the veil. God grant
that in my day, at least, that curtain may not rise. God grant that,
on my vision, never may be opened what lies behind. When my
eyes shall be turned to behold for the last time the sun in heaven,
may I not see him shining on the broken and dishonored fragments of a once glorious Union; on states dissevered, discordant,
belligerent; on a land rent with civil feuds, or drenched, it may
be, in fraternal blood! Let their last feeble and lingering glance
rather behold the gorgeous ensign of the republic, now known
and honored throughout the earth, still full high advanced, its arms
and trophies streaming in their original luster, not a stripe erased
or polluted, nor a single star obscured, bearing for its motto no
such miserable interrogatory as, What is all this worth? nor those
other words of delusion and folly, Liberty first, and Union afterward; but everywhere, spread all over in characters of living light,
blazing on all its ample folds, as they float over the sea and over
the land, and in every wind under the whole heavens, that other
sentiment, dear to every true American heart—Liberty *and* Union,
now and forever, one and inseparable!

SINK OR SWIM

By
DANIEL WEBSTER

SINK OR SWIM, live or die, survive or perish, I give my hand and
my heart to this vote. It is true, indeed, that in the beginning, we
aimed not at independence. But there is a divinity which shapes
our ends. The injustice of England has driven us to arms; and

blinded to her own interest, she has obstinately persisted, till independence is now within our grasp. We have but to reach forth to it, and it is ours. Why, then, should we defer the Declaration? Is any man so weak as now to hope for a reconciliation with England, which shall leave either safety to the country and its liberties, or security to his own life and his own honour? Are not you, sir, who sit in that chair,—is not he, our venerable colleague, near you—are you not both already the proscribed and predestined objects of punishment and of vengeance? Cut off from all hope of royal clemency, what are you, what can you be, while the power of England remains, but outlaws? If we postpone independence, do we mean to carry on or to give up the war? Do we mean to submit to the measures of Parliament, Boston Port Bill and all? Do we mean to submit, and consent that we ourselves shall be ground to powder, and our country and its rights trodden down in the dust? I know we do not mean to submit. We never shall submit. Do we intend to violate that most solemn obligation ever entered into by men,—that plighting, before God, of our sacred honour to Washington, when, putting him forth to incur the dangers of war, as well as the political hazards of the times, we promise to adhere to him, in every extremity, with our fortunes and our lives? I know there is not a man here who would not rather see a general conflagration sweep over the land, or an earthquake sink it, than one jot or tittle of that plighted faith fall to the ground. For myself, having twelve months ago, in this place, moved you, that George Washington be appointed commander of the forces raised, or to be raised, for defence of American liberty, may my right hand forget her cunning, and my tongue cleave to the roof of my mouth, if I hesitate or waver in the support I give him. The war, then, must go on. We must fight it through. And if the war must go on, why put off longer the Declaration of Independence? That measure will strengthen us. It will give us character abroad. The nations will then treat with us, which they never can do while we acknowledge ourselves subjects in arms against our sovereign. Nay, I maintain that England herself will sooner treat for peace with us on the footing of independence, than consent, by re-

pealing her acts, to acknowledge that her whole conduct towards
us has been a course of injustice and oppression. Her pride will
be less wounded by submitting to that course of things which now
predestinates our independence, than by yielding the points in
controversy to her rebellious subjects. The former she would regard as the result of fortune; the latter, she would feel as her own
deep disgrace. Why, then, do we not, as soon as possible, change
this from a civil to a national war? And since we must fight it
through, why not put ourselves in a state to enjoy all the benefits
of victory, if we gain the victory? If we fail, it can be no worse for
us. But we shall not fail. The cause will raise up armies; the cause
will create navies. The people, the people, the people, if we are
true to them, will carry us, and will carry themselves, gloriously
through this struggle. I care not how fickle other people have been
found. I know the people of these colonies; and I know that resistance to British aggression is deep and settled in their hearts,
and cannot be eradicated.

The Declaration of Independence will inspire the people with
increased courage. Instead of a long and bloody war for the
restoration of privileges, for redress of grievances, for chartered
immunities, held under a British king, set before them the glorious object of entire independence, and it will breathe into them
anew the spirit of life. Read this declaration at the head of the
army; every sword will be drawn from its scabbard, and the solemn
vow uttered to maintain it, or perish on the field of honour. Publish it from the pulpit; religion will approve it, and the love of
religious liberty will cling around it, resolved to stand with it, or
fall with it. Send it to the public halls; proclaim it there; let them
hear it who heard the first roar of the enemy's cannon—let them
see it, who saw their brothers and their sons fall on the field of
Bunker Hill, and in the streets of Lexington and Concord,—and
the very walls will cry out in its support.

Sir, I know the uncertainty of human affairs, but I see, I see
clearly, through this day's business. You and I, indeed, may rue it.
We may not live to see the time when this Declaration shall be
made good. We may die; die colonists; die slaves; die, it may be,

ignominiously and on the scaffold. Be it so. Be it so. If it be the pleasure of Heaven that my country shall require the poor offering of my life, the victim shall be ready at the appointed hour of sacrifice, come when that hour may. But while I do live, let me have a country, or at least the hope of a country, and that a free country.

But whatever may be our fate, be assured, be assured that this Declaration will stand. It may cost treasure, and it may cost blood; but it will stand, and it will richly compensate for both. Through the thick gloom of the present, I see the brightness of the future, as the sun in heaven. We shall make this a glorious, an immortal day. When we are in our graves, our children will honour it. They will celebrate it with thanksgiving, with festivity, with bonfires and illuminations. On its annual return, they will shed tears, copious, gushing tears; not of subjection and slavery, not of agony and distress, but of exultation, of gratitude, and of joy.

Sir, before God, I believe the hour is come. My judgment approves this measure, and my whole heart is in it. All that I have, and all that I am, and all that I hope in this life, I am now ready here to stake upon it; and I leave off as I began, that, live or die, survive or perish, I am for the Declaration. It is my living sentiment, and by the blessing of God, it shall be my dying sentiment, —Independence *now,* and INDEPENDENCE FOREVER.

TO THE AMERICAN TROOPS BEFORE
THE BATTLE OF LONG ISLAND

By
GEORGE WASHINGTON

THE time is now near at hand which must probably determine whether Americans are to be freemen or slaves; whether they are to have any property they can call their own; whether their houses and farms are to be pillaged and destroyed, and themselves consigned to a state of wretchedness from which no human efforts will deliver them. The fate of unborn millions will now depend, under God, on the courage and conduct of this army. Our cruel and unrelenting enemy leaves us only the choice of a brave resistance, or the most abject submission. We have, therefore, to resolve to conquer or to die.

Our own, our country's honour, calls upon us for a vigorous and manly exertion; and if we now shamefully fail, we shall become infamous to the whole world. Let us, then, rely on the goodness of our cause, and the aid of the Supreme Being, in whose hands victory is, to animate and encourage us to great and noble actions. The eyes of all our countrymen are now upon us; and we shall have their blessings and praises, if happily we are the instruments of saving them from the tyranny meditated against them. Let us, therefore, animate and encourage each other, and show the whole world that a freeman contending for liberty on his own ground is superior to any slavish mercenary on earth.

Liberty, property, life and honour, are all at stake. Upon your courage and conduct rest the hopes of our bleeding and insulted country. Our wives, children and parents, expect safety from us only; and they have every reason to believe that Heaven will crown with success so just a cause. The enemy will endeavour to intimidate by show and appearance; but remember they have been repulsed on various occasions by a few brave Americans. Their cause is bad,—their men are conscious of it; and, if opposed with firmness and coolness on their first onset, with our advantage of works, and knowledge of the ground, the victory is most assuredly ours. Every good soldier will be silent and attentive, wait for orders, and reserve his fire until he is sure of doing execution.

CAPTURING TICONDEROGA

By

ETHAN ALLEN

EVER since I arrived to a state of manhood, and acquainted myself with the general history of mankind, I have felt a sincere passion for liberty. The history of nations doomed to perpetual slavery, in consequence of yielding up to tyrants their natural-born liberties, I read with a sort of philosophical horror; so that the first systematical and bloody attempt at Lexington, to enslave America, thoroughly electrified my mind, and fully determined me to take part with my country: And while I was wishing for an opportunity to signalize myself in its behalf, directions were privately sent to me from the then colony (now State) of Connecticut, to raise the Green Mountain boys; (and if possible) with them to surprise and take the fortress Ticonderoga. This enterprize I cheerfully undertook; and, after first guarding all the passes that led thither, to cut off all intelligence between the garrison and the country, made a forced march from Bennington, and arrived at the lake opposite to Ticonderoga, on the evening of the ninth day of May, 1775, with two hundred and thirty valiant Green Mountain Boys; and it was with the utmost difficulty that I procured boats to cross the lake: However, I landed eighty three men near the garrison, and sent the boats back for the rear guard commanded by Col. Seth Warner; but the day began to dawn, and I found myself under a necessity to attack the fort, before the rear could cross the lake; and, as it was viewed hazardous, I harangued the officers and soldiers, in the manner following; "Friends and fellow soldiers, you have, for a number of years past, been a scourge and terror to arbitrary power. Your valour has been famed abroad, and acknowledged, as appears by the advice and orders to me (from the General Assembly of Connecticut) to surprize and take the garrison now before us. I now propose to advance before you, and in per-

son conduct you through the wicket-gate; for we must this morning either quit our pretensions to valour or possess ourselves of
this fortress in a few minutes; and, in as much as it is a desperate
attempt, (which none but the bravest of men dare undertake) I do
not urge it on any contrary to his will. You that will undertake
voluntarily, poise your firelocks."

The men being (at this time) drawn up in three ranks, each
poised his firelock. I ordered them to face to the right; and, at the
head of the center-file, marched them immediately to the wicket-
gate aforesaid, where I found a centry posted, who instantly
snapped his fusee at me: I run immediately toward him, and he
retreated through the covered way into the parade within the garrison, gave a halloo, and ran under a bomb-proof. My party who
followed me into the fort, I formed on the parade in such a manner as to face the two barracks which faced each other. The garrison being asleep, (except the centries) we gave three huzzas which
greatly surprized them. One of the centries made a pass at one of
my officers with a charged bayonet, and slightly wounded him:
My first thought was to kill him with my sword; but in an instant,
altered the design and fury of the blow, to a slight cut on the side
of the head; upon which he dropped his gun, and asked quarter,
which I readily granted him; and demanded of him the place
where the commanding officer kept; he shewed me a pair of stairs
in the front of a barrack, on the west part of the garrison, which
led up to a second story in said barrack, to which I immediately
repaired, and ordered the commander (Capt Delaplace) to come
forth instantly, or I would sacrifice the whole garrison; at which
the Capt came immediately to the door with his breeches in his
hand, when I ordered him to deliver to me the fort instantly, who
asked me by what authority I demanded it: I answered him, "In
the name of the great Jehovah, and the Continental Congress."
(The authority of the Congress being very little known at that time)
he began to speak again; but I interrupted him, and with my
drawn sword over his head, again demanded an immediate surrender of the garrison; to which he then complied, and ordered
his men to be forthwith paraded without arms, as he had given up

the garrison: In the mean time some of my officers had given orders, and in consequence thereof, sundry of the barrack doors were beat down, and about one third of the garrison imprisoned, which consisted of the said commander, a Lieut. Feltham, a conducter of artillery, a gunner, two serjeants, and forty four rank and file; about one hundred pieces of cannon, one 13 inch mortar, and a number of swivels. This surprize was carried into execution in the gray of the morning on the 10th day of May, 1775. The sun seemed to rise that morning with a superior lustre; and Ticonderoga and its dependencies smiled on its conquerors, who tossed about the flowing bowl, and wished success to Congress, and the liberty and freedom of America.

From LETTER OF LAFAYETTE TO WASHINGTON

"Paris, March 17th, 1790.

"Our revolution is getting on as well as it can with a nation that has attained its liberty at once, and is still liable to mistake licentiousness for freedom. The Assembly have more hatred to the ancient system, than experience in the proper organization of a new and constitutional government. The ministers are lamenting their loss of power, and afraid to use that, which they have; and, as every thing has been destroyed, and not much of the new building is yet above ground, there is room for criticisms and calumnies. To this it may be added, that we still are pestered by two parties, the aristocratic, that is panting for a counter revolution, and the factious, which aims at the division of the empire and destruction of all authority, and perhaps of the lives of the reigning branch; both of which parties are fomenting troubles.

"After I have confessed all this, I will tell you with the same candor, that we have made an admirable and almost incredible destruction of all abuses and prejudices; that every thing not directly useful to, or coming from, the people has been levelled; that, in the topographical, moral, and political situation of France, we have made more changes in ten months, than the most saguine patriots could have imagined; that our internal troubles and anarchy are much exaggerated; and that, upon the whole, this revolution, in which nothing will be wanting but energy of government as it was in America, will implant liberty and make it flourish throughout the world; while we must wait for a convention in a few years to mend some defects, which are not now perceived by men just escaped from aristocracy and despotism.

"Give me leave, my dear General, to present you with a picture of the Bastille, just as it looked a few days after I had ordered its demolition, with the main key of the fortress of despotism. It is a tribute, which I owe as a son to my adopted father, as an aid-de-camp to my general, as a missionary of liberty to its patriarch."

TREATY OF PEACE WITH GREAT BRITAIN

September 3, 1783

The surrender of Cornwallis at Yorktown, October 19, 1781, brought an end to the British effort to subdue the American colonies. February 27, 1782, a motion urging King George to end the war passed the House of Commons; a month later Lord North resigned, and the Rockingham Ministry entered into negotiations for a definitive peace. Congress appointed John Adams, Benjamin Franklin, John Jay, Henry Laurens, and Thomas Jefferson to conduct the negotiations, but Jefferson did not leave America, and Laurens was released from prison too late to take part in the peace conferences. The chief burden of the negotiations fell upon Franklin, and the treaty is largely a tribute to his shrewdness, persistence, and sagacity. On the Treaty, see the scholarly account by J. B. Scott, in S. F. Bemis, ed. *American Secretaries of State*, Vol. I, chs. iv–v; A. C. McLaughlin, *Confederation and Constitution,* chs. i–ii; E. G. Petty, Lord Fitzmaurice, *Life of William, Earl of Shelburne,* Vol. III.

... ART. I.—His Britannic Majesty acknowledges the said United States, viz. New Hampshire, Massachusetts Bay, Rhode Island, and Providence Plantations, Connecticut, New York, New Jersey, Pennsylvania, Delaware, Maryland, Virginia, North Carolina, South Carolina, and Georgia, to be free, sovereign and independent States; that he treats with them as such, and for himself, his heirs and successors, relinquishes all claims to the Government, proprietary and territorial rights of the same, and every part thereof.

ART. II.—And that all disputes which might arise in future, on the subject of the boundaries of the said United States may be prevented, it is hereby agreed and declared, that the following are, and shall be their boundaries, viz.: From the northwest angle of Nova Scotia, viz.: that angle which is formed by a line drawn due north from the source of Saint Croix River to the Highlands; along the said Highlands which divide those rivers that empty themselves into the river St. Lawrence, from those which fall into the Atlantic Ocean, to the northwesternmost head of Connecticut River; thence down along the middle of that river, to the forty-fifth degree of north latitude; from thence, by a line due west on said latitude, until it strikes the river Iroquois or Cataraquy; thence along the middle of said river into Lake Ontario, through the middle of said lake until it strikes the communication by water between that lake and Lake Erie; thence along the middle of said communication into Lake Erie, through the middle of said lake until it arrives at the water communication between that lake and Lake Huron; thence along the middle of said water communication into the Lake Huron; thence through the middle of said lake to the water communication between that lake and Lake Superior; thence through Lake Superior northward of the Isles Royal and Phelipeaux, to the Long Lake; thence through the middle of said Long Lake, and the water communication between it and the Lake of the Woods, to the said Lake of the Woods; thence through the said lake to the most northwestern point thereof, and from thence on a due west course to the river Mississippi; thence by a line to be drawn along the middle of the said river Mississippi

until it shall intersect the northernmost part of the thirty-first
degree of north latitude. South, by a line to be drawn due east
from the determination of the line last mentioned, in the latitude
of thirty-one degrees north of the Equator, to the middle of the
river Appalachicola or Catahouche; thence along the middle
thereof to its junction with the Flint River; thence straight to the
head of St. Mary's River; and thence down along the middle of St.
Mary's River to the Atlantic Ocean. East, by a line to be drawn
along the middle of the river St. Croix, from its mouth in the Bay
of Fundy to its source, and from its source directly north to the
aforesaid Highlands, which divide the rivers that fall into the
Atlantic Ocean from those which fall into the river St. Lawrence;
comprehending all islands within twenty leagues of any part of
the shores of the United States, and lying between lines to be
drawn due east from the points where the aforesaid boundaries
between Nova Scotia on the one part, and East Florida on the
other, shall respectively touch the Bay of Fundy and the Atlantic
Ocean; excepting such islands as now are, or heretofore have been,
within the limits of the said province of Nova Scotia.

ART. III.—It is agreed that the people of the United States shall
continue to enjoy unmolested the right to take fish of every kind
on the Grand Bank, and on all the other banks of Newfoundland;
also in the Gulph of Saint Lawrence, and at all other places in the
sea where the inhabitants of both countries used at any time
heretofore to fish. And also that the inhabitants of the United
States shall have liberty to take fish of every kind on such part of
the coast of Newfoundland as British fishermen shall use (but
not to dry or cure the same on that island) and also on the coasts,
bays and creeks of all other of His Britannic Majesty's dominions
in America; and that the American fishermen shall have liberty to
dry and cure fish in any of the unsettled bays, harbours and creeks
of Nova Scotia, Magdalen Islands, and Labrador, so long as the
same shall remain unsettled; but so soon as the same or either of
them shall be settled, it shall not be lawful for the said fishermen
to dry or cure fish at such settlements, without a previous agree-

ment for that purpose with the inhabitants, proprietors or possessors of the ground.

Art. IV.—It is agreed that creditors on either side shall meet with no lawful impediment to the recovery of the full value in sterling money, of all *bona fide* debts heretofore contracted.

Art. V.—It is agreed that the Congress shall earnestly recommend it to the legislatures of the respective States, to provide for the restitution of all estates, rights and properties which have been confiscated, belonging to real British subjects, and also of the estates, rights and properties of persons resident in districts in the possession of His Majesty's arms, and who have not borne arms against the said United States. And that persons of any other description shall have free liberty to go to any part or parts of any of the thirteen United States, and therein to remain twelve months, unmolested in their endeavours to obtain the restitution of such of their estates, rights and properties as may have been confiscated; and that Congress shall also earnestly recommend to the several States a reconsideration and revision of all acts or laws regarding the premises, so as to render the said laws or acts perfectly consistent, not only with justice and equity, but with that spirit of conciliation which, on the return of the blessings of peace, should universally prevail. And that Congress shall also earnestly recommend to the several States, that the estates, rights and properties of such last mentioned persons, shall be restored to them, they refunding to any persons who may be now in possession, the *bona fide* price (where any has been given) which such persons may have paid on purchasing any of the said lands, rights or properties, since the confiscation. And it is agreed, that all persons who have any interest in confiscated lands, either by debts, marriage settlements or otherwise, shall meet with no lawful impediment in the prosecution of their just rights.

Art. VI.—That there shall be no future confiscations made, nor any prosecutions commenced against any person or persons for, or by reason of the part which he or they may have taken in the present war; and that no person shall, on that account, suffer any future loss or damage, either in his person, liberty or property;

and that those who may be in confinement on such charges, at the time of the ratification of the treaty in America, shall be immediately set at liberty, and the prosecutions so commenced be discontinued.

ART. VII.—There shall be a firm and perpetual peace between His Britannic Majesty and the said States, and between the subjects of the one and the citizens of the other, wherefore all hostilities, both by sea and land, shall from henceforth cease; All prisoners on both sides shall be set at liberty, and His Britannic Majesty shall, with all convenient speed, and without causing any destruction, or carrying away any negroes or other property of the American inhabitants, withdraw all his armies, garrisons and fleets from the said United States, and from every post, place and harbour within the same; leaving in all fortifications the American artillery that may be therein; And shall also order and cause all archives, records, deeds and papers, belonging to any of the said States, or their citizens, which, in the course of the war, may have fallen into the hands of his officers, to be forthwith restored and deliver'd to the proper States and persons to whom they belong.

ART. VIII.—The navigation of the river Mississippi, from its source to the ocean, shall forever remain free and open to the subjects of Great Britain, and the citizens of the United States.

ART. IX.—In case it should so happen that any place or territory belonging to Great Britain or to the United States, should have been conquer'd by the arms of either from the other, before the arrival of the said provisional articles in America, it is agreed, that the same shall be restored without difficulty, and without requiring any compensation. . . .

GENERAL WASHINGTON'S RESIGNATION

December 23, 1783

MR. PRESIDENT,—The great events on which my resignation depended having at length taken place, I have now the honor of offering my sincere congratulations to Congress, and of presenting myself before them to surrender into their hands the trust committed to me, and to claim the indulgence of retiring from the service of my country.

Happy in the confirmation of our independence and sovereignty, and pleased with the opportunity afforded the United States of becoming a respectable nation, I resign with satisfaction the appointment I accepted with diffidence,—a diffidence in my abilities to accomplish so arduous a task, which, however, was superseded by a confidence in the rectitude of our cause, the support of the supreme power of the Union, and the patronage of Heaven.

The successful termination of the war has verified the most sanguine expectations; and my gratitude for the interposition of Providence, and the assistance I have received from my countrymen, increases with every review of the momentous contest. While I repeat my obligations to the Army in general, I should do injustice to my own feelings not to acknowledge, in this place, the peculiar services and distinguished merits of the gentlemen who have been attached to my person during the war. It was impossible the choice of confidential officers to compose my family should have been more fortunate. Permit me, Sir, to recommend in particular those who have continued in the service to the present moment, as worthy of the favorable notice and patronage of Congress.

I consider it an indispensable duty to close this last solemn act of my official life by commending the interests of our beloved country to the protection of Almighty God; and those who have the superintendence of them, to His holy keeping.

Having now finished the work assigned me, I retire from the great theatre of action; and, bidding an affectionate farewell to this august body, under whose orders I have so long acted, I here offer my commission, and take my leave of all the employments of public life.

G. WASHINGTON

POST–REVOLUTION TO 1815

ENGLAND AND AMERICA IN 1782

O THOU, that sendest out the man
   To rule by land and sea,
Strong mother of a Lion-line,
Be proud of those strong sons of thine
   Who wrench'd their rights from thee!

What wonder if in noble heat
   Those men thine arms withstood,
Retaught the lesson thou had'st taught,
And in thy spirit with thee fought,—
   Who sprang from English blood!

But thou rejoice with liberal joy,
   Lift up thy rocky face,
And shatter, when the storms are black,
In many a streaming torrent back,
   The seas that shock thy base!

Whatever harmonies of law
   The growing world assume,
Thy work is thine—the single note
From that deep chord which Hampden smote
   Will vibrate to the doom.

ALFRED TENNYSON

AMERICA TO GREAT BRITAIN

ALL hail! thou noble land,
   Our Fathers' native soil!
Oh, stretch thy mighty hand,
   Gigantic grown by toil,
O'er the vast Atlantic wave to our shore!
   For thou with magic might
   Canst reach to where the light
   Of Phœbus travels bright
     The world o'er!

The Genius of our clime,
   From his pine-embattled steep,
Shall hail the guest sublime;
   While the Tritons of the deep
With their conchs the kindred league shall proclaim.
   Then let the world combine—
   O'er the main our naval line
   Like the milky-way shall shine
     Bright in fame!

Though ages long have past
   Since our Fathers left their home,
The pilot in the blast,
   O'er untraveled seas to roam,
Yet lives the blood of England in our veins!
   And shall we not proclaim
   That blood of honest fame
   Which no tyranny can tame
     By its chains?

While the language free and bold
   Which the bard of Avon sung,
In which our Milton told
   How the vault of heaven rung

When Satan, blasted, fell with his host;—
  While this, with reverence meet,
  Ten thousand echoes greet,
  From rock to rock repeat
    Round our coast;—

While the manners, while the arts,
  That mould a nation's soul,
Still cling around our hearts,—
  Between let Ocean roll,
Our joint communion breaking with the Sun:
  Yet still from either beach
  The voice of blood shall reach,
  More audible than speech,
    "We are One."
                            WASHINGTON ALLSTON

BRITONS AND GUESTS

WE FOUGHT you once—but that was long ago!
  We fought you once, O Briton hearts of oak;
  Away from you—from parent stock—we broke.
Be glad we did! Because from every blow
We hurled in that old day a force did grow
  That now shall stead you, level stroke by stroke—
  So Heaven help us, who but late awoke,
The charge upon our common race to know!

And we will stand with you, the world to save—
  To make it safe for Freedom (as we free have been).
Have you not seen our mutual banners wave
As one upon the wind—a sight most brave! . . .
  We once did fight you—ev'n as next of kin
  May cleave apart, at end to closer win!
                            EDITH M. THOMAS

THE FLAG OF THE CONSTELLATION

THE stars of the morn
  On our banner borne,
With the Iris of Heaven are blended;
  The hand of our sires,
  First mingled those fires,
And by us they shall be defended.
  Then hail the true
  Red, White and Blue,
The flag of the Constellation;
  It sails as it sailed,
  By our forefathers hailed,
O'er battles that made us a nation.

What hand so bold
  As strike from its fold
One star or one stripe of its bright'ning,
  For him be those stars
  Each a fiery Mars,
And each stripe be as terrible lightning.
  Then hail the true
  Red, White and Blue,
The flag of the Constellation;
  It sails as it sailed,
  By our forefathers hailed,
O'er battles that made us a nation.

Its meteor form
  Shall ride the storm
Till the fiercest of foes surrender;
  The storm gone by,
  It shall gild the sky,

A rainbow of peace and of splendor.
    Then hail the true
    Red, White and Blue,
The flag of the Constellation;
    It sails as it sailed,
    By our forefathers hailed,
O'er battles that made us a nation.

    Peace, peace to the world,
    Is our motto unfurled,
Though we shun not the field that is gory;
    At home or abroad,
    Fearing none but our God,
We will carve our own pathway to glory.
    Then hail the true
    Red, White and Blue,
The flag of the Constellation;
    It sails as it sailed,
    By our forefathers hailed,
O'er battles that made us a nation.

THOMAS BUCHANAN READ

HOW WE BURNED THE PHILADELPHIA

By the beard of the Prophet the Bashaw swore
  He would scourge us from the seas;
Yankees should trouble his soul no more—
By the Prophet's beard the Bashaw swore,
  Then lighted his hookah, and took his ease,
And troubled his soul no more.

The moon was dim in the western sky,
  And a mist fell soft on the sea,
As we slipped away from the Siren brig
  And headed for Tripoli.

Behind us the hulk of the Siren lay,
    Before us the empty night;
And when again we looked behind
    The Siren was gone from our sight.

Nothing behind us, and nothing before,
    Only the silence and rain,
As the jaws of the sea took hold of our bows
    And cast us up again.

Through the rain and the silence we stole along,
    Cautious and stealthy and slow,
For we knew the waters were full of those
    Who might challenge the Mastico.

But nothing we saw till we saw the ghost
    Of the ship we had come to see,
Her ghostly lights and her ghostly frame
    Rolling uneasily.

And as we looked, the mist drew up
    And the moon threw off her veil,
And we saw the ship in the pale moonlight,
    Ghostly and drear and pale.

Then spoke Decatur low and said:
    "To the bulwarks' shadow all!
But the six who wear the Tripoli dress
    Shall answer the sentinel's call."

"What ship is that?" cried the sentinel.
    "No ship," was the answer free;
"But only a Malta ketch in distress
    Wanting to moor in your lee.

"We have lost our anchor, and wait for day
    To sail into Tripoli town.
And the sea rolls fierce and high to-night,
    So cast a cable down."

Then close to the frigate's side we came,
    Made fast to her unforbid—
Six of us bold in the heathen dress,
    The rest of us lying hid.

But one who saw us hiding there
    "Americano!" cried.
Then straight we rose and made a rush
    Pellmell up the frigate's side.

Less than a hundred men were we,
    And the heathen were twenty score;
But a Yankee sailor in those old days
    Liked odds of one to four.

And first we cleaned the quarter-deck,
    And then from stern to stem
We charged into our enemies
    And quickly slaughtered them.

All around was the dreadful sound
    Of corpses striking the sea,
And the awful shrieks of dying men
    In their last agony.

The heathen fought like devils all,
    But one by one they fell,
Swept from the deck by our cutlasses
    To the water, and so to hell.

Some we found in the black of the hold,
    Some to the fo'c'sle fled,
But all in vain; we sought them out
    And left them lying dead;

Till at last no soul but Christian souls
    Upon that ship was found;
The twenty score were dead, and we,
    The hundred, safe and sound.

And, stumbling over the tangled dead,
    The deck a crimson tide,
We fired the ship from keel to shrouds
    And tumbled over the side.

Then out to sea we sailed once more
    With the world as light as day,
And the flames revealed a hundred sail
    Of the heathen there in the bay.

All suddenly the red light paled,
    And the rain rang out on the sea;
Then—a dazzling flash, a deafening roar,
    Between us and Tripoli!

Then, nothing behind us, and nothing before,
    Only the silence and rain;
And the jaws of the sea took hold of our bows
    And cast us up again.

By the beard of the Prophet the Bashaw swore
    He would scourge us from the seas;
Yankees should trouble his soul no more—
By the Prophet's beard the Bashaw swore,
    Then lighted his hookah and took his ease,
And troubled his soul no more.

                        BARRETT EASTMAN

OLD IRONSIDES

Written with reference to the proposed breaking up
of the famous U. S. frigate *Constitution*.

AY, TEAR her tattered ensign down!
  Long has it waved on high,
And many an eye has danced to see
  That banner in the sky;
Beneath it rung the battle-shout,
  And burst the cannon's roar:
The meteor of the ocean air
  Shall sweep the clouds no more!

Her deck, once red with heroes' blood,
  Where knelt the vanquished foe,
When winds were hurrying o'er the flood
  And waves were white below,
No more shall feel the victor's tread,
  Or know the conquered knee:
The harpies of the shore shall pluck
  The eagle of the sea!

O better that her shattered hulk
  Should sink beneath the wave!
Her thunders shook the mighty deep,
  And there should be her grave:
Nail to the mast her holy flag,
  Set every threadbare sail,
And give her to the god of storms,
  The lightning and the gale!

                    OLIVER WENDELL HOLMES

PERRY'S VICTORY ON LAKE ERIE

BRIGHT was the morn,—the waveless bay
Shone like a mirror to the sun;
'Mid greenwood shades and meadows gay,
The matin birds their lays begun:
While swelling o'er the gloomy wood
Was heard the faintly-echoed roar,—
The dashing of the foamy flood,
That beat on Erie's distant shore.

The tawny wanderer of the wild
Paddled his painted birch canoe,
And, where the wave serenely smiled,
Swift as the darting falcon, flew;
He rowed along that peaceful bay,
And glanced its polished surface o'er,
Listening the billow far away,
That rolled on Erie's lonely shore.

What sounds awake my slumbering ear?
What echoes o'er the waters come?
It is the morning gun I hear,
The rolling of the distant drum.
Far o'er the bright illumined wave
I mark the flash,—I hear the roar,
That calls from sleep the slumbering brave,
To fight on Erie's lonely shore.

See how the starry banner floats,
And sparkles in the morning ray:
While sweetly swell the fife's gay notes
In echoes o'er the gleaming bay:
Flash follows flash, as through yon fleet

Columbia's cannons loudly roar,
And valiant tars the battle greet,
That storms on Erie's echoing shore.

O, who can tell what deeds were done,
When Britain's cross, on yonder wave,
Sunk 'neath Columbia's dazzling sun,
And met in Erie's flood its grave?
Who tell the triumphs of that day,
When, smiling at the cannon's roar,
Our hero, 'mid the bloody fray,
Conquered on Erie's echoing shore?

Though many a wounded bosom bleeds
For sire, for son, for lover dear,
Yet Sorrow smiles amid her weeds,—
Affliction dries her tender tear;
Oh! she exclaims, with glowing pride,
With ardent thoughts that wildly soar,
My sire, my son, my lover died,
Conquering on Erie's bloody shore!

Long shall my country bless that day,
When soared our Eagle to the skies;
Long, long in triumph's bright array,
That victory shall proudly rise:
And when our country's lights are gone,
And all its proudest days are o'er,
How will her fading courage dawn,
To think on Erie's bloody shore!

———————

By THE spirits of the dead,
Who sunk to death in Erie's wave,—
By the hearts that nobly bled,—
By the free, unconquered brave,—

We will draw the freeman's sword,
When the Briton threats our shore;
Mingle freedom's battle-word
Proudly with the cannon's roar.

We have faced, will face again,
Death and slaughter;—shall we fly?
Shall we leave the tented plain,—
Leave it, when the foe is nigh?

Come, invader! here we stand,
On the border of the wave;
Ere thou touch our native land,
Thou shalt lay us in the grave.

Here we stand, and here we die;
Bring thy ships, thy rockets bring;
Here our nation's flag shall fly,
Here shall wave our Eagle's wing.

Range in battle-line thy fleet,—
Ravage—burn—destroy; but know,
Though we perish, thou shalt meet—
Meet in every form a foe.

Sons of freedom! seize the gun,
Level well the marksman's eye,
Tell them how the deed is done,
Tell how sure our bullets fly.

Draw a sword, the brave may wield,
Draw it, when the Britons come,
"Hurry, hurry to the field,"
With the fife and rolling drum.

Point thy cannons on the foe,
Bid their lightnings flash afar,

Far and wide his thousands strow
With thy thunder-bolts of war.

Mingle boldly in the fray,
Shrink not at the sight of blood,
Think how, on his fatal day,
Firm, undaunted, Lawrence stood.

See! his spirit strides the wave,
Calls you where he nobly fell,—
Victory's summons to the brave,
To the foe his funeral knell.

By that soul of ardent flame,
By that soul that could not yield,
Hurry to the field of fame,—
Hurry to the battle-field.

JAMES GATES PERCIVAL

THE BLUE HEN'S CHICKENS

Commodore Thomas Macdonough, victor in the
Battle of Lake Champlain, September, 1814, hailed
from Delaware, whose best fighting men were known
from Revolutionary days as "The Blue Hen's
Chickens."

SOU'-SOU'EAST of the Woods of Penn
Lies the Nest of the Old Blue Hen—
The garden spot beyond compare
Known as the State of Delaware.
Dutchman, Yankee, Finn, and Swede
Filled the land with a stalwart breed,
Cleared the forest, sowed the maize,
Back in the old Colonial days;

Then, in "the times that tried men's souls,"
Put their names on the muster-rolls
And marched away with courage stout
To drive King George's Redcoats out.

North with the Delaware Regiment
Captain Jonathan Caldwell went,
Taking along to amuse his men,
Sundry chicks of an Old Blue Hen.—
Yes, they had their minor crimes;
Men "fought cocks" in those wicked times,
And the best-plucked birds from the Gulf to Maine
Were the fighting cocks of the Old Blue strain;
And like those birds, the books declare,
Were the men who marched from the Delaware;
For fight they could, and fight like the dickens,—
So the Army called them, "The Blue Hen's Chickens!"

    *   *   *   *   *   *   *

Once again was the land at grips
With mad King George's troops and ships:
Macdonough sailed on Lake Champlain—
A fighting cock of the Old Blue strain.
His fleet, new-built of lakeside pine
And oak, he ranged in battle line
Where Plattsburg's headland rears its crag;
The *Saratoga* bore his flag.
The foe came down; the fight was hot;
Port and starboard crashed the shot;
Heavy broadsides, stroke on stroke,
Battered the Flagship's walls of oak,—

When,—a bolt from a British sloop
Broke the bars of the chicken coop!
Forth upon the blood-stained deck
Strutted a Bird with arching neck.

Up he flew to the splintering spars
Under the Flag of Fifteen Stars
And crowed and crowed and crowed again,
For *he* was a Cock of the Old Blue Hen!
And the grimy sailors down below
Laughed and cheered to hear him crow,
And kept the rapid guns aflame
Till down the British ensign came!

*   *   *   *   *   *   *

Bravely flung to the autumn breeze
Floats the Flag on the lakes and seas
From bending masts and dipping spars,
And two score-eight are its Clustered Stars.
Two score-eight, in their silver sheen,
Cluster the Stars that were once Thirteen;
And there's Peace in the East, Peace in the West,
From the Golden Gate to the Blue Hen's Nest
There is Peace. And the Peace that ye hold so dear
Was won by men who laughed at Fear;
So may we have, in time of need,
More Fighting Cocks of the Blue Hen's breed!

                                        ARTHUR GUITERMAN

WHAT IS AN AMERICAN?

By
J. HECTOR ST. JOHN DE CRÈVECŒUR

WHAT ATTACHMENT can a poor European emigrant have for a
country where he had nothing? The knowledge of the language,
the love of a few kindred as poor as himself, were the only cords
that tied him. His country is now that which gives him his land,
bread, protection, and consequence. . . . What then is the American, this new man? He is neither a European nor the descendant

of a European; hence that strange mixture of blood which you will find in no other country. I could point out to you a family whose grandfather was an Englishman, whose wife was Dutch, whose son married a French woman, and whose present four sons have now four wives of different nations. He is an American who, leaving behind him all his ancient prejudices and manners, receives new ones from the new mode of life he has embraced, the new government he obeys, and the new rank he holds. He becomes an American by being received in the broad lap of our great *alma mater*. Here individuals of all nations are melted into a new race of men whose labors and posterity will one day cause great changes in the world. Americans are the western pilgrims, who are carrying along with them the great mass of arts, sciences, vigor, and industry which began long since in the East. They will finish the great circle. The Americans were once scattered all over Europe. Here they are incorporated into one of the finest systems of population which has ever appeared and which will hereafter become distinct by the power of the different climates they inhabit. The American ought therefore to love this country much better than that in which either he or his forefathers were born. Here the rewards of his industry follow with equal steps the progress of his labor. His labor is founded on the basis of nature, *self-interest:* can it want a stronger allurement? Wives and children, who before in vain demanded of him a morsel of bread, now, fat and frolicsome, gladly help their father to clear those fields whence exuberant crops are to rise, to feed and to clothe them all, without any part being claimed either by a despotic prince, a rich abbot, or a mighty lord. Here religion demands but little of him—a small voluntary salary to the minister, and gratitude to God—can he refuse these? The American is a new man who acts on new principles; he must therefore entertain new ideas and form new opinions. From involuntary idleness, servile dependence, penury, and useless labor, he has passed to toils of a very different nature, rewarded by ample subsistence.

This is an American.

CRÈVECŒUR, *Letters from an American Farmer, 1782*

From WASHINGTON'S FAREWELL ADDRESS

September 17, 1796

AGAINST the insidious wiles of foreign influence (I conjure you to believe me, fellow-citizens) the jealousy of a free people ought to be *constantly* awake, since history and experience prove that foreign influence is one of the most baneful foes of republican government. But that jealousy, to be useful, must be impartial, else it becomes the instrument of the very influence to be avoided, instead of a defense against it. Excessive partiality for one foreign nation and excessive dislike of another cause those whom they actuate to see danger only on one side, and serve to veil and even second the arts of influence on the other. Real patriots who may resist the intrigues of the favorite are liable to become suspected and odious, while its tools and dupes usurp the applause and confidence of the people to surrender their interests.

The great rule of conduct for us in regard to foreign nations is, in extending our commercial relations to have with them as little *political* connection as possible. So far as we have already formed engagements let them be fulfilled with perfect good faith. Here let us stop.

Europe has a set of primary interests which to us have none or a very remote relation. Hence she must be engaged in frequent controversies, the causes of which are essentially foreign to our concerns. Hence, therefore, it must be unwise in us to implicate ourselves by artificial ties in the ordinary vicissitudes of her politics or the ordinary combinations and collisions of her friendships or enmities.

Our detached and distant situation invites and enables us to pursue a different course. If we remain one people, under an efficient government, the period is not far off when we may defy material injury from external annoyance; when we may take such an attitude as will cause the neutrality we may at any time resolve upon to be scrupulously respected; when belligerent nations, under the impossibility of making acquisitions upon us, will not lightly hazard the giving us provocation; when we may choose peace or war, as our interest, guided by justice, shall counsel.

Why forego the advantages of so peculiar a situation? Why quit our own to stand upon foreign ground? Why, by interweaving our destiny with that of any part of Europe, entangle our peace and prosperity in the toils of European ambition, rivalship, interest, humor, or caprice?

It is our true policy to steer clear of permanent alliances with any portion of the foreign world, so far, I mean, as we are now at liberty to do it; for let me not be understood as capable of patronizing infidelity to existing engagements. I hold the maxim no less applicable to public than to private affairs that honesty is always the best policy. I repeat, therefore, let those engagements be observed in their genuine sense. But in my opinion it is unnecessary and would be unwise to extend them.

WELCOME OF THE HEBREW CONGREGATION, NEWPORT, RHODE ISLAND, U.S.A., TO GEORGE WASHINGTON

"SIR,

"Permit the Children of the Stock of Abraham to approach you with the most cordial affection and esteem for your person and merits, and to join with your fellow citizens in welcoming you to Newport.

"Deprived as we heretofore have been of the invaluable rights of free citizens, we now (with a deep sense of gratitude to the Almighty Disposer of all events) behold a Government erected by the Majesty of the people—a Government which to bigotry gives no sanction, to persecution no assistance, but generously affording to all, liberty of conscience, and immunities of citizenship, deeming every one, of whatever Nation, tongue, or language, equal parts of the great Government Machine. This so ample and extensive

Federal Union, whose basis is Philanthropy, Mutual Confidence, and Public Virtue, we cannot but acknowledge to be the work of the great God, Who ruleth in the Armies of Heaven, and among the inhabitants of the earth, doing whatever seemcth Him good.

"For all the blessings of civil and religious liberty which we enjoy under an equal and benign administration, we desire to send up our thanks to the Ancient of Days, the great Preserver of men, beseeching Him that the Angel who conducted our forefathers through the Wilderness into the Promised Land may graciously conduct you through all the difficulties and dangers of this mortal life. And when, like Joshua, full of days and full of honour, you are gathered to your Fathers, may you be admitted into the Heavenly Paradise to partake of the water of life and the tree of immortality.

"Done and signed by order of the Hebrew Congregation in Newport, Rhode Island, August 17th, 1790.

Moses Seixas"

NECESSITY OF UNION BETWEEN THE STATES

By
John Jay

It has often given me pleasure to observe that independent America was not composed of detached and distant territories, but that one connected, fertile, wide-spreading country was the portion of our western sons of liberty. Providence has, in a particular manner, blessed it with a variety of soils and productions, and watered it with innumerable streams for the delight and accommodation of its inhabitants. A succession of navigable waters forms a kind of chain round its borders, as if to bind it together; while the most noble rivers in the world, running at convenient distances, present them with highways for the easy communication of friendly aids, and the mutual transportation and exchange of their various commodities.

With equal pleasure I have as often taken notice, that Providence has been pleased to give this one connected country to one united people; a people descended from the same ancestors, speaking the same language, professing the same religion, attached to the same principles of government, very similar in their manners and customs; and who, by their joint counsels, arms and efforts, fighting side by side, through a long and bloody war, have nobly established their general liberty and independence.

This country and this people seem to have been made for each other; and it appears as if it were the design of Providence, that an inheritance so proper and convenient for a band of brethren united to each other by the strongest ties, should never be split into a number of unsocial, jealous and alien sovereignties.

RESOLUTIONS
ON THE DEATH OF GEORGE WASHINGTON
IN THE HOUSE OF REPRESENTATIVES

By
JOHN MARSHALL

THE DEEP and wide-spreading grief, occasioned by this melancholy event, assembled a great concourse of people, for the purpose of paying the last tribute of respect to the first of Americans. On Wednesday, the 18th of December, attended by military honours and the ceremonies of religion, his body was deposited in the family vault at Mount Vernon.

So short was his illness, that, at the seat of government, the intelligence of his death preceded that of his indisposition. It was first communicated by a passenger in the stage to an acquaintance whom he met in the street, and the report quickly reached the house of representatives, which was then in session. The utmost dismay and affliction were displayed for a few minutes, after which a member stated in his place the melancholy information which had been received. This information, he said, was not certain, but there was too much reason to believe it true.

"After receiving intelligence," he added, "of a national calamity so heavy and afflicting, the house of representatives can be but ill fitted for public business." He therefore moved an adjournment. Both houses adjourned until the next day.

On the succeeding day, as soon as the orders were read, the same member addressed the chair, and afterwards offered the following resolutions:

"Resolved, that this house will wait upon the president, in condolence of this mournful event.

"Resolved, that the speaker's chair be shrouded with black, and that the members and officers of the house wear black during the session.

"Resolved, that a committee, in conjunction with one from the senate, be appointed to consider on the most suitable manner of paying honour to the memory of the Man first in war, first in peace, and first in the hearts of his fellow-citizens."

THE FATHER OF HIS COUNTRY

By
HENRY LEE

A FUNERAL ORATION IN HONOR OF THE MEMORY OF
GEORGE WASHINGTON

FIRST in war—first in peace—and first in the hearts of his countrymen, he was second to none in the humble and endearing scenes of private life; pious, just, humane, temperate and sincere; uniform, dignified and commanding, his example was as edifying to all around him, as were the effects of that example lasting.

To his equals he was condescending, to his inferiors kind, and to the dear object of his affections exemplarily tender; correct throughout, vice shuddered in his presence, and virtue always felt his fostering hand; the purity of his private character gave effulgence to his public virtues.

His last scene comported with the whole tenor of his life—although in extreme pain, not a sigh, not a groan escaped him; and with undisturbed serenity he closed his well-spent life. Such was the man America has lost—such was the man for whom our nation mourns.

Methinks I see his august image, and I hear falling from his venerable lips these deep-sinking words:

"Cease, Sons of America, lamenting our separation: go on, and confirm by your wisdom the fruits of our joint councils, joint efforts, and common dangers; reverence religion, diffuse knowledge throughout your land, patronize the arts and sciences; let Liberty and Order be inseparable companions. Control party spirit, the bane of free governments; observe good faith to, and cultivate peace with all nations, shut up every avenue to foreign influence, contract rather than extend national connection, rely on yourselves only: be Americans in thought, word, and deed;—thus will you give immortality to that union which was the constant object of my terrestrial labors; thus will you preserve undisturbed to the latest posterity the felicity of a people to me most dear, and thus will you supply (if my happiness is now aught to you) the only vacancy in the round of pure bliss high Heaven bestows."

SOLILOQUY IN THE WHITE HOUSE

By
JOHN QUINCY ADAMS

Feb. 28, 1829. The month has been remarkable, as the last of my public service; and the preceding pages will show that the business of my office crowds upon me with accumulation as it draws near its end. Three days more and I shall be restored to private life and left to an old age of retirement, though certainly not of repose. I go into it with a combination of parties and of public men against my character and reputation such as I believe never before was exhibited against any man since this Union existed. Posterity will scarcely believe it, but so it is, that this combination against me has been formed, and is now exulting in triumph over me, for the devotion of my life and of all the faculties of my soul to the Union, and to the improvement, physical, moral, and intellectual of my country. The North assails me for my fidelity to the Union; the South, for my ardent aspirations of improvement. Yet "bate I not a jot of heart and hope." Passion, prejudice, envy, and jealousy will pass. The cause of Union and of improvement will remain, and I have duties to it and to my country yet to discharge.

SUPPOSED ANSWER TO TALLEYRAND

WAR be it, then; millions for defense, sir, but not one cent for tribute!

CHARLES COTESWORTH PINCKNEY

From THOMAS JEFFERSON'S
FIRST INAUGURAL ADDRESS

March 4, 1801

ABOUT TO ENTER, fellow-citizens, on the exercise of duties which comprehend everything dear and valuable to you, it is proper you should understand what I deem the essential principles of our Government, and consequently those which ought to shape its Administration. I will compress them within the narrowest compass they will bear, stating the general principle, but not all its limitations. Equal and exact justice to all men, of whatever state or persuasion, religious or political; peace, commerce, and honest friendship with all nations, entangling alliances with none; the support of the State governments in all their rights, as the most competent administrations for our domestic concerns and the surest bulwarks against antirepublican tendencies; the preservation of the General Government in its whole constitutional vigor, as the sheet anchor of our peace at home and safety abroad; a jealous care of the right of election by the people—a mild and safe corrective of abuses which are lopped by the sword of revolution where peaceable remedies are unprovided; absolute acquiescence in the decisions of the majority, the vital principle of republics, from which is no appeal but to force, the vital principle and immediate parent of despotism; a well-disciplined militia, our best reliance in peace and for the first moments of war, till regulars may relieve them; the supremacy of the civil over the military authority; economy in the public expense, that labor may be lightly burthened; the honest payment of our debts and sacred preservation of the public faith; encouragement of agriculture, and of commerce as its handmaid; the diffusion of information and arraignment of all abuses at the bar of the public reason; freedom of religion; freedom of the press, and freedom of person under the protection of the habeas corpus, and trial by juries impartially selected. These principles form the bright constellation which has gone before us and guided our steps through an age of revolution and reformation. The wisdom of our sages and blood of our heroes have been devoted to their attainment. They should be the creed of our political faith, the text of civic instruction, the touchstone by which to try the services of those we trust; and should we wander from them in moments of error or of alarm, let us hasten to retrace our steps and to regain the road which alone leads to peace, liberty, and safety.

TOAST TO CELEBRATE VICTORY
OVER BARBARY PIRATES

MY COUNTRY! In her intercourse with foreign nations, may she ever be right; but, right or wrong, my country!

STEPHEN DECATUR

DISPATCH TO GENERAL HARRISON
AFTER LAKE ERIE

WE HAVE MET the enemy and they are ours: two ships, two brigs, one schooner, and one sloop.

Yours, with great respect and esteem,

O. H. PERRY

1815–1860

TRIBUTE TO AMERICA

THERE is a people mighty in its youth,
   A land beyond the oceans of the west,
Where, though with rudest rites, Freedom and Truth
   Are worshipt. From a glorious mother's breast,
    Who, since high Athens fell, among the rest
Sate like the Queen of Nations, but in woe,
   By inbred monsters outraged and opprest,
Turns to her chainless child for succor now,
It draws the milk of Power in Wisdom's fullest flow.

That land is like an eagle, whose young gaze
   Feeds on the noontide beam, whose golden plume
Floats moveless on the storm, and on the blaze
   Of sunrise gleams when Earth is wrapt in gloom;
    An epitaph of glory for thy tomb
Of murdered Europe may thy fame be made,
   Great People! As the sands shalt thou become;
Thy growth is swift as morn when night must fade;
The multitudinous Earth shall sleep beneath thy shade.

Yes, in the desert, there is built a home
   For Freedom! Genius is made strong to rear
The monuments of man beneath the dome
   Of a new Heaven; myriads assemble there
    Whom the proud lords of man, in rage or fear,
Drive from their wasted homes. The boon I pray
   Is this—that Cythna shall be convoyed there,—
Nay, start not at the name—America!

PERCY BYSSHE SHELLEY

BOSTON HYMN

THE WORD of the Lord by night
  To the watching Pilgrims came,
As they sat by the seaside,
  And filled their hearts with flame.

God said, I am tired of kings,
  I suffer them no more;
Up to my ear the morning brings
  The outrage of the poor.

Think ye I made this ball
  A field of havoc and war,
Where tyrants great and tyrants small
  Might harry the weak and poor?

My angel—his name is Freedom—
  Choose him to be your king;
He shall cut pathways east and west,
  And fend you with his wing.

Lo! I uncover the land,
  Which I hid of old time in the West,
As the sculptor uncovers the statue
  When he has wrought his best;

I show Columbia, of the rocks
  Which dip their foot in the seas,
And soar to the air-borne flocks
  Of clouds and the boreal fleece.

I will divide my goods;
  Call in the wretch and slave;
None shall rule but the humble,
  And none but Toil shall have.

I will have never a noble.
  No lineage counted great;
Fishers and choppers and ploughmen
  Shall constitute a state.

Go, cut down trees in the forest
  And trim the straightest boughs;
Cut down trees in the forest
  And build me a wooden house.

Call the people together,
  The young men and the sires,
The digger in the harvest-field,
  Hireling and him that hires;

And here in a pine state-house
  They shall choose men to rule
In every needful faculty,
  In church and state and school.

Lo, now! if these poor men
  Can govern the land and sea,
And make just laws below the sun,
  As planets faithful be.

And ye shall succor men;
  'T is nobleness to serve;
Help them who cannot help again:
  Beware from right to swerve.

I break your bonds and masterships,
  And I unchain the slave:
Free be his heart and hand henceforth
  As wind and wandering wave.

I cause from every creature
  His proper good to flow;
As much as he is and doeth,
  So much he shall bestow.

But, laying hands on another,
   To coin his labor and sweat,
He goes in pawn to his victim
   For eternal years in debt.

To-day unbind the captive,
   So only are ye unbound;
Lift up a people from the dust,
   Trump of their rescue, sound!

Pay ransom to the owner
   And fill the bag to the brim.
Who is the owner? The slave is owner,
   And ever was. Pay him.

O North! give him beauty for rags,
   And honor, O South! for his shame;
Nevada! coin thy golden crags
   With Freedom's image and name.

Up! and the dusky race
   That sat in darkness long,—
Be swift their feet as antelopes,
   And as behemoth strong.

Come, East and West and North,
   By races, as snowflakes,
And carry my purpose forth,
   Which neither halts nor shakes.

My will fulfilled shall be,
   For, in daylight or in dark,
My thunderbolt has eyes to see
   His way home to the mark.
             RALPH WALDO EMERSON

ODE

Sung in the Town Hall, Concord

July 4, 1857

O TENDERLY the haughty day
  Fills his blue urn with fire;
One morn is in the mighty heaven,
  And one in our desire.

The cannon booms from town to town,
  Our pulses beat not less,
The joy-bells chime their tidings down,
  Which children's voices bless.

For He that flung the broad blue fold
  O'er-mantling land and sea,
One third part of the sky unrolled
  For the banner of the free.

The men are ripe of Saxon kind
  To build an equal state,—
To take the statute from the mind
  And make of duty fate.

United States! the ages plead,—
  Present and Past in under-song,—
Go put your creed into your deed,
  Nor speak with double tongue.

For sea and land don't understand
  Nor skies without a frown
See rights for which the one hand fights
  By the other cloven down.

Be just at home; then write your scroll
    Of honor o'er the sea,
And bid the broad Atlantic roll
    A ferry of the free.

And henceforth there shall be no chain,
    Save underneath the sea
The wires shall murmur through the main
    Sweet songs of liberty.

The conscious stars accord above,
    The waters wild below,
And under, through the cable wove,
    Her fiery errands go.

For He that worketh high and wise,
    Nor pauses in his plan,
Will take the sun out of the skies
    Ere freedom out of man.
                    RALPH WALDO EMERSON

HOW CYRUS LAID THE CABLE

COME, listen all unto my song;
    It is no silly fable;
'T is all about the mighty cord
    They call the Atlantic Cable.

Bold Cyrus Field he said, says he,
    "I have a pretty notion
That I can run a telegraph
    Across the Atlantic Ocean."

Then all the people laughed, and said
  They'd like to see him do it;
He might get half-seas over, but
  He never could go through it.

To carry out his foolish plan
  He never would be able;
He might as well go hang himself
  With his Atlantic Cable.

But Cyrus was a valiant man,
  A fellow of decision;
And heeded not their mocking words,
  Their laughter and derision.

Twice did his bravest efforts fail,
  And yet his mind was stable;
He wa'n't the man to break his heart
  Because he broke his cable.

"Once more, my gallant boys!" he cried;
  "Three times!—you know the fable
(I'll make it *thirty*," muttered he,
  "But I will lay the cable!").

Once more they tried,—hurrah! hurrah!
  What means this great commotion?
The Lord be praised! the cable's laid
  Across the Atlantic Ocean!

Loud ring the bells,—for, flashing through
  Six hundred leagues of water,
Old Mother England's benison
  Salutes her eldest daughter!

O'er all the land the tidings speed,
  And soon, in every nation,
They'll hear about the cable with
  Profoundest admiration!

Now, long live President and Queen;
  And long live gallant Cyrus;
And may his courage, faith, and zeal
  With emulation fire us;

And may we honor evermore
  The manly, bold, and stable;
And tell our sons, to make them brave,
  How Cyrus laid the cable!

JOHN GODFREY SAXE

OH! SUSANNA

I COME from Alabama
  Wid my banjo on my knee,
I'm g'wan to Lousiana,
  My true love for to see;
It rained all night and day I left,
  The weather it was dry,
The sun so hot I froze to death;
  Susanna, don't you cry.

Chorus

Oh! Susanna,
  Don't you cry for me,
I come from Alabama
  Wid my banjo on my knee.

I jumped aboard de telegraph
  And trabbeled down de ribber,
De lectric fluid magnified,
  And killed five hundred nigger;
De bullgine bust, de horse run off,
  I really thought I'd die;
I shut my eyes to hold my breath,
  Susanna, don't you cry.

Chorus
Oh! Susanna, *etc.*

I had a dream de udder night,
  When eberyting was still;
I thought I saw Susanna,
  A coming down de hill;
De buckwheat-cake was in her mouth,
  De tear was in her eye,
Says I, I'm coming from de South,
  Susanna, don't you cry.

Chorus
Oh! Susanna, *etc.*

Oh! when I gets to New Orleans
  I'll look all round and round,
And when I find Susanna
  I'll fall right on de ground;
But if I do not find her,
  Dis darkey'll surely die,
And when I'm dead and buried,
  Susanna, don't you cry.

Chorus
Oh! Susanna, *etc.*

STEPHEN FOSTER

DANIEL BOONE

DANIEL BOONE at twenty-one
Came with his tomahawk, knife and gun
Home from the French and Indian War
To North Carolina and the Yadkin shore.
He married his maid with a golden band,
Builded his house and cleared his land;
But the deep woods claimed their son again
And he turned his face from the homes of men.
Over the Blue Ridge, dark and lone,
The Mountains of Iron, the Hills of Stone,
Braving the Shawnee's jealous wrath,
He made his way on the Warrior's Path.
Alone he trod the shadowed trails;
But he was the lord of a thousand vales
As he roved Kentucky, far and near,
Hunting the buffalo, elk and deer.
What joy to see, what joy to win
So fair a land for his kith and kin,
Of streams unstained and woods unhewn!
"Elbowroom!" laughed Daniel Boone.

On the Wilderness Road that his axmen made
The settlers flocked to the first stockade;
The deerskin shirts and the coonskin caps
Filed through the glens and the mountain gaps;
And hearts were high in the fateful spring
When the land said "Nay!" to the stubborn king.
While the men of the East of farm and town
Strove with the troops of the British Crown,
Daniel Boone from a surge of hate
Guarded a nation's westward gate.

Down on the fort in a wave of flame
The Shawnee horde and the Mingo came,
And the stout logs shook in a storm of lead;
But Boone stood firm and the savage fled.
Peace! And the settlers flocked anew,
The farm lands spread, the town lands grew;
But Daniel Boone was ill at ease
When he saw the smoke in his forest trees.
"There'll be no game in the country soon.
Elbowroom!" cried Daniel Boone.

Straight as a pine at sixty-five—
Time enough for a man to thrive—
He launched his bateau on Ohio's breast
And his heart was glad as he oared it west;
There were kindly folk and his own true blood
Where great Missouri rolls his flood;
New woods, new streams and room to spare,
And Daniel Boone found comfort there.
Yet far he ranged toward the sunset still,
Where the Kansas runs and the Smoky Hill,
And the prairies toss, by the south wind blown;
And he killed his bear on the Yellowstone.
But ever he dreamed of new domains
With vaster woods and wider plains;
Ever he dreamed of a world-to-be
Where there are no bounds and the soul is free.
At four-score-five, still stout and hale,
He heard a call to a farther trail;
So he turned his face where the stars are strewn;
"Elbowroom!" sighed Daniel Boone.

Down the Milky Way in its banks of blue
Far he has paddled his white canoe
To the splendid quest of the tameless soul—
He has reached the goal where there is no goal.

Now he rides and rides an endless trail
On the Hippogriff of the flaming tail
Or the Horse of the Stars with the golden mane,
As he rode the first of the blue-grass strain.
The joy that lies in the Search he seeks
On breathless hills with crystal peaks;
He makes his camp on heights untrod,
The steps of the Shrine, alone with God.
Through the woods of the vast, on the plains of Space
He hunts the pride of the Mammoth race
And the Dinosaur of the triple horn,
The manticore and the Unicorn,
As once by the broad Missouri's flow
He followed the elk and the buffalo.
East of the Sun and west of the Moon,
"Elbowroom!" laughs Daniel Boone.

ARTHUR GUITERMAN

JIM BLUDSO

WALL, no! I can't tell whar he lives,
    Because he don't live, you see;
Leastways, he's got out of the habit
    Of livin' like you and me.
Whar have you been for the last three year
    That you haven't heard folks tell
How Jimmy Bludso passed in his checks
    The night of the Prairie Belle?

He weren't no saint,—them engineers
    Is all pretty much alike,—
One wife in Natchez-under-the-Hill
    And another one here, in Pike;

A keerless man in his talk, was Jim,
  And an awkward hand in a row,
But he never flunked, and he never lied,—
  I reckon he never knowed how.

And this was all the religion he had,—
  To treat his engine well;
Never be passed on the river;
  To mind the pilot's bell;
And if ever the Prairie Belle took fire,—
  A thousand times he swore
He'd hold her nozzle agin the bank
  Till the last soul got ashore.

All boats has their day on the Mississip,
  And her day come at last,—
The Movastar was a better boat,
  But the Belle she *wouldn't* be passed.
And so she come tearin' along that night—
  The oldest craft on the line—
With a nigger squat on her safety-valve,
  And her furnace crammed, rosin and pine.

The fire bust out as she clared the bar,
  And burnt a hole in the night,
And quick as a flash she turned, and made
  For that willer-bank on the right.
There was runnin' and cursin', but Jim yelled out,
  Over all the infernal roar,
"I'll hold her nozzle agin the bank
  Till the last galoot's ashore."

Through the hot, black breath of the burnin' boat
  Jim Bludso's voice was heard,
And they all had trust in his cussedness,
  And knowed he would keep his word.

And, sure's you're born, they all got off
  Afore the smoke-stacks fell,—
And Bludso's ghost went up alone
  In the smoke of the Prairie Belle.

He weren't no saint,—but at jedgment
  I'd run my chance with Jim,
'Longside of some pious gentlemen
  That wouldn't shook hands with him.
He seen his duty, a dead-sure thing,—
  And went for it thar and then;
And Christ ain't a going to be too hard
  On a man that died for men.

JOHN HAY

THE OREGON TRAIL

THE grizzled trapper of the log stockade,
Gaudy in buckskin sewn with beads and bells,
Hawk-eyed, his ears still echoing the yells
Of fierce Dakotas riding on their raid;
The coulee's murmur in the willows' shade;
The glaring prairie; Indian village smells;
Dust of the bison herd; the miracles
Of hardihood whereby the West was made;

Half fabulous from page on page they rise,
Traced by an ailing hand, with failing eyes,
Till, dark upon a clear and golden sky,
The heroic Ogallalah lifts his lance
And hurls, where war plumes in the distance dance,
His doomed and unintelligible cry.

WILLIAM ROSE BENÉT

OREGON TRAIL: 1851

Out they came from Liberty, out across the plains,
Two-stepping, single-footing, hard-boiled and easy-shooting,
Whips cracking; oaths snapping. . . .
                                Hear those banjos wail—
Emigratin' westward on the Oregon Trail.

.   .   .   .

Squishing thru the mudholes; drunken with the rain,
Turn your face to heaven, boy!—and punch those bulls again;
Onward to the sunset; Hallelujah! Sing!
Don't let nothing stop yuh! Not a consarned thing!
White sails of schooners, snapping in the wind,
Oregon ahead of us—t' hell with them behind!
Free land in Oregon!
                        Thru the prairie gale
Emigrating westward on the free land trail.

Hell blasted heathens, Rickarees and Sioux,
Aim across the wagon-wheel and drill the varmints thru.
Line 'em up, line 'em out, pray the tugs'll hold,
Wheels a-screeching glory thru the sunset's gold;
Keep y'r musket handy, trigger on the cock,
Peel y'r eyes, kid, if you'd see old Independence Rock!
Took our luck right in our hands; can't afford to fail—
Hittin' f'r the westward on the bone-strewed trail.

Milt's woman had a kid. Nary doctor nigh,
Milt thought he'd lose 'em; figured that they'd die;
God's mercy pulled 'em thru; Hallelujah, sing!
Put y'r faith in God, friends, and conquer everything!

Line them millin' leaders out, get the bulls a-going—
Got to get to Oregon!
                        West winds blowing
Bitter from the Stonies, looming blue ahead,
Wagons bogged in prairie mud, teams stuck fast,
Heave the tumbled baggage off, clean the wagon bed,
Sweat and curse and on again, freed at last,
On again and damn the rain, buck the wind and hail—
Emigratin' westward on the Oregon Trail.

.   .   .   .

Onward thru the mountains, lifting to the blue,
Up and thru the rock cuts, weaving to the pass;
Old Ezra stopped here, where his spirit flew,
Left his little gran'child, such a pretty lass;
Ben's agoin' to take her; that'll make him eight,—
God sure'll bless him for his kindly thought,
Hitch up and roll again. Hi, 's getting late
And this old defile ain't no place t'be caught;
No time for sorrowing, tear-eyed and pale—
Got to keep a-movin' on the Oregon Trail.

.   .   .   .

Can't see the wagon-tracks; trail's pinched out;
Nothing but the snow peaks and shale-rock slopes,
Outspan the bull-teams; we'll heave them wagons
Upside and over with the rawhide ropes—
God damn the mountains! God damn the snow-crusts!—
Pounding thru the chill wind, shirts sweat-black,
God! But I wisht I was back down in Liberty!
Pull, there, you quitter! for y'u can't turn back—
Top of the mountains now, keen in the starlight,
Sunup's a-comin' on the western sea,
Yellow beams of glory-glow, floodin' the snow peaks—
There lies Oregon! Glory to Thee!

Punch up the bull-teams, tune up the banjo,
Hallelujah! Praise God, kneeling in the snow,
Land of the dripping fir, land of the homestead,
Oregon! Oregon! Beckoning below—
All out from Liberty, out across the ranges,
Two-stepping, single-footing, hard-boiled and glory-singing,
Whips cracking, oaths snapping, bull-teams slogging on,
Babes a-borning, men a-dying, trail shouts ringing—
Here come the conquerors
                    (And there lie the frail)
Roaring to the sunset on the Oregon Trail!

JAMES MARSHALL

THE KANSAS EMIGRANTS

July, 1854

WE CROSS the prairie as of old
    The pilgrims crossed the sea,
To make the West, as they the East,
    The homestead of the free!

We go to rear a wall of men
    On Freedom's southern line,
And plant beside the cotton-tree
    The rugged Northern pine!

We're flowing from our native hills
    As our free rivers flow:
The blessing of our Mother-land
    Is on us as we go.

We go to plant her common schools
    On distant prairie swells,
And give the Sabbaths of the wild
    The music of her bells.

Upbearing, like the Ark of old,
    The Bible in our van,
We go to test the truth of God
    Against the fraud of man.

No pause, nor rest, save where the streams
    That feed the Kansas run,
Save where our Pilgrim gonfalon
    Shall flout the setting sun!

We'll tread the prairie as of old
    Our fathers sailed the sea,
And make the West, as they the East,
    The homestead of the free!
                    JOHN GREENLEAF WHITTIER

THE FOUNDERS OF OHIO

THE footsteps of a hundred years
    Have echoed, since o'er Braddock's Road
Bold Putnam and the Pioneers
    Led History the way they strode.

On wild Monongahela stream
    They launched the Mayflower of the West,
A perfect State their civic dream,
    A New World their pilgrim quest.

When April robed the Buckeye trees
    Muskingum's bosky shore they trod;
They pitched their tents, and to the breeze
    Flung freedom's star-flag, thanking God.

As glides the Oyo's solemn flood,
  So fleeted their eventful years;
Resurgent in their children's blood,
  They still live on—the Pioneers.

Their fame shrinks not to names and dates
  On votive stone, the prey of time;—
Behold where monumental States
  Immortalize their lives sublime!
                    WILLIAM HENRY VENABLE

OUT WHERE THE WEST BEGINS

OUT WHERE the handclasp's a little stronger,
Out where the smile dwells a little longer,
  That's where the West begins;
Out where the sun is a little brighter,
Where the snows that fall are a trifle whiter,
Where the bonds of home are a wee bit tighter,—
  That's where the West begins.

Out where the skies are a trifle bluer,
Out where friendship's a little truer,
  That's where the West begins;
Out where a fresher breeze is blowing,
Where there's laughter in every streamlet flowing,
Where there's more of reaping and less of sowing,—
  That's where the West begins.

Out where the world is in the making,
Where fewer hearts in despair are aching,
  That's where the West begins;
Where there's more of singing and less of sighing,

We primeval forests felling,
We the rivers stemming, vexing we and piercing deep the mines
          within,
We the surface broad surveying, we the virgin soil upheaving,
          Pioneers! O pioneers!

Colorado men are we,
From the peaks gigantic, from the great sierras and the high pla-
          teaus,
From the mine and from the gully, from the hunting trail we come,
          Pioneers! O pioneers!

From Nebraska, from Arkansas,
Central inland race are we, from Missouri, with the continental
          blood intervein'd,
All the hands of comrades clasping, all the Southern, all the
          Northern,
          Pioneers! O pioneers!

O resistless restless race!
O beloved race in all! O my breast aches with tender love for all!
O I mourn and yet exult, I am rapt with love for all,
          Pioneers! O pioneers!

Raise the mighty mother mistress,
Waving high the delicate mistress, over all the starry mistress,
          (bend your heads all,)
Raise the fang'd and warlike mistress, stern, impassive, weapon'd
          mistress,
          Pioneers! O pioneers!

See my children, resolute children,
By those swarms upon our rear we must never yield or falter,
Ages back in ghostly millions frowning there behind us urging,
          Pioneers! O pioneers!

On and on the compact ranks,
With accessions ever waiting, with the places of the dead quickly
       fill'd,
Through the battle, through defeat, moving yet and never stop-
       ping,
        Pioneers! O pioneers!

O to die advancing on!
Are there some of us to droop and die? has the hour come?
Then upon the march we fittest die, soon and sure the gap is fill'd,
        Pioneers! O pioneers!

All the pulses of the world,
Falling in they beat for us, with the Western movement beat,
Holding single or together, steady moving to the front, all for us,
        Pioneers! O pioneers!

Life's involv'd and varied pageants,
All the forms and shows, all the workmen at their work,
All the seamen and the landsmen, all the masters with their slaves,
        Pioneers! O pioneers!

All the hapless silent lovers,
All the prisoners in the prisons, all the righteous and the wicked,
All the joyous, all the sorrowing, all the living, all the dying,
        Pioneers! O pioneers!

I too with my soul and body,
We, a curious trio, picking, wandering on our way,
Through these shores amid the shadows, with the apparitions
       pressing,
        Pioneers! O pioneers!

Lo, the darting bowling orb!
Lo, the brother orbs around, all the clustering suns and planets,
All the dazzling days, all the mystic nights with dreams,
        Pioneers! O pioneers!

These are of us, they are with us,
All for primal needed work, while the followers there in embryo
      wait behind,
We to-day's procession heading, we the route for travel clearing,
      Pioneers! O pioneers!

O you daughters of the West!
O you young and elder daughters! O you mothers and you wives!
Never must you be divided, in our ranks you move united,
      Pioneers! O pioneers!

Minstrels latent on the prairies!
(Shrouded bards of other lands, you may rest, you have done your
      work,)
Soon I hear you coming warbling, soon you rise and tramp amid
      us,
      Pioneers! O pioneers!

Not for delectations sweet,
Not the cushion and the slipper, not the peaceful and the studious,
Not the riches safe and palling, not for us the tame enjoyment,
      Pioneers! O pioneers!

Do the feasters gluttonous feast?
Do the corpulent sleepers sleep? have they lock'd and bolted
      doors?
Still be ours the diet hard, and the blanket on the ground,
      Pioneers! O pioneers!

Has the night descended?
Was the road of late so toilsome? did we stop discouraged nodding
      on our way?
Yet a passing hour I yield you in your tracks to pause oblivious,
      Pioneers! O pioneers!

Till with sound of trumpet,
Far, far off the daybreak call—hark! how loud and clear I hear it
      wind,
Swift! to the head of the army!—swift! spring to your places,
      Pioneers! O pioneers!

                    WALT WHITMAN

A CLEARY PIONEER

You talk of the deeds of the old pioneers
   and laud them to the skies,
But never a word of the woman
   or the grave wherein she lies
Who's asleep out here on the hillside,
   where people as they pass,
Oft catch a glimpse of the little grave
   half hidden in the grass,
That holds the first white woman
   who trod this golden land,
Who brighten'd the hopes of many
   by extending the helping hand,
Who went through all that you did—
   camp'd on the same old trail—
Mush'd in the lead in the wild stampede
   and laughed at the icy gale.

There's a picket-fence around her,
   but no sign of slab or stone,
To tell the name of the sleeper
   or explain why she's alone—
Alone out here on the hillside
   in a little fenc'd-off plot,
Slumbering on in silence,
   by everyone forgot,

With none to plant a flower
  or shed a single tear
As tribute to the grit and nerve
  of this Cleary pioneer,
Who went through all that you did—
  camp'd on the same old trail—
Mush'd in the lead in the wild stampede
  and laugh'd at the icy gale.

FRED CREWE

PRAIRIE BIRTH

I was born on the prairie:
  I know how a partridge rises
Like a bullet out of the grain fields.
  I have watched the coveys of quail
Running along the road
  In front of a loaded wagon
And the wagons hurrying to the barn
  Ahead of the rattling hail.

Here the valleys lift
  Toward pine-swept peaks above them;
I hold my peace when their dwellers
  Disparage the level sod.
Canyon and cliff are vast;
  My heart is glad that men love them.
But no less for me on the prairie
  Has rested the hand of God.

GRACE STONE COATES

THE STONE CROP

THOSE lean and salty sires of ours
   Who pinched their houses small
And made the big New England barns
   Sowed one crop best of all.

They pulled the stumps and sowed to oats;
   They picked stones from a field
As thick with stones as mince with meat
   And made the gravel yield.

But not in oat-fields, not in corn
   They sowed their richest seed,
But in the little barren lots
   Too hard for vim or greed.

They cut off hunks of their poor land
   Where the thistles choke
And hungry ledges bleach bone-white
   The shells the wise crows broke.

"These Devil's acres thick with thorns,
   With junipers and briars,
Will do to build the schoolhouse on,"
   Said our saving sires.

They ran against the Scripture truth
   And Sermon on the Mount,
They scattered seedlings of their loins
   On soil of no account.

And they lay down in graves to sleep
  And never had the glee
Of seeing such a crop spring up
  As spread from sea to sea.

They did not know that hungry soil
  Which tinged the asters blue
Could breed the blue and burning eyes
  That saw the grim game through.

Their little lads grew all to stone
  On granite wastes they manned
And got the grit to grow into
  The backbone of the land.

Ohio, Illinois, and on
  Across the prairies west,
Wastes and wilds could not choke down
  The seed that loved rock best.

                ROBERT P. TRISTRAM COFFIN

JOHNNY APPLESEED

A BALLAD OF THE OLD NORTHWEST

A MIDNIGHT cry appalls the gloom,
  The puncheon door is shaken:
"Awake! arouse! and flee the doom!
  Man, woman, child, awaken!

"Your sky shall glow with fiery beams
  Before the morn breaks ruddy!
The scalpknife in the moonlight gleams,
  Athirst for vengeance bloody!"

Alarumed by the dreadful word
  Some warning tongue thus utters,
The settler's wife, like mother bird,
  About her young ones flutters.

Her first-born, rustling from a soft
  Leaf-couch, the roof close under,
Glides down the ladder from the loft,
  With eyes of dreamy wonder.

The pioneer flings open wide
  The cabin door, naught fearing;
The grim woods drowse on every side,
  Around the lonely clearing.

"Come in! come in! nor like an owl
  Thus hoot your doleful humors;
What fiend possesses you to howl
  Such crazy, coward rumors?"

The herald strode into the room;
  That moment, through the ashes,
The back-log struggled into bloom
  Of gold and crimson flashes.

The glimmer lighted up a face,
  And o'er a figure dartled,
So eerie, of so solemn grace,
  The bluff backwoodsman startled.

The brow was gathered to a frown,
  The eyes were strangely glowing,
And, like a snow-fall drifting down,
  The stormy beard went flowing.

The tattered cloak that round him clung
  Had warred with foulest weather;
Across his shoulders broad were flung
  Brown saddlebags of leather.

One pouch with hoarded seed was packed,
  From Penn-land cider-presses;
The other garnered book and tract
  Within its creased recesses.

A glance disdainful and austere,
  Contemptuous of danger,
Cast he upon the pioneer,
  Then spake the uncouth stranger:

"Heed what the Lord's anointed saith;
  Hear one who would deliver
Your bodies and your souls from death;
  List ye to John the Giver.

"Thou trustful boy, in spirit wise
  Beyond thy father's measure,
Because of thy believing eyes
  I share with thee my treasure.

"Of precious seed this handful take;
  Take next this Bible Holy:
In good soil sow both gifts, for sake
  Of Him, the meek and lowly.

"Farewell! I go!—the forest calls
  My life to ceaseless labors;
Wherever danger's shadow falls
  I fly to save my neighbors.

"I save; I neither curse nor slay;
  I am a voice that crieth
In night and wilderness. Away!
  Whoever doubteth, dieth!"

The prophet vanished in the night,
  Like some fleet ghost belated:
Then, awe-struck, fled with panic fright
  The household, evil-fated.

They hurried on with stumbling feet,
  Foreboding ambuscado;
Bewildered hope told of retreat
  In frontier palisado.

But ere a mile of tangled maze
  Their bleeding hands had broken,
Their home-roof set the dark ablaze,
  Fulfilling doom forespoken.

The savage death-whoop rent the air!
  A howl of rage infernal!
The fugitives were in Thy care,
  Almighty Power eternal!

Unscathed by tomahawk or knife,
  In bosky dingle nested,
The hunted pioneer, with wife
  And babes, hid unmolested.

The lad, when age his locks of gold
  Had changed to silver glory,
Told grandchildren, as I have told,
  This western wildwood story.

Told how the fertile seeds had grown
  To famous trees, and thriven;
And oft the Sacred Book was shown,
  By that weird Pilgrim given.

Remember Johnny Appleseed,
  All ye who love the apple;
He served his kind by Word and Deed,
  In God's grand greenwood chapel.
                    WILLIAM HENRY VENABLE.

CROSSING THE PLAINS

WHAT great yoked brutes with briskets low,
With wrinkled necks like buffalo,
With round, brown, liquid, pleading eyes,
That turned so slow and sad to you,
That shone like love's eyes soft with tears,
That seemed to plead, and make replies,
The while they bowed their necks and drew
The creaking load; and looked at you.
Their sable briskets swept the ground,
Their cloven feet kept solemn sound.

Two sullen bullocks led the line,
Their great eyes shining bright like wine;
Two sullen captive kings were they,
That had in time held herds at bay,
And even now they crushed the sod
With stolid sense of majesty,
And stately stepped and stately trod,
As if 't were something still to be
Kings even in captivity.
                    JOAQUIN MILLER

THE REVENGE OF RAIN-IN-THE-FACE

In that desolate land and lone,
Where the Big Horn and Yellowstone
  Roar down their mountain path,
By their fires the Sioux Chiefs
Muttered their woes and griefs
  And the menace of their wrath.

"Revenge!" cried Rain-in-the-Face,
"Revenge upon all the race
  Of the White Chief with yellow hair!"
And the mountains dark and high
From their crags reëchoed the cry
  Of his anger and despair.

In the meadow, spreading wide
By woodland and river-side
  The Indian village stood;
All was silent as a dream,
Save the rushing of the stream
  And the blue-jay in the wood.

In his war paint and his beads,
Like a bison among the reeds,
  In ambush the Sitting Bull
Lay with three thousand braves
Crouched in the clefts and caves,
  Savage, unmerciful!

Into the fatal snare
The White Chief with yellow hair
  And his three hundred men

Dashed headlong, sword in hand;
But of that gallant band
   Not one returned again.

The sudden darkness of death
Overwhelmed them like the breath
   And smoke of a furnace fire:
By the river's bank, and between
The rocks of the ravine,
   They lay in their bloody attire.

But the foemen fled in the night,
And Rain-in-the-Face, in his flight,
   Uplifted high in air
As a ghastly trophy, bore
The brave heart, that beat no more,
   Of the White Chief with yellow hair.

Whose was the right and the wrong?
Sing it, O funeral song,
   With a voice that is full of tears,
And say that our broken faith
Wrought all this ruin and scathe,
   In the Year of a Hundred Years.
                HENRY WADSWORTH LONGFELLOW

THE DEFENCE OF THE ALAMO

March 6, 1835

SANTA ANA came storming, as a storm might come;
   There was rumble of cannon; there was rattle of blade;
There was cavalry, infantry, bugle and drum—
   Full seven thousand in pomp and parade.

The chivalry, flower of Mexico;
And a gaunt two hundred in the Alamo!

And thirty lay sick, and some were shot through;
   For the siege had been bitter, and bloody, and long.
"Surrender, or die!"—"Men, what will *you* do?"
   And Travis, great Travis, drew sword, quick and strong;
Drew a line at his feet. . . . "Will you come? Will you go?
I die with my wounded, in the Alamo."

The Bowie gasped, "Lead me over that line!"
   Then Crockett, one hand to the sick, one hand to his gun,
Crossed with him; then never a word or a sign
   Till all, sick or well, all, all save but one,
One man. Then a woman stepped, praying, and slow
Across; to die at her post in the Alamo.

Then that one coward fled, in the night, in that night
   When all men silently prayed and thought
Of home; of to-morrow; of God and the right,
   Till dawn; and with dawn came Travis's cannon-shot,
In answer to insolent Mexico,
From the old bell-tower of the Alamo.

Then came Santa Ana; a crescent of flame!
   Then the red escalade; then the fight hand to hand;
Such an unequal fight as never had name
   Since the Persian hordes butchered that doomed Spartan band.
All day—all day and all night; and the morning? so slow,
Through the battle smoke mantling the Alamo.

Now silence! Such silence! Two thousand lay dead
   In a crescent outside! And within? Not a breath
Save the gasp of a woman, with gory gashed head,
   All alone, all alone there, waiting for death;
And she but a nurse. Yet when shall we know
Another like this of the Alamo?

Shout "Victory, victory, victory ho!"
  I say 't is not always to the hosts that win!
I say that the victory, high or low,
  Is given the hero who grapples with sin,
Or legion or single; just asking to know
When duty fronts death in his Alamo.

                JOAQUIN MILLER

THE FIGHT AT SAN JACINTO

"Now for a brisk and cheerful fight!"
  Said Harman, big and droll,
As he coaxed his flint and steel for a light,
  And puffed at his cold clay bowl;
"For we are a skulking lot," says he,
  "Of land-thieves hereabout,
And the bold señores, two to one,
  Have come to smoke us out."

Santa Anna and Castrillon,
  Almonte brave and gay,
Portilla red from Goliad,
  And Cos with his smart array.
Dulces and cigaritos,
  And the light guitar, ting-tum!
Sant' Anna courts siesta—
  And Sam Houston taps his drum.

The buck stands still in the timber—
  "Is 't the patter of nuts that fall?"
The foal of the wild mare whinnies—
  "Did he hear the Comanche call?"
In the brake by the crawling bayou
  The slinking she-wolves howl,
And the mustang's snort in the river sedge
  Has startled the paddling fowl.

A soft low tap, and a muffled tap,
  And a roll not loud nor long—
We would not break Sant' Anna's nap,
  Nor spoil Almonte's song.
Saddles and knives and rifles!
  Lord! but the men were glad
When Deaf Smith muttered "Alamo!"
  And Karnes hissed "Goliad!"

The drummer tucked his sticks in his belt,
  And the fifer gripped his gun.
Oh, for one free, wild Texan yell,
  And we took the slope in a run!
But never a shout nor a shot we spent,
  Nor an oath nor a prayer that day,
Till we faced the bravos, eye to eye,
  And then we blazed away.

Then we knew the rapture of Ben Milam,
  And the glory that Travis made,
With Bowie's lunge and Crockett's shot,
  And Fannin's dancing blade;
And the heart of the fighter, bounding free
  In his joy so hot and mad—
When Millard charged for Alamo,
  Lamar for Goliad.

Deaf Smith rode straight, with reeking spur,
  Into the shock and rout:
"I've hacked and burned the bayou bridge,
  There's no sneak's back-way out!"
Muzzle or butt for Goliad,
  Pistol and blade and fist!
Oh, for the knife that never glanced,
  And the gun that never missed!

Dulces and cigaritos,
　　Song and the mandolin!
That gory swamp was a gruesome grove
　　To dance fandangos in.
We bridged the bog with the sprawling herd
　　That fell in that frantic rout;
We slew and slew till the sun set red,
　　And the Texan star flashed out.
　　　　　　　　　　JOHN WILLIAMSON PALMER

MONTEREY

WE WERE not many, we who stood
　　Before the iron sleet that day:
Yet many a gallant spirit would
Give half his years if but he could
　　Have been with us at Monterey.

Now here, now there, the shot is hail'd
　　In deadly drifts of fiery spray,
Yet not a single soldier quail'd
When wounded comrades round them wail'd
　　Their dying shout at Monterey.

And on—still on our column kept
　　Through walls of flame its withering way;
Where fell the dead, the living stept,
Still charging on the guns which swept
　　The slippery streets of Monterey.

The foe himself recoil'd aghast,
　　When, striking where he strongest lay,
We swoop'd his flanking batteries past,
And braving full their murderous blast,
　　Storm'd home the towers of Monterey.

Our banners on those turrets wave,
  And there our evening bugles play:
Where orange-boughs above their grave
Keep green the memory of the brave
  Who fought and fell at Monterey.

We are not many—we who press'd
  Beside the brave who fell that day—
But who of us has not confess'd
He'd rather share their warrior rest
  Than not have been at Monterey?

CHARLES FENNO HOFFMAN

THE WINNING OF THE WEST

By
THEODORE ROOSEVELT

BACKWOODS society was simple, and the duties and rights of each member of the family were plain and clear. The man was the armed protector and provider, the bread-winner; the woman was the housewife and child-bearer. They married young and their families were large, for they were strong and healthy, and their success in life depended on their own stout arms and willing hearts. There was everywhere great equality of conditions. Land was plenty and all else scarce; so courage, thrift, and industry were sure of their reward. All had small farms, with the few stock necessary to cultivate them; the farms being generally placed in the hollows, the division lines between them, if they were close together, being the tops of the ridges and the watercourses, especially the former. The buildings of each farm were usually at its lowest point, as if in the centre of an amphitheatre.

   *   *   *   *   *   *   *

These armed hunters, wood-choppers, and farmers were their own soldiers. They built and manned their own forts; they did their own fighting under their own commanders. There were no regiments of regular troops along the frontier. In the event of an Indian inroad each borderer had to defend himself until there was time for them all to gather together to repel or avenge it. Every man was accustomed to the use of arms from his childhood; when a boy was twelve years old he was given a rifle and made a fort-soldier, with a loophole where he was to stand if the station was attacked. The war was never-ending, for even the times of so-called peace were broken by forays and murders; a man might grow from babyhood to middle age on the border, and yet never remember a year in which some one of his neighbors did not fall a victim to the Indians.

There was everywhere a rude military organization, which included all the able-bodied men of the community. Every settlement had its colonels and captains; but these officers, both in their training and in the authority they exercised, corresponded much more nearly to Indian chiefs than to the regular army men whose titles they bore. They had no means whatever of enforcing their orders, and their tumultuous and disorderly levies of sinewy riflemen were hardly as well disciplined as the Indians themselves. The superior officer could advise, entreat, lead, and influence his men, but he could not command them, or, if he did, the men obeyed him only just so far as it suited them. If an officer planned a scout or campaign, those who thought proper accompanied him, and the others stayed at home, and even those who went out came back if the fit seized them, or perchance followed the lead of an insubordinate junior officer whom they liked better than they did his superior. There was no compulsion to perform military duties beyond dread of being disgraced in the eyes of the neighbors, and there was no pecuniary reward for performing them; nevertheless the moral sentiment of a backwoods community was too robust to tolerate habitual remisses in military affairs, and the coward and laggard were treated with utter scorn, and were generally in the end either laughed out, or "hated out," of the neighborhood, or else got rid of in a still more summary manner. Among people naturally brave and reckless, this public opinion acted fairly effectively, and there was generally but little shrinking from military service.

THE DEFENSE OF THE ALAMO

By
WILLIAM BARRET TRAVIS

COMMANDANCY of the Alamo, Bexar, February 24, 1836.—
To the people of Texas and all Americans in the world.

Fellow citizens and compatriots: I am besieged by a thousand or more of the Mexicans under Santa Anna. I have sustained a continual bombardment and cannonade for twenty-four hours and have not lost a man. The enemy has demanded a surrender at discretion; otherwise the garrison are to be put to the sword if the fort is taken. I have answered the demand with a cannon shot, and our flag still waves proudly from the walls. *I shall never surrender nor retreat*. Then, I call on you in the name of liberty, of patriotism, and everything dear to the American character, to come to our aid with all dispatch. The enemy is receiving reinforcements daily and will no doubt increase to three or four thousand in four or five days. If this call is neglected, I am determined to sustain myself as long as possible and die like a soldier who never forgets what is due to his own honor and that of his country. VICTORY OR DEATH.

WILLIAM BARRET TRAVIS
Lieutenant Colonel Commandant

P.S. The Lord is on our side. When the enemy appeared in sight we had not three bushels of corn. We have since found in deserted houses eighty or ninety bushels and got into the walls twenty or thirty head of beeves.

EPITAPH ON THE ALAMO

"THERMOPOLAE had its messenger of defeat, but the Alamo had none."

THE COVERED WAGON

By

JESSE APPLEGATE

FROM six to seven o'clock is a busy time; breakfast is to be eaten, the tents struck, the wagons loaded and the teams yoked and brought up in readiness to be attached to their respective wagons. All know when, at seven o'clock, the signal to march sounds, that those not ready to take their places in the line of march must fall into the dusty rear for the day. There are sixty wagons. They have been divided into fifteen divisions or platoons of four wagons each, and each platoon is entitled to lead in its turn. The leading platoon today will be the rear one tomorrow, and will bring up the rear unless some teamster through indolence or negligence has lost his place in the line, and is condemned to that uncomfortable post. It is within ten minutes of seven; the corral but now a strong barricade is everywhere broken, the teams being attached to the wagons. The women and children have taken their places in them. The pilot (a borderer who has passed his life on the verge of civilization and has been chosen to his post of leader from his knowledge of the savage and his experience in travel through roadless wastes) stands ready, in the midst of his pioneers and aids, to mount and lead the way. Ten or fifteen young men, not today on duty, form another cluster. They are ready to start on a buffalo hunt, all well mounted and well armed, as they need to be, for the unfriendly Sioux have driven the buffalo out of the Platte, and the hunters must ride fifteen or twenty miles to find them. The cow drivers are hastening, as they get ready, to the rear of their charge, to collect and prepare them for the day's march.

It is on the stroke of seven; the rush to and fro, the cracking of whips, the loud command to oxen, and what seemed to be the inextricable confusion of the last ten minutes has ceased. Fortunately every one has been found and every teamster is at his post. The clear notes of a trumpet sound in the front; the pilot and his guards mount their horses, the leading divisions of the wagons move out of the encampment, and take up the line of march; the rest fall into their places with the precision of clockwork, until the spot so lately full of life sinks back into that solitude that seems to reign over the broad plain and rushing river as the caravan draws its lazy length towards the distant El Dorado. . . .

NOTES ON A JOURNEY IN AMERICA

By
Morris Birbeck

McConnel's town, May 23, 1817.—The road we have been traveling terminates at this place, where it strikes the great turnpike from Philadelphia to Pittsburgh; and with the road ends the line of stages by which we have been traveling, a circumstance of which we knew nothing until our arrival here, having entered ourselves passengers at George Town for Pittsburgh, by the Pittsburgh stage, as it professed to be.

So here we are, nine in number, one hundred and thirty miles of mountain country between us and Pittsburgh. We learn that the stages which pass daily from Philadelphia and Baltimore are generally full and that there are now many persons at Baltimore waiting for places. No vehicles of any kind are to be hired, and here we must either stay or *walk* off. The latter we prefer, and separating each our bundle from the little that we have of traveling stores, we are about to undertake our mountain pilgrimage—accepting the alternative most cheerfully after the dreadful shaking of the last hundred miles by stage. . . .

We have now fairly turned our backs on the old world and find ourselves in the very stream of emigration. Old America seems to be breaking up and moving westward. We are seldom out of sight, as we travel on this grand track towards the Ohio, of family groups, behind and before us, some with a view to a particular spot, close to a brother, perhaps, or a friend who has gone before and reported well of the country. Many, like ourselves, when they arrive in the wilderness, will find no lodge prepared for them.

A small wagon (so light that you might almost carry it, yet strong enough to bear a good load of bedding, utensils and provisions, and a swarm of young citizens, and to sustain marvelous shocks in its passage over these rocky heights) with two small horses, sometimes a cow or two, comprises their all, excepting a little store of hard-earned cash for the land office of the district, where they may obtain a title for as many acres as they possess half-dollars, being one-fourth of the purchase money. The wagon has a tilt, or cover, made of a sheet or perhaps a blanket. The family are seen before, behind, or within the vehicle, according to the road or weather or perhaps the spirits of the party.

The New Englanders, they say, may be known by the cheerful air of the women advancing in front of the vehicle, the Jersey people by their being fixed steadily within it, whilst the Pennsylvanians creep lingering behind, as though regretting the homes they have left. A cart and single horse frequently afford the means of transfer, sometimes a horse and packsaddle. Often the back of the poor pilgrim bears all his effects, and his wife follows, naked-footed, bending under the hopes of the family. . . .

"OUR INTELLECTUAL DECLARATION OF INDEPENDENCE"

By
RALPH WALDO EMERSON

THUS far, our holiday has been simply a friendly sign of the survival of the love of letters amongst a people too busy to give to letters any more. As such it is precious as the sign of an indestructible instinct. Perhaps the time is already come when it ought to be, and will be, something else; when the sluggard intellect of this continent will look from under its iron lids and fill the postponed expectation of the world with something better than the exertions of mechanical skill. Our day of dependence, our long apprenticeship to the learning of other lands, draws to a close. The millions that around us are rushing into life, cannot always be fed on the sere remains of foreign harvests. Events, actions arise, that must be sung, that will sing themselves. Who can doubt that poetry will revive and lead in a new age, as the star in the constellation Harp, which now flames in our zenith, astronomers announce, shall one day be the pole-star for a thousand years?

From THE MONROE DOCTRINE

AT THE proposal of the Russian Imperial Government, made through the minister of the Emperor residing here, a full power and instructions have been transmitted to the minister of the United States at St. Petersburg to arrange by amicable negotiation the respective rights and interests of the two nations on the northwest coast of this continent. A similar proposal had been made by His Imperial Majesty to the Government of Great Britain, which has likewise been acceded to. The Government of the United States has been desirous by this friendly proceeding of manifesting the great value which they have invariably attached to the friendship of the Emperor and their solicitude to cultivate the best understanding with his Government. In the discussions to which this interest has given rise and in the arrangement by which they may terminate, the occasion has been judged proper for asserting, as a principle in which the rights and interests of the United States are involved, that the American continents, by the free and independent condition which they have assumed and maintain, are henceforth not to be considered as subjects for future colonization by any European powers.

It was stated at the commencement of the last session that a great effort was then making in Spain and Portugal to improve the condition of the people of those countries, and that it appeared to be conducted with extraordinary moderation. It need scarcely be remarked that the result has been so far very different from what was then anticipated. Of events in that quarter of the Globe, with which we have so much intercourse and from which we derive our origin, we have always been anxious and interested spectators. The citizens of the United States cherish sentiments the most friendly in favor of the liberty and happiness of their fellow men on that side of the Atlantic. In the wars of European powers in matters relating to themselves we have never taken any part, nor does it comport with our policy to do so. It is only when our rights are invaded or seriously menaced that we resent injuries or make preparation for our defense. With the movements in this hemisphere we are of necessity more immediately connected, and by causes which must be obvious to all enlightened and impartial observers. The political system of the allied powers is essentially different in this respect from that of America. This difference proceeds from that which exists in their respective governments; and to the defense of our own, which has been achieved by the loss of so much blood and treasure, and matured by the wisdom of their most enlightened citizens, and under which we have enjoyed unexampled felicity, this whole nation is devoted. We owe it, therefore, to candor and to the amicable relations existing between the United States and those powers to declare that we should consider any attempt on their part to extend their system to any portion of this hemisphere as dangerous to our peace and safety. With the existing colonies or dependencies of any European power we have not interfered and shall not interfere. But with the governments who have declared their independence and maintained it, and whose independence we have, on great consideration and on just principles, acknowledged, we could not view any interposition for the purpose of oppressing them, or controlling in any other manner their destiny, by any European power in any other light than as the manifestation of an unfriendly disposition toward the United States.

From ANDREW JACKSON'S INAUGURAL ADDRESS

As LONG as our Government is administered for the good of the people, and is regulated by their will; as long as it secures to us the rights of persons and of property, liberty of conscience and of the press, it will be worth defending.

THE DEATH OF JOHN ADAMS

By
PHILIP HONE

FEBRUARY 24, 1848.—*Death of Mr. Adams.* John Quincy Adams is no more. Full of age and honors, the termination of his eventful career accorded with the character of its progress. He died, as he must have wished to die, breathing his last in the Capitol, stricken down by the angel of death on the field of his civil glory—employed in the service of the people, in the people's senate house, standing by the Constitution at the side of its altar, and administering in the temple of liberty the rites which he had assisted in establishing.

At twenty minutes past one o'clock on Monday, the 21st, Mr. Adams, being in his seat in the House of Representatives (from which he was never absent during its session), attempted to rise (as was supposed, to speak), but sank back upon his seat and fell upon his side. Those nearest caught him in their arms. Mr. Grinnell bathed his temples with ice water, when he rallied for an instant. The House immediately adjourned in the utmost consternation, as did the Senate, when informed of the melancholy event. His last words were characterized by that concise eloquence for which he was remarkable: *"This is the last of earth: I am content."* Dr. Fries of Ohio, a member, raised him in his arms and bore him to the Speaker's room, where he lay, with occasional indications of consciousness, until last evening, a few minutes before seven o'clock, when he breathed his last. The intelligence of his death came to Albany by the telegraph.

THE CIVIL WAR

GLORY HALLELUJAH! OR JOHN BROWN'S BODY

JOHN BROWN's body lies a-mould'ring in the grave,
John Brown's body lies a-mould'ring in the grave,
John Brown's body lies a-mould'ring in the grave,
　His soul is marching on!
　Chorus—Glory! Glory Hallelujah!
　　　　Glory! Glory Hallelujah!
　　　　Glory! Glory Hallelujah!
　　　　His soul is marching on.

He's gone to be a soldier in the army of the Lord!
　His soul is marching on.

John Brown's knapsack is strapped upon his back.
　His soul is marching on.

His pet lambs will meet him on the way,
　And they'll go marching on.

They'll hang Jeff Davis on a sour apple tree,
　As they go marching on.

Now for the Union let's give three rousing cheers,
　As we go marching on.
　　　　Hip, hip, hip, hip, Hurrah!
　　　　　　CHARLES SPRAGUE HALL

HOW OLD BROWN TOOK HARPER'S FERRY

JOHN BROWN in Kansas settled, like a steadfast Yankee farmer,
  Brave and godly, with four sons, all stalwart men of might.
There he spoke aloud for freedom, and the Border-strife grew
    warmer,
    Till the Rangers fired his dwelling, in his absence, in the night;
        And Old Brown,
        Osawatomie Brown,
Came homeward in the morning to find his house burned down.

Then he grasped his trusty rifle and boldly fought for freedom;
  Smote from border unto border the fierce, invading band;
And he and his brave boys vowed—so might Heaven help and
    speed 'em!—
    They would save those grand old prairies from the curse that
    blights the land;
        And Old Brown,
        Osawatomie Brown,
Said, "Boys, the Lord will aid us!" and he shoved his ramrod down.

And the Lord *did* aid these men, and they labored day and even,
  Saving Kansas from its peril; and their very lives seemed
    charmed,
Till the ruffians killed one son, in the blessed light of Heaven,—
    In cold blood the fellows slew him, as he journeyed all unarmed;
        Then Old Brown,
        Osawatomie Brown,
Shed not a tear, but shut his teeth, and frowned a terrible frown!

Then they seized another brave boy,—not amid the heat of battle,
  But in peace, behind his ploughshare,—and they loaded him
    with chains,

And with pikes, before their horses, even as they goad their cattle,
 Drove him cruelly, for their sport, and at last blew out his brains;
  Then Old Brown,
  Osawatomie Brown,
Raised his right hand up to Heaven, calling Heaven's vengeance
 down.

And he swore a fearful oath, by the name of the Almighty,
 He would hunt this ravening evil that had scathed and torn
 him so;
He would seize it by the vitals; he would crush it day and night;
 he
 Would so pursue its footsteps, so return it blow for blow,
  That Old Brown,
  Osawatomie Brown,
Should be a name to swear by, in backwoods or in town!

Then his beard became more grizzled, and his wild blue eye grew
 wilder,
 And more sharply curved his hawk's-nose, snuffing battle from
 afar;
And he and the two boys left, though the Kansas strife waxed
 milder,
 Grew more sullen, till was over the bloody Border War,
  And Old Brown,
  Osawatomie Brown,
Had gone crazy, as they reckoned by his fearful glare and frown.

So he left the plains of Kansas and their bitter woes behind him,
 Slipt off into Virginia, where the statesmen all are born,
Hired a farm by Harper's Ferry, and no one knew where to find
 him,
 Or whether he'd turned parson, or was jacketed and shorn;
  For Old Brown,
  Osawatomie Brown,
Mad as he was, knew texts enough to wear a parson's gown.

He bought no ploughs and harrows, spades and shovels, and such
    trifles;
  But quietly to his rancho there came, by every train,
Boxes full of pikes and pistols, and his well-beloved Sharp's rifles;
  And eighteen other madmen joined their leader there again.
        Says Old Brown,
        Osawatomie Brown,
"Boys, we've got an army large enough to march and take the
    town!

"Take the town, and seize the muskets, free the negroes and then
    arm them;
  Carry the County and the State, ay, and all the potent South.
On their own heads be the slaughter, if their victims rise to harm
    them—
These Virginians! who believed not, nor would heed the warn-
    ing mouth."
        Says Old Brown,
        Osawatomie Brown,
"The world shall see a Republic, or my name is not John Brown."

'T was the sixteenth of October, on the evening of a Sunday:
  "This good work," declared the captain, "shall be on a holy
    night!"
It was on a Sunday evening, and before the noon of Monday,
  With two sons, and Captain Stephens, fifteen privates—black
    and white,
        Captain Brown,
        Osawatomie Brown,
Marched across the bridged Potomac, and knocked the sentry
    down;

Took the guarded armory-building, and the muskets and the can-
    non;
  Captured all the county majors and the colonels, one by one;

Scared to death each gallant scion of Virginia they ran on,
  And before the noon of Monday, I say, the deed was done.
      Mad Old Brown,
      Osawatomie Brown,
With his eighteen other crazy men, went in and took the town.

Very little noise and bluster, little smell of powder made he;
  It was all done in the midnight, like the Emperor's *coup d'état.*
"Cut the wires! Stop the rail-cars! Hold the streets and bridges!"
  said he,
  Then declared the new Republic, with himself for guiding star,—
      This Old Brown,
      Osawatomie Brown;
And the bold two thousand citizens ran off and left the town.

Then was riding and railroading and expressing here and thither;
  And the Martinsburg Sharpshooters and the Charlestown
    Volunteers,
And the Sheperdstown and Winchester militia hastened whither
  Old Brown was said to muster his ten thousand grenadiers.
      General Brown!
      Osawatomie Brown!
Behind whose rampant banner all the North was pouring down.

But at last, 't is said, some prisoners escaped from Old Brown's
  durance,
  And the effervescent valor of the Chivalry broke out,
When they learned that nineteen madmen had the marvellous as-
  surance—
  Only nineteen—thus to seize the place and drive them straight
    about;
      And Old Brown,
      Osawatomie Brown,
Found an army come to take him, encamped around the town.

But to storm, with all the forces I have mentioned, was too risky;
   So they hurried off to Richmond for the Government Marines,
Tore them from their weeping matrons, fired their souls with
      Bourbon whiskey,
   Till they battered down Brown's castle with their ladders and
      machines;
         And Old Brown,
         Osawatomie Brown,
Received three bayonet stabs, and a cut on his brave old crown.

Tallyho! the old Virginia gentry gather to the baying!
   In they rushed and killed the game, shooting lustily away;
And whene'er they slew a rebel, those who come too late for slay-
      ing,
   Not to lose a share of glory, fired their bullets in his clay;
         And Old Brown,
         Osawatomie Brown,
Saw his sons fall dead beside him, and between them laid him
      down.

How the conquerors wore their laurels; how they hastened on the
      trial;
   How Old Brown was placed, half dying, on the Charlestown
      court-house floor;
How he spoke his grand oration, in the scorn of all denial;
   What the brave old madman told them,—these are known the
      country o'er.
         "Hang Old Brown,
         Osawatomie Brown,"
Said the judge, "and all such rebels!" with his most judicial
      frown.

But, Virginians, don't do it! for I tell you that the flagon,
   Filled with blood of Old Brown's offspring, was first poured by
      Southern hands;

And each drop from Old Brown's life-veins, like the red gore of
    the dragon,
  May spring up a vengeful Fury, hissing through your slave-worn
    lands!
        And Old Brown,
        Osawatomie Brown,
May trouble you more than ever, when you've nailed his coffin
    down!

EDMUND CLARENCE STEDMAN

THE SIGNIFICANCE OF JOHN BROWN

From *John Brown's Body*

OUT of his body grows revolving steel,
Out of his body grows the spinning wheel
Made up of wheels, the new, mechanic birth,
No longer bound by toil
To the unsparing soil
Or the old furrow-line,
The great, metallic beast
Expanding West and East,
His heart a spinning coil,
His juices burning oil,
His body serpentine.
Out of John Brown's strong sinews the tall skyscrapers grow,
Out of his heart the chanting buildings rise,
Rivet and girder, motor and dynamo,
Pillar of smoke by day and fire by night,
The steel-faced cities reaching at the skies,
The whole enormous and rotating cage
Hung with hard jewels of electric light,
Smoky with sorrow, black with splendor, dyed
Whiter than damask for a crystal bride

With metal suns, the engine-handed Age,
The genie we have raised to rule the earth,
Obsequious to our will
But servant-master still,
The tireless serf already half a god—

John Brown's body lies a-mouldering in the grave.
Spread over it the bloodstained flag of his song,
For the sun to bleach, the wind and the birds to tear,
The snow to cover over with a pure fleece
And the New England cloud to work upon
With the grey absolution of its slow, most lilac-smelling rain,
Until there is nothing there
That ever knew a master or a slave
Or, brooding on the symbol of a wrong,
Threw down the irons in the field of peace.
John Brown is dead, he will not come again,
A stray ghost-walker with a ghostly gun.
Let the strong metal rust
In the enclosing dust
And the consuming coal
That was the furious soul
And still like iron groans,
Anointed with the earth,
Grow colder than the stones
While the white roots of grass and little weeds
Suck the last hollow wildfire from the singing bones.

Bury the South together with this man,
Bury the bygone South.
Bury the minstrel with the honey-mouth,
Bury the broadsword virtues of the clan,
Bury the unmachined, the planters' pride,
The courtesy and the bitter arrogance,
The pistol-hearted horsemen who could ride

Like jolly centaurs under the hot stars.
Bury the whip, bury the branding-bars,
Bury the unjust thing
That some tamed into mercy, being wise,
But could not starve the tiger from its eyes
Or make it feed where beasts of mercy feed.
Bury the fiddle-music and the dance,
The sick magnolias of the false romance
And all the chivalry that went to seed
Before its ripening.

And with these things, bury the purple dream
Of the America we have not been,
The tropic empire, seeking the warm sea,
The last foray of aristocracy
Based not on dollars or initiative
Or any blood for what that blood was worth
But on a certain code, a manner of birth,
A certain manner of knowing how to live,
The pastoral rebellion of the earth
Against machines, against the Age of Steam,
The Hamiltonian extremes against the Franklin mean,
The genius of the land
Against the metal hand,
The great, slave-driven bark,
Full-oared upon the dark,
With gilded figurehead,
With fetters for the crew
And spices for the few,
The passion that is dead,
The pomp we never knew,
Bury this, too.

                              STEPHEN VINCENT BENÉT

BATTLE-HYMN OF THE REPUBLIC

MINE EYES have seen the glory of the coming of the Lord:
He is tramping out the vintage where the grapes of wrath are
    stored;
He hath loosed the fateful lightning of his terrible swift sword:
    His truth is marching on.

I have seen him in the watch-fires of a hundred circling camps;
They have builded him an altar in the evening dews and damps;
I can read his righteous sentence by the dim and flaring lamps:
    His day is marching on.

I have read a fiery gospel, writ in burnished rows of steel:
"As ye deal with my contemners, so with you my grace shall deal;
Let the Hero, born of woman, crush the serpent with his heel,
    Since God is marching on."

He has sounded forth the trumpet that shall never call retreat;
He is sifting out the hearts of men before his judgment-seat:
O, be swift, my soul, to answer him! be jubilant, my feet!
    Our God is marching on.

In the beauty of the lilies Christ was born across the sea,
With the glory in his bosom that transfigures you and me;
As he died to make men holy, let us die to make men free,
    While God is marching on.

                                        JULIA WARD HOWE

[A sixth stanza, as follows, was written by the author, but is seldom quoted.]

He is coming like the glory of the morning on the wave,
He is wisdom to the mighty, he is honor to the brave,
So the world shall be his footstool, and the soul of wrong his slave,
    Our God is marching on!

THE BATTLE-CRY OF FREEDOM

Yes, we'll rally round the flag, boys, we'll rally once again,
  Shouting the battle-cry of freedom,
We will rally from the hill-side, we'll gather from the plain,
  Shouting the battle-cry of freedom.

Chorus—The Union forever, hurrah! boys, hurrah!
      Down with the traitor, up with the star,
        While we rally round the flag, boys, rally once again,
          Shouting the battle-cry of freedom.

We are springing to the call of our brothers gone before,
  Shouting the battle-cry of freedom,
And we'll fill the vacant ranks with a million freemen more,
  Shouting the battle-cry of freedom.

We will welcome to our numbers the loyal, true, and brave,
  Shouting the battle-cry of freedom,
And altho' they may be poor, not a man shall be a slave,
  Shouting the battle-cry of freedom.

So we're springing to the call from the East and from the West,
  Shouting the battle-cry of freedom,
And we'll hurl the rebel crew from the land we love the best,
  Shouting the battle-cry of freedom.

                          George Frederick Root

JONATHAN TO JOHN

IT don't seem hardly right, John,
　When both my hands was full,
To stump me to a fight, John,—
　Your cousin, tu, John Bull!
　　Ole Uncle S. sez he, "I guess
　　We know it now," sez he,
　"The Lion's paw is all the law,
　　Accordin' to J. B.,
　　Thet's fit for you an' me!"

You wonder why we're hot, John?
　Your mark wuz on the guns,
The neutral guns, thet shot, John,
　Our brothers an' our sons:
　　Ole Uncle S. sez he, "I guess
　　There's human blood," sez he,
　"By fits an' starts, in Yankee hearts,
　　Though 't may surprise J. B.
　　More 'n it would you an' me."

Ef *I* turned mad dogs loose, John,
　On *your* front-parlor stairs,
Would it jest meet your views, John,
　To wait an' sue their heirs?
　　Ole Uncle S. sez he, "I guess,
　　I on'y guess," sez he,
　"Thet ef Vattel on *his* toes fell,
　　'T would kind o' rile J. B.,
　　Ez wal ez you an' me!"

Who made the law thet hurts, John,
　Heads I win—ditto tails?

"J. B." was on his shirts, John,
  Onless my memory fails.
    Ole Uncle S. sez he, "I guess
     (I'm good at thet)," sez he,
"Thet sauce for goose ain't *jest* the juice
    For ganders with J. B.,
    No more 'n with you or me!"

When your rights was our wrongs, John,
  You didn't stop for fuss,—
Britanny's trident prongs, John,
  Was good 'nough law for us.
    Ole Uncle S. sez he, "I guess,
     Though physic 's good," sez he,
"It does n't foller thet he can swaller
    Prescriptions signed 'J. B.,'
    Put up by you an' me."

We own the ocean, tu, John:
  You mus'n' take it hard,
Ef we can't think with you, John,
  It's jest your own back yard.
    Ole Uncle S. sez he, "I guess
     Ef *thet's* his claim," sez he,
"The fencin'-stuff 'll cost enough
    To bust up friend J. B.,
    Ez wal ez you an' me!"

Why talk so dreffle big, John,
  Of honor when it meant
You did n't care a fig, John,
  But jest for *ten per cent?*
    Ole Uncle S. sez he, "I guess
     He's like the rest," sez he:
"When all is done, it's number one
    Thet's nearest to J. B.,
    Ez wal ez t' you an' me!"

We give the critters back, John,
  Cos Abram thought 't was right;
It warn't your bullyin' clack, John,
  Provokin' us to fight.
    Ole Uncle S. sez he, "I guess
    We've a hard row," sez he,
"To hoe jest now; but thet, somehow,
    May happen to J. B.,
    Ez wal ez you an' me!"

We ain't so weak an' poor, John,
  With twenty million people,
An' close to every door, John,
  A school-house an' a steeple.
    Ole Uncle S. sez he, "I guess
    It is a fact," sez he,
"The surest plan to make a Man
    Is, think him so, J. B.,
    Ez much ez you or me!"

Our folks believe in Law, John;
  An' it's fer her sake, now,
They've left the axe an' saw, John,
  The anvil an' the plough.
    Ole Uncle S. sez he, "I guess,
    Ef 't warn't fer law," sez he,
"There'd be one shindy from here to Indy;
    An' *thet* don't suit J. B.
    (When 't ain't 'twixt you an' me!)"

We know we've got a cause, John,
  Thet's honest, just, an' true;
We thought 't would win applause, John,
  If nowheres else, from you.
    Ole Uncle S. sez he, "I guess
    His love of right," sez he,

"Hangs by a rotton fibre o' cotton:
    There's natur' in J. B.,
    Ez wal ez in you an' me!"

The South says, *"Poor folks down!"* John,
    An' *"All men up!"* say we,—
White, yaller, black, an' brown, John:
    Now which is your idee?
        Ole Uncle S. sez he, "I guess
        John preaches wal," sez he;
"But, sermon thru, an' come to *du,*
        Why, there's the old J. B.
        A-crowdin' you an' me!"

Shall it be love, or hate, John?
    It's you thet's to decide;
Ain't *your* bonds held by Fate, John,
    Like all the world's beside?
        Ole Uncle S. sez he, "I guess
        Wise men forgive," sez he,
"But not forgit; an' some time yit
        Thet truth may strike J. B.,
        Ez wal ez you an' me!"

God means to make this land, John,
    Clear thru, from sea to sea,
Believe an' understand, John,
    The *wuth* o' bein' free.
        Ole Uncle S. sez he, "I guess
        God's price is high," sez he;
"But nothin' else than wut he sells
        Wears long, an' thet J. B.
        May larn, like you an' me!"
                            JAMES RUSSELL LOWELL

SUMTER

So THEY *will* have it!
     The Black Witch (curse on her)
     Always had won her
Greediest demand—for we gave it—
     All but our honor!

Thirty hours thundered
     Siege-guns and mortars—
     (Flames in the quarters!)
One to a hundred
     Stood our brave Forters!

No more of parties!—
     Let them all moulder—
     Here's work that's bolder!
Forward, my hearties!
     Shoulder to shoulder.

Sight o'er the trunnion—
     Send home the rammer—
     Linstock and hammer!
Speak for the Union!
     Tones that won't stammer!

Men of Columbia,
     Leal hearts from Annan,
     Brave lads of Shannon!
We are all one to-day—
     On with the cannon!
                    HENRY HOWARD BROWNELL

FREDERICKSBURG

THE increasing moonlight drifts across my bed,
And on the churchyard by the road, I know
It falls as white and noiselessly as snow. . . .
'Twas such a night two weary summers fled;
The stars, as now, were waning overhead.
Listen! Again the shrill-lipped bugles blow
Where the swift currents of the river flow
Past Fredericksburg; far off the heavens are red
With sudden conflagration: on yon height,
Linstock in hand, the gunners hold their breath;
A signal-rocket pierces the dense night,
Flings its spent stars upon the town beneath:
Hark!—the artillery massing on the right,
Hark!—the black squadrons wheeling down to Death!

THOMAS BAILEY ALDRICH

BARBARA FRIETCHIE

UP FROM the meadows rich with corn,
Clear in the cool September morn,

The clustered spires of Frederick stand
Green-walled by the hills of Maryland.

Round about them orchards sweep,
Apple and peach tree fruited deep,

Fair as the garden of the Lord
To the eyes of the famished rebel horde,

On that pleasant morn of the early fall
When Lee marched over the mountain-wall;

Over the mountains winding down,
Horse and foot, into Frederick town.

Forty flags with their silver stars,
Forty flags with their crimson bars,

Flapped in the morning wind: the sun
Of noon looked down, and saw not one.

Up rose old Barbara Frietchie then,
Bowed with her fourscore years and ten;

Bravest of all in Frederick town,
She took up the flag the men hauled down;

In her attic window the staff she set,
To show that one heart was loyal yet.

Up the street came the rebel tread,
Stonewall Jackson riding ahead.

Under his slouched hat left and right
He glanced; the old flag met his sight.

"Halt!"—the dust-brown ranks stood fast.
"Fire!"—out blazed the rifle-blast.

It shivered the window, pane and sash;
It rent the banner with seam and gash.

Quick, as it fell, from the broken staff
Dame Barbara snatched the silken scarf.

She leaned far out on the window-sill,
And shook it forth with a royal will.

"Shoot, if you must, this old gray head,
But spare your country's flag," she said.

A shade of sadness, a blush of shame,
Over the face of the leader came;

The nobler nature within him stirred
To life at that woman's deed and word;

"Who touches a hair of yon gray head
Dies like a dog! March on!" he said.

All day long through Frederick street
Sounded the tread of marching feet:

All day long that free flag tost
Over the heads of the rebel host.

Ever its torn folds rose and fell
On the loyal winds that loved it well;

And through the hill-gaps sunset light
Shone over it with a warm good-night.

Barbara Frietchie's work is o'er,
And the Rebel rides on his raids no more.

Honor to her! and let a tear
Fall, for her sake, on Stonewall's bier.

Over Barbara Frietchie's grave,
Flag of Freedom and Union, wave!

Peace and order and beauty draw
Round thy symbol of light and law;

And ever the stars above look down
On thy stars below in Frederick town!

JOHN GREENLEAF WHITTIER

BEAUREGARD

OUR trust is now in thee,
        Beauregard!
In thy hand the God of Hosts
        Hath placed the sword;
And the glory of thy fame
Has set the world aflame—
Hearts kindle at thy name,
        Beauregard!

The way that lies before
        Is cold and hard;
We are led across the desert
        By the Lord!
But the cloud that shines by night
To guide our steps aright,
Is the pillar of thy might,
        Beauregard!

Thou hast watched the southern heavens
        Evening starred,
And chosen thence thine emblems,
        Beauregard;
And upon thy banner's fold
Is that starry cross enrolled,
Which no Northman shall behold
        Shamed or scarred.

By the blood that crieth loudly
    From the sword,
We have sworn to keep around it
    Watch and ward,
And the standard of thine hand
Yet shall shine above a land,
Like its leader, free and grand,
    Beauregard!
              Mrs. C. A. Warfield

THE CUMBERLAND

At anchor in Hampton Roads we lay,
  On board of the Cumberland, sloop-of-war;
And at times from the fortress across the bay
    The alarum of drums swept past,
    Or a bugle blast
  From the camp on the shore.

Then far away to the south uprose
  A little feather of snow-white smoke,
And we knew that the iron ship of our foes
    Was steadily steering its course
    To try the force
  Of our ribs of oak.

Down upon us heavily runs,
  Silent and sullen, the floating fort;
Then comes a puff of smoke from her guns,
    And leaps the terrible death,
    With fiery breath,
  From each open port.

We are not idle, but send her straight
  Defiance back in a full broadside!
As hail rebounds from a roof of slate,
    Rebounds our heavier hail
    From each iron scale
  Of the monster's hide.

"Strike your flag!" the rebel cries
  In his arrogant old plantation strain.
"Never!" our gallant Morris replies:
    "It is better to sink than to yield!"
    And the whole air pealed
  With the cheers of our men.

Then, like a kraken huge and black,
  She crushed our ribs in her iron grasp!
Down went the Cumberland all a wrack,
    With a sudden shudder of death,
    And the cannon's breath
  For her dying gasp.

Next morn, as the sun rose over the bay,
  Still floated our flag at the mainmast head.
Lord, how beautiful was Thy day!
    Every waft of the air
    Was a whisper of prayer,
  Or a dirge for the dead.

Ho! brave hearts that went down in the seas!
  Ye are at peace in the troubled stream;
Ho! brave land! with hearts like these,
    Thy flag, that is rent in twain,
    Shall be one again,
  And without a seam!
                    HENRY WADSWORTH LONGFELLOW

THE RIVER FIGHT

April 18, 1862

Do you know of the dreary land,
If land such region may seem,
Where 't is neither sea nor strand,
Ocean, nor good, dry land,
But the nightmare marsh of a dream?
Where the Mighty River his death-road takes,
'Mid pools and windings that coil like snakes,
A hundred leagues of bayous and lakes,
To die in the great Gulf Stream?

No coast-line clear and true,
Granite and deep-sea blue,
On that dismal shore you pass,
Surf-worn boulder or sandy beach,—
But ooze-flats as far as the eye can reach,
With shallows of water-grass;
Reedy Savannahs, vast and dun,
Lying dead in the dim March sun;
Huge, rotting trunks and roots that lie
Like the blackened bones of shapes gone by,
And miles of sunken morass.

No lovely, delicate thing
Of life o'er the waste is seen
But the cayman couched by his weedy spring,
And the pelican, bird unclean,
Or the buzzard, flapping with heavy wing,
Like an evil ghost o'er the desolate scene.

Ah! many a weary day
With our Leader there we lay.
In the sultry haze and smoke,
Tugging our ships o'er the bar,
Till the spring was wasted far,
Till his brave heart almost broke.
For the sullen river seemed
As if our intent he dreamed,—
All his sallow mouths did spew and choke.

But ere April fully passed
All ground over at last
And we knew the die was cast,—
Knew the day drew nigh
To dare to the end one stormy deed,
Might save the land at her sorest need,
Or on the old deck to die!

Anchored we lay,—and a morn the more,
To his captains and all his men
Thus wrote our old commodore
(He wasn't Admiral then):—
"GENERAL ORDERS:
Send your to'gallant masts down,
Rig in each flying jib-boom!
Clear all ahead for the loom
Of traitor fortress and town,
Or traitor fleet bearing down.

"In with your canvas high;
We shall want no sail to fly!
Topsail, foresail, spanker, and jib
(With the heart of oak in the oaken rib),
Shall serve us to win or die!

"Trim every sail by the head
(So shall you spare the lead),

Lest if she ground, your ship swing round,
Bows in shore, for a wreck.
See your grapnels all clear with pains,
And a solid kedge in your port main-chains,
With a whip to the main yard:
Drop it heavy and hard
When you grapple a traitor deck!

"On forecastle and on poop
Mount guns, as best you may deem.
If possible, rouse them up
(For still you must bow the stream).
Also hoist and secure with stops
Howitzers firmly in your tops,
To fire on the foe abeam.

"Look well to your pumps and hose;
Have water tubs fore and aft,
For quenching flame in your craft,
And the gun crew's fiery thirst.
See planks with felt fitted close,
To plug every shot-hole tight.
Stand ready to meet the worst!
For, if I have reckoned aright,
They will serve us shot,
Both cold and hot,
Freely enough to-night.

"Mark well each signal I make
(Our life-long service at stake,
And honor that must not lag!),—
Whate'er the peril and awe,
In the battle's fieriest flaw,
Let never one ship withdraw
Till the orders come from the flag!"

Would you hear of the river fight?
It was two of a soft spring night;
God's stars looked down on all;
And all was clear and bright
But the low fog's clinging breath;
Up the River of Death
Sailed the great Admiral.

On our high poop-deck he stood,
And round him ranged the men
Who have made their birthright good
Of manhood once and again,—
Lords of helm and of sail,
Tried in tempest and gale,
Bronzed in battle and wreck.
Bell and Bailey grandly led
Each his line of the Blue and Red;
Wainwright stood by our starboard rail;
Thornton fought the deck.
And I mind me of more than they,
Of the youthful, steadfast ones,
That have shown them worthy sons
Of the seamen passed away.
Tyson conned our helm that day;
Watson stood by his guns.

What thought our Admiral then,
Looking down on his men?
Since the terrible day
(Day of renown and tears!),—
When at anchor the Essex lay,—
Holding her foes at bay,—
When a boy by Porter's side he stood,
Till deck and plank-sheer were dyed with blood;
'T is half a hundred years,—
Half a hundred years to a day!

Who could fail with him?
Who reckon of life or limb?
Not a pulse but beat the higher!
There had you seen, by the starlight dim,
Five hundred faces strong and grim:
The Flag is going under fire!
Right up by the fort,
With her helm hard aport,
The Hartford is going under fire!

The way to our work was plain.
Caldwell had broken the chain
(Two hulks swung down amain
Soon as 't was sundered).
Under the night's dark blue,
Steering steady and true,
Ship after ship went through,
Till, as we hove in view,
"Jackson" out-thundered!

Back echoed "Philip!" ah! then
Could you have seen our men.
How they sprung in the dim night haze,
To their work of toil and of clamor!
How the boarders, with sponge and rammer
And their captains, with cord and hammer,
Kept every muzzle ablaze.
How the guns, as with cheer and shout—
Our tackle-men hurled them out—
Brought up on the water-ways!

First, as we fired at their flash,
'T was lightning and black eclipse,
With a bellowing roll and crash.
But soon, upon either bow,
What with forts and fire-rafts and ships

(The whole fleet was hard at it now),
All pounding away!—and Porter
Still thundering with shell and mortar,—
'T was the mighty sound and form!

(Such you see in the far South,
After long heat and drought,
As day draws nigh to even,
Arching from north to south,
Blinding the tropic sun,
The great black bow comes on,
Till the thunder-veil is riven,—
When all is crash and levin,
And the cannonade of heaven
Rolls down the Amazon!)

But, as we worked along higher,
Just where the river enlarges,
Down came a pyramid of fire,—
It was one of your long coal barges.
(We had often had the like before.)
'T was coming down on us to larboard,
Well in with the eastern shore;
And our pilot, to let it pass round
(You may guess we never stopped to sound),
Giving us a rank sheer to starboard,
Ran the Flag hard and fast aground!

'T was nigh abreast of the Upper Fort,
And straightway a rascal ram
(She was shaped like the Devil's dam)
Puffed away for us, with a snort,
And shoved it, with spiteful strength,
Right alongside of us to port.
It was all of our ship's length,—

A huge, crackling Cradle of the Pit!
Pitch-pine knots to the brim,
Belching flame red and grim,
What a roar came up from it!

Well, for a little it looked bad:
But these things are, somehow, shorter,
In the acting than in the telling;
There was no singing out or yelling,
Or any fussing and fretting,
No stampede, in short;
But there we were, my lad,
All afire on our port quarter,
Hammocks ablaze in the netting,
Flames spouting in at every port,
Our fourth cutter burning at the davit
(No chance to lower away and save it).

In a twinkling, the flames had risen
Halfway to maintop and mizzen.
Darting up the shrouds like snakes!
Ah, how we clanked at the brakes,
And the deep, steaming pumps throbbed under,
Sending a ceaseless flow.
Our topmen, a dauntless crowd,
Swarmed in rigging and shroud:
There ('t was a wonder!)
The burning ratlines and strands
They quenched with their bare, hard hands;
But the great guns below
Never silenced their thunder.

At last, by backing and sounding,
When we were clear of grounding,
And under headway once more,
The whole rebel fleet came rounding

The point. If we had it hot before,
'T was now from shore to shore,
One long, loud, thundering roar,—
Such crashing, splintering, and pounding,
And smashing as you never heard before!

But that we fought foul wrong to wreck,
And to save the land we loved so well,
You might have deemed our long gun-deck
Two hundred feet of hell!
For above all was battle,
Broadside, and blaze, and rattle,
Smoke and thunder alone
(But, down in the sick-bay,
Where our wounded and dying lay,
There was scarce a sob or a moan).

And at last, when the dim day broke,
And the sullen sun awoke,
Drearily blinking
O'er the haze and the cannon smoke,
That ever such morning dulls,—
There were thirteen traitor hulls
On fire and sinking!

Now, up the river!—though mad Chalmette
Sputters a vain resistance yet,
Small helm we gave her our course to steer,—
'T was nicer work than you well would dream,
With cant and sheer to keep her clear
Of the burning wrecks that cumbered the stream.

The Louisiana, hurled on high,
Mounts in thunder to meet the sky!
Then down to the depths of the turbid flood,—
Fifty fathom of rebel mud!

The Mississippi comes floating down,
A mighty bonfire from off the town;
And along the river, on stocks and ways,
A half-hatched devil's brood is ablaze,—
The great Anglo-Norman is all in flames
(Hark to the roar of her trembling frames!),
And the smaller fry that Treason would spawn
Are lighting Algiers like an angry dawn!

From stem to stern, how the pirates burn,
Fired by the furious hands that built!
So to ashes forever turn
The suicide wrecks of wrong and guilt!

But as we neared the city,
By field and vast plantation
(Ah! millstone of our nation!),
With wonder and with pity,
What crowds we there espied
Of dark and wistful faces,
Mute in their toiling places,
Strangely and sadly eyed,
Haply 'mid doubt and fear,
Deeming deliverance near
(One gave the ghost of a cheer!).

And on that dolorous strand,
To greet the victor brave,
One flag did welcome wave—
Raised, ah me! by a wretched hand,
All outworn on our cruel land,—
The withered hand of a slave!

But all along the levee,
In a dark and drenching rain
(By this 't was pouring heavy),

Stood a fierce and sullen train,
A strange and frenzied time!
There were scowling rage and pain,
Curses, howls, and hisses,
Out of Hate's black abysses,—
Their courage and their crime
All in vain—all in vain!

For from the hour that the Rebel Stream
With the Crescent City lying abeam,
Shuddered under our keel,
Smit to the heart with self-struck sting,
Slavery died in her scorpion-ring
And Murder fell on his steel.

'T is well to do and dare;
But ever may grateful prayer
Follow, as aye it ought,
When the good fight is fought,
When the true deed is done.
Aloft in heaven's pure light
(Deep azure crossed on white),
Our fair Church pennant waves
O'er a thousand thankful braves,
Bareheaded in God's bright sun.

Lord of mercy and frown,
Ruling o'er sea and shore,
Send us such scene once more!
All in line of battle
When the black ships bear down
On tyrant fort and town,
'Mid cannon cloud and rattle;
And the great guns once more

Thunder back the roar
Of the traitor walls ashore,
And the traitor flags come down.
                        HENRY HOWARD BROWNELL

THE BAY FIGHT

Mobile Harbor, August 5, 1864

THREE days through sapphire seas we sailed,
  The steady Trade blew strong and free,
The Northern Light his banners paled,
The Ocean Stream our channels wet,
  We rounded low Canaveral's lee,
And passed the isles of emerald set
  In blue Bahama's turquoise sea.

By reef and shoal obscurely mapped,
  The hauntings of the gray sea-wolf,
The palmy Western Key lay lapped
  In the warm washing of the Gulf.

But weary to the hearts of all
  The burning glare, the barren reach
  Of Santa Rosa's withered beach,
And Pensacola's ruined wall.

And weary was the long patrol,
  The thousand miles of shapeless strand,
From Brazos to San Blas that roll
  Their drifting dunes of desert sand.

Yet coastwise as we cruised or lay,
  The land-breeze still at nightfall bore,
By beach and fortress-guarded bay,
  Sweet odors from the enemy's shore,

Fresh from the forest solitudes,
  Unchallenged of his sentry lines,—
The bursting of his cypress buds,
  And the warm fragrance of his pines.

Ah, never braver bark and crew,
  Nor bolder Flag a foe to dare,
Had left a wake on ocean blue
  Since Lion-Heart sailed Trenc-le-mer!

But little gain by that dark ground
  Was ours, save, sometime, freer breath
For friend or brother strangely found,
  'Scaped from the drear domain of death.

And little venture for the bold,
  Or laurel for our valiant Chief,
  Save some blockaded British thief,
Full fraught with murder in his hold,

Caught unawares at ebb or flood,
  Or dull bombardment, day by day,
  With fort and earthwork, far away,
Low couched in sullen leagues of mud.

A weary time,—but to the strong
  The day at last, as ever, came;
And the volcano, laid so long,
  Leaped forth in thunder and in flame!

"Man your starboard battery!"
Kimberly shouted;—
The ship, with her hearts of oak,
Was going, 'mid roar and smoke,
On to victory;
None of us doubted,
No, not our dying—
Farragut's Flag was flying!

Gaines growled low on our left,
Morgan roared on our right;
Before us, gloomy and fell,
With breath like the fume of hell,
Lay the dragon of iron shell,
Driven at last to the fight!

Ha, old ship! do they thrill,
The brave two hundred scars
You got in the River-Wars?
That were leeched with clamorous skill
(Surgery savage and hard),
Splinted with bolt and beam,
Probed in scarfing and seam,
Rudely linted and tarred
With oakum and boiling pitch,
And sutured with splice and hitch,
At the Brooklyn Navy Yard!

Our lofty spars were down,
To bide the battle's frown
(Wont of old renown)—
But every ship was drest
In her bravest and her best,
As if for a July day;
Sixty flags and three,
As we floated up the bay—

At every peak and mast-head flew
The brave Red, White, and Blue,—
We were eighteen ships that day.

With hawsers strong and taut,
The weaker lashed to port,
On we sailed two by two—
That if either a bolt should feel
Crash through caldron or wheel,
Fin of bronze, or sinew of steel,
Her mate might bear her through.

Forging boldly ahead,
The great Flag-Ship led,
Grandest of sights!
On her lofty mizzen flew
Our leader's dauntless Blue,
That had waved o'er twenty fights.
So we went with the first of the tide,
Slowly, 'mid the roar
Of the rebel guns ashore
And the thunder of each full broadside.

Ah, how poor the prate
Of statute and state
We once held these fellows!
Here on the flood's pale green,
Hark how he bellows,
Each bluff old Sea-Lawyer!
Talk to them, Dahlgren,
Parrott, and Sawyer!

On, in the whirling shade
Of the cannon's sulphury breath,
We drew to the Line of Death
That our devilish Foe had laid,—

Meshed in a horrible net,
And baited villainous well,
Right in our path were set
Three hundred traps of hell!

And there, O sight forlorn!
There, while the cannon
Hurtled and thundered
(Ah, what ill raven
Flapped o'er the ship that morn!),—
Caught by the under-death,
In the drawing of a breath
Down went dauntless Craven,
He and his hundred!

A moment we saw her turret,
A little heel she gave,
And a thin white spray went o'er her,
Like the crest of a breaking wave;—
In that great iron coffin,
The channel for their grave,
The fort their monument
(Seen afar in the offing),
Ten fathom deep lie Craven
And the bravest of our brave.

Then in that deadly track
A little the ships held back,
Closing up in their stations;—
There are minutes that fix the fate
Of battles and of nations
(Christening the generations),
When valor were all too late.
If a moment's doubt be harbored;—
From the main-top, bold and brief,
Came the word of our grand old chief:

"Go on!"—'t was all he said,—
Our helm was put to starboard,
And the Hartford passed ahead.

Ahead lay the Tennessee,
On our starboard bow he lay,
With his mail-clad consorts three
(The rest had run up the bay);
There he was, belching flame from his bow,
And the steam from his throat's abyss
Was a Dragon's maddened hiss;
In sooth a most cursed craft!—
In a sullen ring, at bay,
By the Middle-Ground they lay,
Raking us fore and aft.

Trust me, our berth was hot,
Ah, wickedly well they shot—
How their death-bolts howled and stung!
And the water-batteries played
With their deadly cannonade
Till the air around us rung;
So the battle raged and roared;—
Ah, had you been aboard
To have seen the fight we made!
How they leapt, the tongues of flame,
From the cannon's fiery lip!
How the broadsides, deck and frame,
Shook the great ship!

And how the enemy's shell
Came crashing, heavy and oft,
Clouds of splinters flying aloft
And falling in oaken showers;—

But ah, the pluck of the crew!
Had you stood on that deck of ours,
You had seen what men may do.

Still, as the fray grew louder,
Boldly they worked and well—
Steadily came the powder,
Steadily came the shell.
And if tackle or truck found hurt,
Quickly they cleared the wreck—
And the dead were laid to port,
All a-row, on our deck.

Never a nerve that failed,
Never a cheek that paled,
Not a tinge of gloom or pallor;—
There was bold Kentucky's grit,
And the old Virginian valor,
And the daring Yankee wit.
There were blue eyes from turfy Shannon,
There were black orbs from palmy Niger,—
But there alongside the cannon,
Each man fought like a tiger!

A little, once, it looked ill,
Our consort began to burn—
They quenched the flames with a will,
But our men were falling still,
And still the fleet were astern.

Right abreast of the Fort
In an awful shroud they lay,
Broadsides thundering away,
And lightning from every port;

Scene of glory and dread!
A storm-cloud all aglow
With flashes of fiery red,
The thunder raging below,
And the forest of flags o'erhead!

So grand the hurly and roar,
So fiercely their broadsides blazed,
The regiments fighting ashore
Forgot to fire as they gazed.

There, to silence the foe,
Moving grimly and slow,
They loomed in that deadly wreath,
Where the darkest batteries frowned,—
Death in the air all round,
And the black torpedoes beneath!

And now, as we looked ahead,
All for'ard, the long white deck
Was growing a strange dull red,—
But soon, as once and again
Fore and aft we sped
(The firing to guide or check),
You could hardly choose but tread
On the ghastly human wreck
(Dreadful gobbet and shred
That a minute ago were men!),

Red, from mainmast to bitts!
Red, on bulwark and wale,
Red, by combing and hatch,
Red, o'er netting and vail!

And ever, with steady con,
The ship forged slowly by,—

And ever the crew fought on,
And their cheers rang loud and high.

Grand was the sight to see
How by their guns they stood,
Right in front of our dead,
Fighting square abreast—
Each brawny arm and chest
All spotted with black and red,
Chrism of fire and blood!

Worth our watch, dull and sterile,
Worth all the weary time,
Worth the woe and the peril,
To stand in that strait sublime!

Fear? A forgotten form!
Death? A dream of the eyes!
We were atoms in God's great storm
That roared through the angry skies.

One only doubt was ours,
One only dread we knew,—
Could the day that dawned so well
Go down for the Darker Powers?
Would the fleet get through?
And ever the shot and shell
Came with the howl of hell,
The splinter-clouds rose and fell,
And the long line of corpses grew,—
Would the fleet win through?

They are men that never will fail
(How aforetime they've fought!),
But Murder may yet prevail,—
They may sink as Craven sank.

Therewith one hard fierce thought,
Burning on heart and lip,
Ran like fire through the ship;
Fight her, to the last plank!

A dimmer renown might strike
If Death lay square alongside,—
But the old Flag has no like,
She must fight, whatever betide;—
When the War is a tale of old,
And this day's story is told,
They shall hear how the Hartford died!

But as we ranged ahead,
And the leading ships worked in,
Losing their hope to win,
The enemy turned and fled—
And one seeks a shallow reach!
And another, winged in her flight,
Our mate, brave Jouett, brings in;—
And one, all torn in the fight,
Runs for a wreck on the beach,
Where her flames soon fire the night.

And the Ram, when well up the Bay,
And we looked that our stems should meet
(He had us fair for a prey),
Shifting his helm midway,
Sheered off, and ran for the fleet;
There, without skulking or sham,
He fought them gun for gun;
And ever he sought to ram,
But could finish never a one.

From the first of the iron shower
Till we sent our parting shell,

'T was just one savage hour
Of the roar and the rage of hell.

With the lessening smoke and thunder,
Our glasses around we aim,—
What is that burning yonder?
Our Philippi—aground and in flame!

Below, 't was still all a-roar,
As the ships went by the shore,
But the fire of the Fort had slacked
(So fierce their volleys had been),—
And now with a mighty din,
The whole fleet came grandly in,
Though sorely battered and wracked.

So, up the Bay we ran,
The Flag to port and ahead,—
And a pitying rain began
To wash the lips of our dead.

A league from the Fort we lay,
And deemed that the end must lag,—
When lo! looking down the Bay,
There flaunted the Rebel Rag;—
The Ram is again under way
And heading dead for the Flag!

Steering up with the stream,
Boldly his course he lay,
Though the fleet all answered his fire,
And, as he still drew nigher,
Ever on bow and beam
Our Monitors pounded away;
How the Chickasaw hammered away!

Quickly breasting the wave,
Eager the prize to win,
First of us all the brave
Monongahela went in
Under full head of steam;—
Twice she struck him abeam,
Till her stem was a sorry work
(She might have run on a crag!),
The Lackawanna hit fair,
He flung her aside like cork,
And still he held for the Flag.

High in the mizzen shroud
(Lest the smoke his sight o'erwhelm),
Our Admiral's voice rang loud;
"Hard-a-starboard your helm!
Starboard, and run him down!"
Starboard it was,—and so,
Like a black squall's lifting frown,
Our mighty bow bore down
On the iron beak of the Foe.

We stood on the deck together,
Men that had looked on death
In battle and stormy weather;
Yet a little we held our breath,
When, with the hush of death,
The great ships drew together.

Our Captain strode to the bow,
Drayton, courtly and wise,
Kindly cynic, and wise
(You hardly had known him now,
The flame of fight in his eyes!),—
His brave heart eager to feel
How the oak would tell on the steel!

But, as the space grew short,
A little he seemed to shun us;
Out peered a form grim and lanky,
And a voice yelled, *"Hard-a-port!*
Hard-a-port!—here's the damned Yankee
Coming right down on us!"

He sheered, but the ships ran foul
With a gnarring shudder and growl;
He gave us a deadly gun;
But as he passed in his pride
(Rasping right alongside!),
The old Flag, in thunder-tones
Poured in her port broadside,
Rattling his iron hide
And cracking his timber-bones!

Just then, at speed on the Foe,
With her bow all weathered and brown,
The great Lackawanna came down
Full tilt, for another blow;—
We were forging ahead,
She reversed—but, for all our pains,
Rammed the old Hartford, instead,
Just for'ard the mizzen chains!

Ah! how the masts did buckle and bend,
And the stout hull ring and reel,
As she took us right on end!
(Vain were engine and wheel,
She was under full steam)—
With the roar of a thunder-stroke
Her two thousand tons of oak
Brought up on us, right abeam!

A wreck, as it looked, we lay
(Rib and plank-sheer gave way
To the stroke of that giant wedge!)—
Here, after all, we go—
The old ship is gone!—ah, no,
But cut to the water's edge.

Never mind then,—at him again!
His flurry now can't last long;
He'll never again see land,—
Try that on *him,* Marchand!
On him again, brave Strong!

Heading square at the hulk,
Full on his beam we bore;
But the spine of the huge Sea-Hog
Lay on the tide like a log,
He vomited flame no more.

By this, he had found it hot;—
Half the fleet, in an angry ring,
Closed round the hideous thing,
Hammering with solid shot,
And bearing down, bow on bow;
He has but a minute to choose,—
Life or renown?—which now
Will the Rebel Admiral lose?

Cruel, haughty, and cold,
He ever was strong and bold;
Shall he shrink from a wooden stem?
He will think of that brave band
He sank in the Cumberland;
Ay, he will sink like them.

Nothing left but to fight
Boldly his last sea-fight!

Can he strike? By Heaven, 't is true!
Down comes the traitor Blue,
And up goes the captive White!

Up went the White! Ah, then
The hurrahs that once and again
Rang from three thousand men
All flushed and savage with fight!
Our dead lay cold and stark;
But our dying, down in the dark,
Answered as best they might,
Lifting their poor lost arms,
And cheering for God and Right!

Ended the mighty noise,
Thunder of forts and ships.
Down we went to the hold,
Oh, our dear dying boys!
How we pressed their poor brave lips
(Ah, so pallid and cold!)
And held their hands to the last
(Those who had hands to hold).

Still thee, O woman heart!
(So strong an hour ago);
If the idle tears must start,
'T is not in vain they flow.

They died, our children dear.
On the drear berth-deck they died,—
Do not think of them here—
Even now their footsteps near
The immortal, tender sphere
(Land of love and cheer!
Home of the Crucified!).

And the glorious deed survives;
Our threescore, quiet and cold,
Lie thus, for a myriad lives
And treasure-millions untold
(Labor of poor men's lives,
Hunger of weans and wives,
Such is war-wasted gold).

Our ship and her fame to-day
Shall float on the storied Stream
When mast and shroud have crumbled away,
And her long white deck is a dream.

One daring leap in the dark,
Three mortal hours, at the most,—
And hell lies stiff and stark
On a hundred leagues of coast.

For the mighty Gulf is ours,—
The bay is lost and won,
An Empire is lost and won!
Land, if thou yet hast flowers,
Twine them in one more wreath
Of tenderest white and red
(Twin buds of glory and death!),
For the brows of our brave dead,
For thy Navy's noblest son.

Joy, O Land, for thy sons,
Victors by flood and field!
The traitor walls and guns
Have nothing left but to yield
(Even now they surrender!).

And the ships shall sail once more,
And the cloud of war sweep on
To break on the cruel shore;—
But Craven is gone,
He and his hundred are gone.

The flags flutter up and down
At sunrise and twilight dim,
The cannons menace and frown,—
But never again for him,
Him and the hundred.

The Dahlgrens are dumb,
Dumb are the mortars;
Never more shall the drum
Beat to colors and quarters,—
The great guns are silent.

O brave heart and loyal!
Let all your colors dip;—
Mourn him proud ship!
From main deck to royal.
God rest our Captain,
Rest our lost hundred!

Droop, flag and pennant!
What is your pride for?
Heaven, that he died for,
Rest our Lieutenant,
Rest our brave threescore!

.   .   .   .

O Mother Land! this weary life
  We led, we lead, is 'long of thee;
Thine the strong agony of strife,
  And thine the lonely sea.

Thine the long decks all slaughter-sprent,
  The weary rows of cots that lie
With wrecks of strong men, marred and rent,
  'Neath Pensacola's sky.

And thine the iron caves and dens
  Wherein the flame our war-fleet drives;
The fiery vaults, whose breath is men's
  Most dear and precious lives!

Ah, ever when with storm sublime
  Dread Nature clears our murky air,
Thus in the crash of falling crime
  Some lesser guilt must share.

Full red the furnace fires must glow
  That melt the ore of mortal kind;
The mills of God are grinding slow,
  But ah, how close they grind!

To-day the Dahlgren and the drum
  Are dread Apostles of His Name;
His kingdom here can only come
  By chrism of blood and flame.

Be strong: already slants the gold
  Athwart these wild and stormy skies:
From out this blackened waste, behold
  What happy homes shall rise!

But see thou well no traitor gloze,
  No striking hands with Death and Shame,
Betray the sacred blood that flows
  So freely for thy name.

And never fear a victor foe—
    Thy children's hearts are strong and high;
Nor mourn too fondly; well they know
    On deck or field to die.

Nor shalt thou want one willing breath,
    Though, ever smiling round the brave,
The blue sea bear us on to death,
    The green were one wide grave.
              HENRY HOWARD BROWNELL

SCOTT AND THE VETERAN

AN OLD and crippled veteran to the War Department came;
He sought the Chief who led him on many a field of fame,—
The Chief who shouted "Forward!" where'er his banner rose,
And bore its stars in triumph behind the flying foes.

"Have you forgotten, General," the battered soldier cried,
"The days of Eighteen Hundred Twelve, when I was at your side?
Have you forgotten Johnson, that fought at Lundy's Lane?
'Tis true, I'm old and pensioned, but I want to fight again."

"Have I forgotten?" said the Chief; "my brave old soldier, No!
And here's the hand I gave you then, and let it tell you so:
But you have done your share, my friend; you're crippled, old, and
    grey,
And we have need of younger arms and fresher blood to-day."

"But, General," cried the veteran, a flush upon his brow,
"The very men who fought with us, they say, are traitors now;
They've torn the flag of Lundy's Lane,—our old red, white, and
    blue;
And while a drop of blood is left, I'll show that drop is true.

"I'm not so weak but I can strike, and I've a good old gun
To get the range of traitors' hearts, and pick them, one by one.
Your Minie rifles, and such arms, it ain't worth while to try:
I couldn't get the hang o' them, but I'll keep my powder dry!"

"God bless you, comrade!" said the Chief; "God bless your loyal
    heart!
But younger men are in the field, and claim to have their part;
They'll plant our sacred banner in each rebellious town,
And woe, henceforth, to any hand that dares to pull it down!"

"But, General,"—still persisting, the weeping veteran cried,
"I'm young enough to follow, so long as you're my guide;
And some, you know, must bite the dust, and that, at least, can I,—
So give the young ones place to fight, but me a place to die!

"If they should fire on Pickens, let the Colonel in command
Put me upon the rampart, with the flag-staff in my hand:
No odds how hot the cannon-smoke, or how the shell may fly;
I'll hold the Stars and Stripes aloft, and hold them till I die!

"I'm ready, General, so you let a post to me be given,
Where Washington can see me, as he looks from highest heaven,
And say to Putnam at his side, or, may be General Wayne:
'There stands old Billy Johnson, that fought at Lundy's Lane!'

"And when the fight is hottest, before the traitors fly,
When shell and ball are screeching and bursting in the sky,
If any shot should hit me, and lay me on my face,
My soul would go to Washington's, and not to Arnold's place!"

                                          BAYARD TAYLOR

THE PICKET-GUARD

November, 1861

"ALL QUIET along the Potomac," they say,
  "Except now and then a stray picket
Is shot, as he walks on his beat to and fro,
  By a rifleman hid in the thicket.
'Tis nothing: a private or two, now and then,
  Will not count in the news of the battle;
Not an officer lost—only one of the men,
  Moaning out, all alone, the death rattle."

All quiet along the Potomac to-night,
  Where the soldiers lie peacefully dreaming;
Their tents in the rays of the clear autumn moon,
  Or the light of the watch-fire, are gleaming.
A tremulous sigh of the gentle night-wind
  Through the forest leaves softly is creeping,
While the stars up above, with their glittering eyes,
  Keep guard, for the army is sleeping.

There's only the sound of the lone sentry's tread
  As he tramps from the rock to the fountain,
And thinks of the two in the low trundle-bed
  Far away in the cot in the mountain.
His musket falls slack; his face, dark and grim,
  Grows gentle with memories tender,
As he mutters a prayer for the children asleep—
  For their mother—may Heaven defend her!

The moon seems to shine just as brightly as then,
  That night, when the love yet unspoken

Leaped up to his lips—when low-murmured vows
  Were pledged to be ever unbroken.
Then drawing his sleeve roughly over his eyes,
  He dashes off tears that are welling,
And gathers his gun closer up to its place
  As if to keep down the heart-swelling.

He passes the fountain, the blasted pine-tree;
  The footstep is lagging and weary;
Yet onward he goes, through the broad belt of light,
  Towards the shade of the forest so dreary.
Hark! was it the night-wind that rustled the leaves?
  Was it moonlight so wondrously flashing?
It looked like a rifle. . . . "Ha! Mary, good-by!"
  The red life-blood is ebbing and plashing.

All quiet along the Potomac to-night—
  No sound save the rush of the river,
While soft falls the dew on the face of the dead—
  The picket's off duty forever!
                              ETHEL LYNN BEERS

OUR COUNTRY'S CALL

LAY down the axe; fling by the spade;
  Leave in its track the toiling plough;
The rifle and the bayonet-blade
  For arms like yours were fitter now;
And let the hands that ply the pen
  Quit the light task, and learn to wield
The horseman's crooked brand, and rein
  The charger on the battle-field.

Our country calls; away! away!
  To where the blood-stream blots the green.
Strike to defend the gentlest sway
  That Time in all his course has seen.
See, from a thousand coverts—see,
  Spring the armed foes that haunt her track;
They rush to smite her down, and we
  Must beat the banded traitors back.

Ho! sturdy as the oaks ye cleave,
  And moved as soon to fear and flight,
Men of the glade and forest! leave
  Your woodcraft for the field of fight.
The arms that wield the axe must pour
  An iron tempest on the foe;
His serried ranks shall reel before
  The arm that lays the panther low.

And ye, who breast the mountain-storm
  By grassy steep or highland lake,
Come, for the land ye love, to form
  A bulwark that no foe can break.
Stand, like your own gray cliffs that mock
  The whirlwind, stand in her defence;
The blast as soon shall move the rock
  As rushing squadrons bear ye thence.

And ye, whose homes are by her grand
  Swift rivers, rising far away,
Come from the depth of her green land,
  As mighty in your march as they;
As terrible as when the rains
  Have swelled them over bank and borne,
With sudden floods to drown the plains
  And sweep along the woods uptorn.

And ye, who throng, beside the deep,
  Her ports and hamlets of the strand,
In number like the waves that leap
  On his long-murmuring marge of sand—
Come like that deep, when, o'er his brim
  He rises, all his floods to pour,
And flings the proudest barks that swim,
  A helpless wreck, against the shore!

Few, few were they whose swords of old
  Won the fair land in which we dwell,
But we are many, we who hold
  The grim resolve to guard it well.
Strike, for that broad and goodly land,
  Blow after blow, till men shall see
That Might and Right move hand in hand,
  And glorious must their triumph be!
                    WILLIAM CULLEN BRYANT

LITTLE GIFFEN

OUT of the focal and foremost fire,
Out of the hospital walls as dire,
Smitten of grape-shot and gangrene
(Eighteenth battle and *he* sixteen)—
Spectre such as you seldom see,
Little Giffen of Tennessee.

"Take him—and welcome!" the surgeons said,
"Little the doctor can help the dead!"
So we took him and brought him where
The balm was sweet on the summer air;
And we laid him down on a wholesome bed—
Utter Lazarus, heel to head!

And we watched the war with bated breath—
Skeleton Boy against skeleton Death.
Months of torture, how many such!
Weary weeks of the stick and 'crutch;
And still a glint in the steel-blue eye
Told of a spirit that wouldn't die.

And didn't. Nay, more! in death's despite
The crippled skeleton learned to write.
"Dear Mother," at first of course; and then
"Dear Captain," inquiring about "the men."
Captain's answer: "Of eighty and five,
Giffen and I are left alive."

Word of gloom from the war one day:
"Johnston's pressed at the front, they say!"
Little Giffen was up and away;
A tear—his first—as he bade good-by,
Dimmed the glint of his steel-blue eye.
"I'll write, if spared!" There was news of the fight;
But none of Giffen—he did not write.

I sometimes fancy that, were I king
Of the princely knights of the Golden Ring,
With the song of the minstrel in mine ear,
And the tender legend that trembles here,
I'd give the best, on his bended knee,
The whitest soul of my chivalry,
For Little Giffen of Tennessee.

FRANCIS ORRERY TICKNOR

KEARNY AT SEVEN PINES

So THAT soldierly legend is still on its journey,—
   That story of Kearny who knew not to yield!
'Twas the day when with Jameson, fierce Berry, and Birney,
   Against twenty thousand he rallied the field.
Where the red volleys poured, where the clamor rose highest,
   Where the dead lay in clumps through the dwarf oak and pine,
Where the aim from the thicket was surest and nighest,—
   No charge like Phil Kearny's along the whole line.

When the battle went ill, and the bravest were solemn,
   Near the dark Seven Pines, where we still held our ground,
He rode down the length of the withering column,
   And his heart at our war-cry leapt up with a bound;
He snuffed, like his charger, the wind of the powder,—
   His sword waved us on and we answered the sign;
Loud our cheer as we rushed, but his laugh rang the louder,
   "There's the devil's own fun, boys, along the whole line!"

How he strode his brown steed! How we saw his blade brighten
   In the one hand still left,—and the reins in his teeth!
He laughed like a boy when the holidays heighten,
   But a soldier's glance shot from his visor beneath.
Up came the reserves to the mellay infernal,
   Asking where to go in,—through the clearing or pine?
"Oh, anywhere! Forward! 'Tis all the same, Colonel:
   You'll find lovely fighting along the whole line!"

Oh, evil the black shroud of night at Chantilly,
   That hid him from sight of his brave men and tried!
Foul, foul sped the bullet that clipped the white lily,
   The flower of our knighthood, the whole army's pride!

Yet we dream that he still,—in that shadowy region
  Where the dead form their ranks at the wan drummer's sign,—
Rides on, as of old, down the length of his legion,
  And the word still is "Forward!" along the whole line.

EDMUND CLARENCE STEDMAN

THE OLD SERGEANT

"Come a little nearer, Doctor,—thank you, let me take the cup:
Draw your chair up,—draw it closer,—just another little sup!
May be you may think I'm better; but I'm pretty well used up:—
  Doctor, you've done all you could do, but I'm just a going up!

"Feel my pulse, sir, if you want to, but it ain't much use to try:"—
"Never say that," said the Surgeon as he smothered down a sigh;
"It will never do, old comrade, for a soldier to say die!"
  "What you *say* will make no difference, Doctor, when you come
    to die.

"Doctor, what has been the matter?" "You were very faint, they
    say;
You must try to get to sleep now." "Doctor, have I been away?"
"Not that anybody knows of!" "Doctor—Doctor, please to stay!
  There is something I must tell you, and you won't have long to
    stay!

"I have got my marching orders, and I'm ready now to go;
Doctor, did you say I fainted?—but it couldn't ha' been so,—
For as sure as I'm a sergeant, and was wounded at Shiloh,
  I've this very night been back there, on the old field of Shiloh!

"This is all that I remember: the last time the Lighter came,
And the lights had all been lowered, and the noises much the same,

He had not been gone five minutes before something called my
    name:
  'ORDERLY SERGEANT—ROBERT BURTON!' just that way it called my
    name.

"And I wondered who could call me so distinctly and so slow,
Knew it couldn't be the Lighter,—he could not have spoken so,—
And I tried to answer, 'Here, sir!' but I couldn't make it go;
    For I couldn't move a muscle, and I couldn't make it go!

"Then I thought: it's all a nightmare, all a humbug and a bore;
Just another foolish grape-vine,[1]—and it won't come any more;
But it came, sir, notwithstanding, just the same way as before:
    'ORDERLY SERGEANT—ROBERT BURTON!'—even plainer than before.

"That is all that I remember, till a sudden burst of light,
And I stood beside the river, where we stood that Sunday night,
Waiting to be ferried over to the dark bluffs opposite,
    When the river was perdition and all hell was opposite!—

"And the same old palpitation came again in all its power,
And I heard a Bugle sounding, as from some celestial Tower;
And the same mysterious voice said: 'IT IS THE ELEVENTH HOUR!
    ORDERLY SERGEANT—ROBERT BURTON—IT IS THE ELEVENTH HOUR!'

"Doctor Austin!—what *day* is this?" "It is Wednesday night, you
    know."
"Yes,—to-morrow will be New Year's, and a right good time
    below!
What *time* is it, Doctor Austin?" "Nearly Twelve." "Then don't
    you go!
    Can it be that all this happened—all this—not an hour ago!

"There was where the gunboats opened on the dark rebellious
    host;
And where Webster semicircled his last guns upon the coast;

[1]Canard.

There were still the two log-houses, just the same, or else their
  ghost,—
  And the same old transport came and took me over—or its
  ghost!

"And the old field lay before me all deserted far and wide;
There was where they fell on Prentiss,—there McClernand met the
  tide;
There was where stern Sherman rallied, and where Hurlbut's
  heroes died,—
  Lower down, where Wallace charged them, and kept charging
  till he died.

"There was where Lew Wallace showed them he was of the canny
  kin,
There was where old Nelson thundered, and where Rousseau
  waded in;
There McCook sent 'em to breakfast, and we all began to win—
  There was where the grape-shot took me, just as we began to
  win.

"Now, a shroud of snow and silence over everything was spread;
And but for this old blue mantle and the old hat on my head,
I should not have even doubted, to this moment, I was dead,—
  For my footsteps were as silent as the snow upon the dead!

"Death and silence!—Death and silence! all around me as I sped!
And, behold, a mighty Tower, as if builded to the dead,
To the Heaven of the heavens lifted up its mighty head,
  Till the Stars and Stripes of Heaven all seemed waving from
  its head!

"Round and mighty-based it towered—up into the infinite—
And I knew no mortal mason could have built a shaft so bright;
For it shone like solid sunshine; and a winding stair of light
Wound around it and around it till it wound clear out of sight!

"And, behold, as I approached it,—with a rapt and dazzled stare,—
Thinking that I saw old comrades just ascending the great Stair,—
Suddenly the solemn challenge broke of, 'Halt, and who goes
    there!'
  'I'm a friend,' I said, 'if you are.' 'Then advance, sir, to the Stair!'

"I advanced!—That sentry, Doctor, was Elijah Ballantyne!—
First of all to fall on Monday, after we had formed the line!—
'Welcome, my old Sergeant, welcome! welcome by that counter-
    sign!'
  And he pointed to the scar there, under this old cloak of mine!

"As he grasped my hand, I shuddered, thinking only of the grave;
But he smiled and pointed upward with a bright and bloodless
    glaive:
'That's the way, sir, to Headquarters.' 'What Headquarters?' 'Of
    the Brave.'
  'But the great Tower?' 'That,' he answered, 'is the way, sir, of
    the Brave!'

"Then a sudden shame came o'er me at his uniform of light;
At my own so old and tattered, and at his so new and bright:
'Ah!' said he, 'you have forgotten the New Uniform to-night,—
  Hurry back, for you must be here at just twelve o'clock to-night!'

"And the next thing I remember, you were sitting *there,* and I—
Doctor—did you hear a footstep? Hark!—God bless you all! Good
    by!
Doctor, please to give my musket and my knapsack, when I die,
To my son—my son that's coming,—he won't get here till I die!

"Tell him his old father blessed him as he never did before,—
And to carry that old musket—hark! a knock is at the door!—
Till the Union— See! it opens!" "Father! father! speak once more!"
  "Bless you!" gasped the old, gray Sergeant, and he lay and said
    no more!

Forceythe Willson

SHERIDAN'S RIDE

October 19, 1864

Up from the South, at break of day,
Bringing to Winchester fresh dismay,
The affrighted air with a shudder bore,
Like a herald in haste to the chieftain's door,
The terrible grumble, and rumble, and roar,
Telling the battle was on once more,
    And Sheridan twenty miles away.

And wider still those billows of war
Thundered along the horizon's bar;
And louder yet into Winchester rolled
The roar of that red sea uncontrolled,
Making the blood of the listener cold,
As he thought of the stake in that fiery fray,
    With Sheridan twenty miles away.

But there is a road from Winchester town,
A good, broad highway leading down:
And there, through the flush of the morning light,
A steed as black as the steeds of night
Was seen to pass, as with eagle flight;
As if he knew the terrible need,
He stretched away with his utmost speed.
Hills rose and fell, but his heart was gay,
    With Sheridan fifteen miles away.

Still sprang from those swift hoofs, thundering south,
The dust like smoke from the cannon's mouth,
Or the trail of a comet, sweeping faster and faster,
Foreboding to traitors the doom of disaster.

The heart of the steed and the heart of the master
Were beating like prisoners assaulting their walls,
Impatient to be where the battle-field calls;
Every nerve of the charger was strained to full play,
    With Sheridan only ten miles away.

Under his spurning feet, the road
Like an arrowy Alpine river flowed,
And the landscape sped away behind
Like an ocean flying before the wind;
And the steed, like a bark fed with furnace ire,
Swept on, with his wild eye full of fire;
But, lo! he is nearing his heart's desire;
He is snuffing the smoke of the roaring fray,
    With Sheridan only five miles away.

The first that the general saw were the groups
Of stragglers, and then the retreating troops;
What was done? what to do? a glance told him both.
Then striking his spurs with a terrible oath,
He dashed down the line, 'mid a storm of huzzas,
And the wave of retreat checked its course there, because
The sight of the master compelled it to pause.
With foam and with dust the black charger was gray;
By the flash of his eye, and the red nostril's play,
He seemed to the whole great army to say:
"I have brought you Sheridan all the way
    From Winchester down to save the day."

Hurrah! hurrah for Sheridan!
Hurrah! hurrah for horse and man!
And when their statues are placed on high
Under the dome of the Union sky,
The American soldier's Temple of Fame,
There, with the glorious general's name,

Be it said, in letters both bold and bright:
"Here is the steed that saved the day
By carrying Sheridan into the fight,
     From Winchester—twenty miles away!"

THOMAS BUCHANAN READ

SHENANDOAH

IN THE Shenandoah Valley, one rider grey and one rider blue, and
the sun on the riders wondering.

Piled in the Shenandoah, riders blue and riders grey, piled with
shovels, one and another, dust in the Shenandoah taking them
quicker than mothers take children done with play.

The blue nobody remembers, the grey nobody remembers, it's all
old and old nowadays in the Shenandoah.

And all is young, a butter of dandelions slung on the turf, climbing
blue flowers of the wishing woodlands wondering: a midnight
purple violet cliams the sun among old heads, among old dreams
of repeating heads of a rider blue and a rider grey in the
Shenandoah.

CARL SANDBURG

WE'RE TENTING TO-NIGHT

WE'RE tenting to-night on the old camp-ground,
     Give us a song to cheer
Our weary hearts, a song of home
     And friends we love so dear.

Many are the hearts that are weary to-night,
   Wishing for the war to cease;
Many are the hearts looking for the right,
   To see the dawn of peace.
Tenting to-night, tenting to-night,
   Tenting on the old camp-ground.

We've been tenting to-night on the old camp-ground,
   Thinking of days gone by,
Of the loved ones at home that gave us the hand,
   And the tear that said "good-bye"!
Many are the hearts that are weary to-night, *etc.*

We are weary of war on the old camp-ground,
   Many are the dead and gone
Of the brave and true who have left their homes,
   Others wounded long.
Many are the hearts that are weary to-night, *etc.*

We've been fighting to-day on the old camp-ground,
   Many are lying near;
Some are dead—and dying are some,
   Many a one in tears.
Many are the hearts that are weary to-night,
   To see the dawn of peace.
Dying to-night, dying to-night,
   Dying on the old camp-ground.

                      WALTER KITTREDGE

MARCHING THROUGH GEORGIA

BRING the good old bugle, boys, we'll sing another song—
Sing it with a spirit that will start the world along—
Sing it as we used to sing it fifty thousand strong,
   While we were marching through Georgia.

Chorus—"Hurrah! Hurrah! we bring the jubilee!
       Hurrah! Hurrah! the flag that makes you free!"
       So we sang the chorus from Atlanta to the sea,
       While we were marching through Georgia.

How the darkeys shouted when they heard the joyful sound!
How the turkeys gobbled which our commissary found!
How the sweet potatoes even started from the ground,
   While we were marching through Georgia.

Yes, and there were Union men who wept with joyful tears,
When they saw the honored flag they had not seen for years;
Hardly could they be restrained from breaking forth in cheers,
   While we were marching through Georgia.

"Sherman's dashing Yankee boys will never reach the coast!"
So the saucy rebels said—and 't was a handsome boast,
Had they not forgot, alas! to reckon on a host,
   While we were marching through Georgia.

So we made a thoroughfare for Freedom and her train,
Sixty miles in latitude—three hundred to the main;
Treason fled before us, for resistance was in vain,
   While we were marching through Georgia.

                  HENRY CLAY WORK

"HOW ARE YOU, SANITARY?"

Down the picket-guarded lane,
Rolled the comfort-laden wain,
Cheered by shouts that shook the plain,
   Soldier-like and merry;
Phrases such as camps may teach,
Sabre-cuts of Saxon speech,
Such as "Bully!" "Them's the peach!"
   "Wade in, Sanitary!"

Right and left the caissons drew
As the car went lumbering through,
Quick succeeding in review
  Squadrons military;
Sunburnt men with beards like frieze,
Smooth-faced boys, and cries like these,—
"U. S. San. Com." "That's the cheese!"
  "Pass in, Sanitary!"

In such cheer it struggled on
Till the battle front was won,
Then the car, its journey done,
  Lo! was stationary;
And where bullets whistling fly,
Came the sadder, fainter cry,
"Help us, brothers, ere we die,—
  Save us, Sanitary!"

Such the work. The phantom flies,
Wrapped in battle clouds that rise;
But the brave—whose dying eyes,
  Veiled and visionary,
See the jasper gates swung wide,
See the parted throng outside—
Hears the voice to those who ride:
  "Pass in, Sanitary!"

                                    BRET HARTE

THREE HUNDRED THOUSAND MORE

WE ARE coming, Father Abraham, three hundred thousand more,
From Mississippi's winding stream and from New England's shore;
We leave our ploughs and workshops, our wives and children dear,
With hearts too full for utterance, with but a silent tear;

We dare not look behind us, but steadfastly before:
We are coming, Father Abraham, three hundred thousand more!

If you look across the hill-tops that meet the northern sky,
Long moving lines of rising dust your vision may descry;
And now the wind, an instant, tears the cloudy veil aside,
And floats aloft our spangled flag in glory and in pride,
And bayonets in the sunlight gleam, and bands brave music pour:
We are coming, Father Abraham, three hundred thousand more!

If you look all up our valleys where the growing harvests shine,
You may see our sturdy farmer boys fast forming into line;
And children from their mother's knees are pulling at the weeds,
And learning how to reap and sow against their country's needs;
And a farewell group stands weeping at every cottage door:
We are coming, Father Abraham, three hundred thousand more!

You have called us, and we're coming, by Richmond's bloody tide
To lay us down, for Freedom's sake, our brothers' bones beside,
Or from foul treason's savage grasp to wrench the murderous
  blade,
And in the face of foreign foes its fragments to parade.
Six hundred thousand loyal men and true have gone before:
We are coming, Father Abraham, three hundred thousand more!

JAMES SLOAN GIBBONS

MUSIC IN CAMP

Two ARMIES covered hill and plain,
    Where Rappahannock's waters
Ran deeply crimsoned with the stain
    Of battle's recent slaughters.

The summer clouds lay pitched like tents
    In meads of heavenly azure;
And each dread gun of the elements
    Slept in its high embrasure.

The breeze so softly blew, it made
    No forest leaf to quiver;
And the smoke of the random cannonade
    Rolled slowly from the river.

And now where circling hills looked down
    With cannon grimly planted,
O'er listless camp and silent town
    The golden sunset slanted.

When on the fervid air there came
    A strain now rich now tender;
The music seemed itself aflame
    With day's departing splendor.

A Federal band which eve and morn
    Played measures brave and nimble,
Had just struck up with flute and horn
    And lively clash of cymbal.

Down flocked the soldiers to the banks;
    Till, margined by its pebbles,
One wooded shore was blue with "Yanks,"
    And one was gray with "Rebels."

Then all was still; and then the band,
    With movement light and tricksy,
Made stream and forest, hill and strand
    Reverberate with "Dixie."

The conscious stream, with burnished glow,
　　Went proudly o'er its pebbles,
But thrilled throughout its deepest flow
　　With yelling of the Rebels,

Again a pause; and then again
　　The trumpet pealed sonorous,
And "Yankee Doodle" was the strain
　　To which the shore gave chorus.

The laughing ripple shoreward flew
　　To kiss the shining pebbles;
Loud shrieked the swarming Boys in Blue
　　Defiance to the Rebels.

And yet once more the bugle sang
　　Above the stormy riot;
No shout upon the evening rang—
　　There reigned a holy quiet.

The sad, slow stream its noiseless flood
　　Poured o'er the glistening pebbles;
All silent now the Yankees stood,
　　All silent stood the Rebels.

No unresponsive soul had heard
　　That plaintive note's appealing,
So deeply "Home, Sweet Home" had stirred
　　The hidden founts of feeling.

Or Blue, or Gray, the soldier sees,
　　As by the wand of fairy,
The cottage 'neath the live-oak trees,
　　The cabin by the prairie.

Tho' cold or warm, his native skies
   Bend in their beauty o'er him;
Seen through the tear-mist in his eyes,
   His loved ones stand before him.

As fades the iris after rain
   In April's tearful weather,
The vision vanished as the strain
   And daylight died together.

But Memory, waked by Music's art,
   Expressed in simple numbers,
Subdued the sternest Yankee's heart,
   Made light the Rebel's slumbers.

And fair the form of Music shines—
   That bright celestial creature—
Who still 'mid War's embattled lines
   Gives this one touch of Nature.
              JOHN R. THOMPSON

THE REVEILLE

HARK! I hear the tramp of thousands,
   And of armèd men the hum;
Lo! a nation's hosts have gathered
   Round the quick-alarming drum,—
        Saying: "Come,
        Freemen, come!
Ere your heritage be wasted," said the quick-alarming drum.

"Let me of my heart take counsel:
   War is not of life the sum;

Who shall stay and reap the harvest
  When the autumn days shall come?"
          But the drum
          Echoed: "Come!
Death shall reap the braver harvest," said the solemn-sounding
  drum.

"But when won the coming battle,
  What of profit springs therefrom?
What if conquest, subjugation,
  Even greater ills become?"
          But the drum
          Answered: "Come!
You must do the sum to prove it," said the Yankee-answering
  drum.

"What if, 'mid the cannons' thunder,
  Whistling shot and bursting bomb,
When my brothers fall around me,
  Should my heart grow cold and numb?"
          But the drum
          Answered: "Come!
Better there in death united than in life a recreant,—Come!"

Thus they answered—hoping, fearing,
  Some in faith and doubting some,
Till a trumpet-voice proclaiming,
  Said: "My chosen people, come!"
          Then the drum,
          Lo! was dumb;
For the great heart of the nation, throbbing, answered: "Lord, we
  come!"

                                                BRET HARTE

THE BONNIE BLUE FLAG

Come, brothers! rally for the right!
   The bravest of the brave
Sends forth her ringing battle-cry
   Beside the Atlantic wave!
She leads the way in honor's path;
   Come, brothers, near and far,
Come rally round the Bonnie Blue Flag
   That bears a single star!

We've borne the Yankee trickery,
   The Yankee gibe and sneer,
Till Yankee insolence and pride
   Know neither shame nor fear;
But ready now with shot and steel
   Their brazen front to mar,
We hoist aloft the Bonnie Blue Flag
   That bears a single star.

Now Georgia marches to the front,
   And close beside her come
Her sisters by the Mexique Sea,
   With pealing trump and drum;
Till answering back from hill and glen
   The rallying cry afar,
A Nation hoists the Bonnie Blue Flag
   That bears a single star.

By every stone in Charleston Bay,
   By each beleaguered town,
We swear to rest not, night nor day,
   But hunt the tyrants down!

Till bathed in valor's holy blood
  The gazing world afar
Shall greet with shouts the Bonnie Blue Flag
  That bears the cross and star!
        ANNIE CHAMBERS KETCHUM

THE CALL TO THE COLORS

"ARE you ready, O Virginia,
  Alabama, Tennessee?
People of the Southland, answer!
  For the land hath need of thee."
"Here!" from sandy Rio Grande,
  Where the Texan horsemen ride;
"Here!" the hunters of Kentucky
  Hail from Chatterawah's side;
Every toiler in the cotton,
  Every rugged mountaineer,
Velvet-voiced and iron-handed,
  Lifts his head to answer, "Here!
Some remain who charged with Pickett,
  Some survive who followed Lee;
They shall lead their sons to battle
  For the flag, if need there be."

"Are you ready, California,
  Arizona, Idaho?
'Come, oh, come, unto the colors!'
  Heard you not the bugle blow?"
Falls a hush in San Francisco
  In the busy hives of trade;
In the vineyards of Sonoma
  Fall the pruning knife and spade;
In the mines of Colorado

Pick and drill are thrown aside;
Idly in Seattle harbor
    Swing the merchants to the tide;
And a million mighty voices
    Throb responsive like a drum,
Rolling from the rough Sierras,
    "You have called us, and we come."

O'er Missouri sounds the challenge—
    O'er the great lakes and the plain;
"Are you ready, Minnesota?
    Are you ready, men of Maine?"
From the woods of Ontonagon,
    From the farms of Illinois,
From the looms of Massachusetts,
    "We are ready, man and boy."
Axemen free, of Androscoggin,
    Clerks who trudge the cities' paves,
Gloucester men who drag their plunder
    From the sullen, hungry waves,
Big-boned Swede and large-limbed German,
    Celt and Saxon swell the call,
And the Adirondacks echo:
    "We are ready, one and all."

Truce to feud and peace to faction!
    All forgot is party zeal
When the war-ships clear for action,
    When the blue battalions wheel.
Europe boasts her standing armies,—
    Serfs who blindly fight by trade;
We have seven million soldiers,
    And a soul guides every blade.
Laborers with arm and mattock,

Laborers with brain and pen,
Railroad prince and railroad brakeman
Build our line of fighting men.
Flag of righteous wars! close mustered
Gleam the bayonets, row on row,
Where thy stars are sternly clustered,
With their daggers towards the foe!
ARTHUR GUITERMAN

THE VIRGINIANS OF THE VALLEY

THE knightliest of the knightly race
That, since the days of old,
Have kept the lamp of chivalry
Alight in hearts of gold;
The kindliest of the kindly band
That, rarely hating ease,
Yet rode with Spotswood round the land,
And Raleigh round the seas;

Who climbed the blue Virginian hills
Against embattled foes,
And planted there, in valleys fair,
The lily and the rose;
Whose fragrance lives in many lands,
Whose beauty stars the earth,
And lights the hearths of happy homes
With loveliness and worth.

We thought they slept!—the sons who kept
The names of noble sires,
And slumbered while the darkness crept
Around their vigil-fires;

But aye the "Golden Horseshoe" knights
    Their old Dominion keep,
Whose foes have found enchanted ground,
    But not a knight asleep!

FRANCIS ORRERY TICKNOR

DIXIE

THE ORIGINAL VERSION

I WISH I was in de land ob cotton,
Old times dar am not forgotten;
    Look away, look away, look away, Dixie land!
In Dixie land whar I was born in,
Early on one frosty mornin',
    Look away, look away, look away, Dixie land!

Chorus—Den I wish I was in Dixie! Hooray! Hooray!
        In Dixie's land we'll took our stand, to lib an' die in Dixie,
        Away, away, away down south in Dixie!
        Away, away, away down south in Dixie!

Old missus marry Will de weaber,
William was a gay deceaber,
When he put his arm around 'er,
He looked as fierce as a forty-pounder.

His face was sharp as a butcher cleaber,
But dat did not seem to greab 'er;
Will run away, missus took a decline, O,
Her face was the color of bacon rhine, O.

While missus libbed, she libbed in clover,
When she died, she died all over;
How could she act de foolish part,
An' marry a man to break her heart?

Buckwheat cakes an' stony batter
Makes you fat or a little fatter;
Here's a health to de next old missus,
An' all de gals dat want to kiss us.

Now if you want to drive 'way sorrow,
Come an' hear dis song to-morrow;
Den hoe it down an' scratch your grabble,
To Dixie's land I'm bound to trabble.

DANIEL DECATUR EMMETT

DIXIE

SOUTHRONS, hear your country call you!
Up, lest worse than death befall you!
    To arms! To arms! To arms, in Dixie!
Lo! all the beacon-fires are lighted,—
Let all hearts be now united!
    To arms! To arms! To arms, in Dixie!
        Advance the flag of Dixie!
            Hurrah! hurrah!
For Dixie's land we take our stand,
        And live and die for Dixie!
            To arms! To arms!
        And conquer peace for Dixie!
            To arms! To arms!
        And conquer peace for Dixie!

Hear the Northern thunders mutter!
Northern flags in South winds flutter!
Send them back your fierce defiance!
Stamp upon the accursed alliance!
Fear no danger! Shun no labor!
Lift up rifle, pike, and sabre!
Shoulder pressing close to shoulder,
Let the odds make each heart bolder!

How the South's great heart rejoices
At your cannons' ringing voices!
For faith betrayed, and pledges broken,
Wrongs inflicted, insults spoken.

Strong as lions, swift as eagles,
Back to their kennels hunt these beagles!
Cut the unequal bonds asunder!
Let them hence each other plunder!

Swear upon your country's altar
Never to submit or falter,
Till the spoilers are defeated,
Till the Lord's work is completed!

Halt not till our Federation
Secures among earth's powers its station!
Then at peace, and crowned with glory,
Hear your children tell the story!

If the loved ones weep in sadness,
Victory soon shall bring them gladness,—
          To arms!
Exultant pride soon vanish sorrow;
Smiles chase tears away to-morrow.

To arms! To arms! To arms, in Dixie!
Advance the flag of Dixie!
Hurrah! hurrah!
For Dixie's land we take our stand,
And live or die for Dixie!
To arms! To arms!
And conquer peace for Dixie!
To arms! To arms!
And conquer peace for Dixie!

ALBERT PIKE

MY MARYLAND

THE despot's heel is on thy shore,
Maryland!
His torch is at thy temple door,
Maryland!
Avenge the patriotic gore
That flecked the streets of Baltimore,
And be the battle-queen of yore,
Maryland, my Maryland!

Hark to an exiled son's appeal,
Maryland!
My Mother State, to thee I kneel,
Maryland!
For life and death, for woe and weal,
Thy peerless chivalry reveal,
And gird thy beauteous limbs with steel,
Maryland, my Maryland!

Thou wilt not cower in the dust,
Maryland!
Thy beaming sword shall never rust,
Maryland!

Remember Carroll's sacred trust,
Remember Howard's warlike thrust,
And all thy slumberers with the just,
   Maryland, my Maryland!

Come! 't is the red dawn of the day,
   Maryland!
Come with thy panoplied array,
   Maryland!
With Ringgold's spirit for the fray,
With Watson's blood at Monterey,
With fearless Lowe and dashing May,
   Maryland, my Maryland!

Dear Mother, burst the tyrant's chain,
   Maryland!
Virginia should not call in vain,
   Maryland!
She meets her sisters on the plain,—
"*Sic semper!*" 't is the proud refrain
That baffles minions back amain,
   Maryland!
Arise in majesty again,
   Maryland, my Maryland!

Come! for thy shield is bright and strong,
   Maryland!
Come! for thy dalliance does thee wrong,
   Maryland!
Come to thine own heroic throng
Stalking with Liberty along,
And chant thy dauntless slogan-song,
   Maryland, my Maryland!

I see the blush upon thy cheek,
   Maryland!
For thou wast ever bravely meek,
   Maryland!
But lo! there surges forth a shriek,
From hill to hill, from creek to creek,
Potomac calls to Chesapeake,
   Maryland, my Maryland!

Thou wilt not yield the Vandal toll,
   Maryland!
Thou wilt not crook to his control,
   Maryland!
Better the fire upon thee roll,
Better the shot, the blade, the bowl,
Than crucifixion of the soul,
   Maryland, my Maryland!

I hear the distant thunder hum,
   Maryland!
The Old Line's bugle, fife, and drum,
   Maryland!
She is not dead, nor deaf, nor dumb;
Huzza! she spurns the Northern scum!
She breathes! She burns! She'll come! She'll come!
   Maryland, my Maryland!
            JAMES RYDER RANDALL

LEE TO THE REAR

DAWN of a pleasant morning in May
Broke through the Wilderness cool and gray;
While perched in the tallest tree-tops, the birds
Were carolling Mendelssohn's "Songs Without Words."

Far from the haunts of men remote,
The brook brawled on with a liquid note;
And Nature, all tranquil and lovely, wore
The smile of the spring, as in Eden of yore.

Little by little, as daylight increased,
And deepened the roseate flush in the East—
Little by little did morning reveal
Two long glittering lines of steel;

Where two hundred thousand bayonets gleam,
Tipped with the light of the earliest beam,
And the faces are sullen and grim to see
In the hostile armies of Grant and Lee.

All of a sudden, ere rose the sun,
Pealed on the silence the opening gun—
A little white puff of smoke there came,
And anon the valley was wreathed in flame.

Down on the left of the Rebel lines,
Where a breastwork stands in a copse of pines,
Before the Rebels their ranks can form,
The Yankees have carried the place by storm.

Stars and Stripes on the salient wave,
Where many a hero has found a grave,
And the gallant Confederates strive in vain
The ground they have drenched with their blood to regain.

Yet louder the thunder of battle roared—
Yet a deadlier fire on the columns poured;
Slaughter infernal rode with Despair,
Furies twain, through the murky air.

Not far off, in the saddle there sat
A gray-bearded man in a black slouched hat;
Not much moved by the fire was he,
Calm and resolute Robert Lee.

Quick and watchful he kept his eye
On the bold Rebel brigades close by,—
Reserves that were standing (and dying) at ease,
While the tempest of wrath toppled over the trees.

For still with their loud, deep, bull-dog bay,
The Yankee batteries blazed away,
And with every murderous second that sped
A dozen brave fellows, alas! fell dead.

The grand old graybeard rode to the space
Where Death and his victims stood face to face,
And silently waved his old slouched hat—
A world of meaning there was in that!

"Follow me! Steady! We'll save the day!"
This was what he seemed to say;
And to the light of his glorious eye
The bold brigades thus made reply:

"We'll go forward, but you must go back"—
And they moved not an inch in the perilous track:
"Go to the rear, and we'll send them to hell!"
And the sound of the battle was lost in their yell.

Turning his bridle, Robert Lee
Rode to the rear. Like waves of the sea,
Bursting the dikes in their overflow,
Madly his veterans dashed on the foe.

And backward in terror that foe was driven,
Their banners rent and their columns riven,
Wherever the tide of battle rolled
Over the Wilderness, wood and wold.

Sunset out of a crimson sky
Streamed o'er a field of ruddier dye,
And the brook ran on with a purple stain,
From the blood of ten thousand foemen slain.

Seasons have passed since that day and year—
Again o'er its pebbles the brook runs clear,
And the field in a richer green is drest
Where the dead of a terrible conflict rest.

Hushed is the roll of the Rebel drum,
The sabres are sheathed, and the cannon are dumb;
And Fate, with his pitiless hand, has furled
The flag that once challenged the gaze of the world;

But the fame of the Wilderness fight abides;
And down into history grandly rides,
Calm and unmoved as in battle he sat,
The gray-bearded man in the black slouched hat.

JOHN R. THOMPSON

MAGNOLIA CEMETERY

SUNG AT CHARLESTON, S. C., OVER THE GRAVES OF THE CONFEDERATE SOLDIERS

SLEEP sweetly in your humble graves,
   Sleep, martyrs of a fallen cause!
Though yet no marble column craves
   The pilgrim here to pause.

In seeds of laurel in the earth
  The blossom of your fame is blown,
And somewhere, waiting for its birth,
  The shaft is in the stone!

Meanwhile, behalf the tardy years
  Which keep in trust your storied tombs,
Behold! your sisters bring their tears,
  And these memorial blooms.

Small tributes! but your shades will smile
  More proudly on these wreaths to-day,
Than when some cannon-moulded pile
  Shall overlook this bay.

Stoop, angels, hither from the skies!
  There is no holier spot of ground
Than where defeated valor lies,
    By mourning beauty crowned!
                              HENRY TIMROD

THE SWORD OF ROBERT LEE

FORTH from its scabbard, pure and bright
  Flashed the sword of Lee!
Far in the front of the deadly fight,
High o'er the brave in the cause of Right,
Its stainless sheen, like a beacon bright,
  Let us to Victory.

Out of its scabbard, where, full long,
  It slumbered peacefully,
Roused from its rest by the battle's song,
Shielding the feeble, smiting the strong,
Guarding the right, avenging the wrong,
  Gleamed the sword of Lee.

Forth from its scabbard, high in air
  Beneath Virginia's sky—
And they who saw it gleaming there,
And knew who bore it, knelt to swear
That were that sword led they would dare
  To follow—and to die.

Out of its scabbard! Never hand
  Waved sword from stain as free,
Nor purer sword led braver band,
Nor braver bled for a brighter land,
Nor brighter land had a cause so grand,
  Nor cause a chief like Lee!

Forth from its scabbard! How we prayed
  That sword might victor be;
And when our triumph was delayed,
And many a heart grew sore afraid,
We still hoped on while gleamed the blade
  Of noble Robert Lee.

Forth from its scabbard all in vain
  Bright flashed the sword of Lee;
'Tis shrouded now in its sheath again,
It sleeps the sleep of our noble slain,
Defeated, yet without a stain,
  Proudly and peacefully.
          ABRAM J. RYAN

LINES ON THE BACK OF A CONFEDERATE NOTE

REPRESENTING nothing on God's earth now,
  And naught in the waters below it,
As the pledge of a nation that's dead and gone,
  Keep it, dear friends, and show it.

Show it to those who will lend an ear
  To the tale that this trifle can tell,
Of a liberty born of a patriot's dream,
  Of a storm-cradled nation that fell.

Too poor to possess the precious ores,
  And too much of a stranger to borrow,
We issued today our promise to pay
  And hoped to redeem on the morrow.

The days rolled by and the weeks became years,
  But our coffers were empty still.
Coin was so rare that the treasury'd quake
  If a dollar dropped into the till.

But the faith that was in us was strong indeed,
  And our poverty well we discerned,
And this little note represented the pay
  That our suffering veterans earned.

They knew it had hardly a value in gold,
  Yet as gold each soldier received it.
It gazed in our eyes with a promise to pay,
  And every true soldier believed it.

But our boys thought little of price or of pay,
  Or of bills that were long past due;
We knew if it brought us our bread today,
  'Twas the best our poor country could do.

Keep it; it tells all our history over,
  From the birth of the dream to its last:
Modest and born of the Angel of Hope,
  Like our hope of success it has passed.
                    MAJOR SAMUEL ALROY JONAS

STONEWALL JACKSON'S WAY

Come, stack arms, men! Pile on the rails,
　Stir up the camp-fire bright;
No growling if the canteen fails,
　We'll make a roaring night.
Here Shenandoah brawls along,
There burly Blue Ridge echoes strong,
To swell the Brigade's rousing song
　Of "Stonewall Jackson's way."

We see him now—the queer slouched hat
　Cocked o'er his eye askew;
The shrewd, dry smile; the speech so pat,
　So calm, so blunt, so true.
The "Blue-Light Elder" knows 'em well;
Says he, "That's Banks—he's fond of shell;
Lord save his soul! we'll give him—" well!
　That's "Stonewall Jackson's way."

Silence! ground arms! kneel all! caps off!
　Old Massa's goin' to pray.
Strangle the fool that dares to scoff!
　Attention! it's his way.
Appealing from his native sod,
In forma pauperis to God:
"Lay bare Thine arm; stretch forth **Thy rod!**
　Amen!" That's "Stonewall's way."

He's in the saddle now. Fall in!
　Steady! the whole brigade!
Hill's at the ford, cut off; we'll win
　His way out, ball and blade!

What matter if our shoes are worn?
What matter if our feet are torn?
"Quick step! we're with him before morn!"
   That's "Stonewall Jackson's way."

The sun's bright lances rout the mists
   Of morning, and, by George!
Here's Longstreet, struggling in the lists,
   Hemmed in an ugly gorge.
Pope and his Dutchmen, whipped before;
"Bay'nets and grape!" hear Stonewall roar;
"Charge, Stuart! Pay off Ashby's score!"
   In "Stonewall Jackson's way."

Ah! Maiden, wait and watch and yearn
   For news of Stonewall's band!
Ah! Widow, read, with eyes that burn,
   That ring upon thy hand.
Ah! Wife, sew on, pray on, hope on;
Thy life shall not be all forlorn;
The foe had better ne'er been born
   That gets in "Stonewall's way."
                    JOHN WILLIAMSON PALMER

RUNNING THE BATTERIES

As Observed From the Anchorage Above Vicksburg, April, 1863

A MOONLESS night—a friendly one;
   A haze dimmed the shadowy shore
As the first lampless boat slid silent on;
   Hist! and we spake no more;
We but pointed, and stilly, to what we saw.

We felt the dew, and seemed to feel
  The secret like a burden laid.
The first boat melts; and a second keel
  Is blent with the foliaged shade—
Their midnight rounds have the rebel officers made?

Unspied as yet. A third—a fourth—
  Gunboat and transport in Indian file
Upon the war-path, smooth from the North;
  But the watch may they hope to beguile?
The manned river-batteries stretch far mile on mile.

A flame leaps out; they are seen;
  Another and another gun roars;
We tell the course of the boats through the screen
  By each further fort that pours,
And we guess how they jump from their beds on those shrouded
    shores.

Converging fires. We speak, though low:
  "That blastful furnace can they thread?"
"Why, Shadrach, Meshach, and Abednego
  Came out all right, we read;
The Lord, be sure, he helps his people, Ned."

How we strain our gaze. On bluffs they shun
  A golden growing flame appears—
Confirms to a silvery steadfast one:
  "The town is afire!" crows Hugh; "three cheers!"
Lot stops his mouth: "Nay, lad, better three tears."

A purposed light; it shows our fleet;
  Yet a little late in its searching ray,
So far and strong that in phantom cheat
  Lank on the deck our shadows lay;
The shining flag-ship stings their guns to furious play.

How dread to mark her near the glare
   And glade of death the beacon throws
Athwart the racing waters there;
   One by one each plainer grows,
Then speeds a blazoned target to our gladdened foes.

The impartial cresset lights as well
   The fixed forts to the boats that run;
And, plunged from the ports, their answers swell
   Back to each fortress dun;
Ponderous words speaks every monster gun.

Fearless they flash through gates of flame,
   The salamanders hard to hit,
Though vivid shows each bulky frame;
   And never the batteries intermit,
Nor the boat's huge guns; they fire and flit.

Anon a lull. The beacon dies.
   "Are they out of that strait accurst?"
But other flames now dawning rise,
   Not mellowly brilliant like the first,
But rolled in smoke, whose whitish volumes burst.

A baleful brand, a hurrying torch
   Whereby anew the boats are seen—
A burning transport all alurch!
   Breathless we gaze; yet still we glean
Glimpses of beauty as we eager lean.

The effulgence takes an amber glow
   Which bathes the hillside villas far;
Affrighted ladies mark the show
   Painting the pale magnolia—
The fair, false, Circe light of cruel War.

The barge drifts doomed, a plague-struck one,
  Shoreward in yawls the sailors fly.
But the gauntlet now is nearly run,
  The spleenful forts by fits reply,
And the burning boat dies down in morning's sky.

All out of range. Adieu, Messieurs!
  Jeers, as it speeds, our parting gun.
So burst we through their barriers
  And menaces every one;
So Porter proves himself a brave man's son.

HERMAN MELVILLE

FARRAGUT

MOBILE BAY, AUGUST 5, 1864

FARRAGUT, Farragut,
    Old Heart of Oak,
Daring Dave Farragut,
    Thunderbolt stroke,
Watches the hoary mist
    Lift from the bay,
Till his flag, glory-kissed,
    Greets the young day.

Far, by gray Morgan's walls,
    Looms the black fleet.
Hark, deck to rampart calls
    With the drums' beat!
Buoy your chains overboard,
    While the steam hums;
Men! to the battlement,
    Farragut comes.

See, as the hurricane
    Hurtles in wrath
Squadrons of clouds amain
    Back from its path!
Back to the parapet,
    To the guns' lips,
Thunderbolt Farragut
    Hurls the black ships.

Now through the battle's roar
    Clear the boy sings,
"By the mark fathoms four,"
    While his lead swings.
Steady the wheelmen five
    "Nor' by East keep her,"
"Steady," but two alive:
    How the shells sweep her!

Lashed to the mast that sways
    Over red decks,
Over the flame that plays
    Round the torn wrecks,
Over the dying lips
    Framed for a cheer,
Farragut leads his ships,
    Guides the line clear.

On by heights cannon-browed,
    While the spars quiver;
Onward still flames the cloud
    Where the hulks shiver.
See, yon fort's star is set,
    Storm and fire past.
Cheer him, lads—Farragut,
    Lashed to the mast!

Oh! while Atlantic's breast
Bears a white sail,
While the Gulf's towering crest
Tops a green vale,
Men thy bold deeds shall tell,
Old Heart of Oak,
Daring Dave Farragut,
Thunderbolt stroke!

WILLIAM TUCKEY MEREDITH

SHILOH

A REQUIEM

SKIMMING lightly, wheeling still,
The swallows fly low
O'er the field in clouded days,
The forest-field of Shiloh—
Over the field where April rain
Solaced the parched ones stretched in pain,
Through the pauses of the night—
That followed the Sunday fight
Around the church of Shiloh,—
The church so lone, the log-built one,
That echoed to many a parting groan
And natural prayer
Of dying foemen mingled there—
Foemen at morn, but friends at eve—
Fame or country least their care:
(What like a bullet can undeceive!)
But now they lie low,
While over them the swallows skim,
And all is hushed at Shiloh.

HERMAN MELVILLE

GETTYSBURG

THERE was no union in the land,
    Though wise men labored long
With links of clay and ropes of sand
    To bind the right and wrong.

There was no temper in the blade
    That once could cleave a chain;
Its edge was dull with touch of trade
    And clogged with rust of gain.

The sand and clay must shrink away
    Before the lava tide:
By blows and blood and fire assay
    The metal must be tried.

Here sledge and anvil met, and when
    The furnace fiercest roared,
God's undiscerning workingmen
    Reforged His people's sword.

Enough for them to ask and know
    The moment's duty clear—
The bayonets flashed it there below,
    The guns proclaimed it here:

To do and dare, and die at need,
    But while life lasts, to fight—
For right or wrong a simple creed,
    But simplest for the right.

They faltered not who stood that day
  And held this post of dread;
Nor cowards they who wore the gray
  Until the gray was red.

For every wreath the victor wears
  The vanquished half may claim;
And every monument declares
  A common pride and fame.

We raise no altar stones to Hate,
  Who never bowed to Fear:
No province crouches at our gate,
  To shame our triumph here.

Here standing by a dead wrong's grave
  The blindest now may see,
The blow that liberates the slave
  But sets the master free!

When ills beset the nation's life
  Too dangerous to bear,
The sword must be the surgeon's knife,
  Too merciful to spare.

O Soldier of our common land,
  'T is thine to bear that blade
Loose in the sheath, or firm in hand,
  But ever unafraid.

When foreign foes assail our right,
  One nation trusts to thee—
To wield it well in worthy fight—
  The sword of Meade and Lee!
           JAMES JEFFREY ROCHE

JOHN BURNS OF GETTYSBURG

HAVE you heard the story that gossips tell
Of Burns of Gettysburg? No? Ah, well:
Brief is the glory that hero earns,
Briefer the story of poor John Burns:
He was the fellow who won renown,—
The only man who didn't back down
When the rebels rode through his native town;
But held his own in the fight next day,
When all his townsfolk ran away.
That was in July, sixty-three,—
The very day that General Lee,
Flower of Southern chivalry,
Baffled and beaten, backward reeled
From a stubborn Meade and a barren field.

I might tell how, but the day before,
John Burns stood at his cottage door,
Looking down the village street,
Where, in the shade of his peaceful vine,
He heard the low of his gathered kine,
And felt their breath with incense sweet;
Or I might say, when the sunset burned
The old farm gable, he thought it turned
The milk that fell like a babbling flood
Into the milk-pail, red as blood!
Or how he fancied the hum of bees
Were bullets buzzing among the trees.
But all such fanciful thoughts as these
Were strange to a practical man like Burns,
Who minded only his own concerns,
Troubled no more by fancies fine
Than one of his calm-eyed, long-tailed kine,—

Quite old-fashioned and matter-of-fact,
Slow to argue, but quick to act.
That was the reason, as some folks say,
He fought so well on that terrible day.

And it was terrible. On the right
Raged for hours the heady fight,
Thundered the battery's double bass,—
Difficult music for men to face;
While on the left—where now the graves
Undulate like the living waves
That all that day unceasing swept
Up to the pits the rebels kept—
Round-shot ploughed the upland glades,
Sown with bullets, reaped with blades;
Shattered fences here and there
Tossed their splinters in the air;
The very trees were stripped and bare;
The barns that once held yellow grain
Were heaped with harvests of the slain;
The cattle bellowed on the plain,
The turkeys screamed with might and main,
The brooding barn-fowl left their rest
With strange shells bursting in each nest.

Just where the tide of battle turns,
Erect and lonely, stood old John Burns.
How do you think the man was dressed?
He wore an ancient long buff vest,
Yellow as saffron,—but his best;
And, buttoned over his manly breast,
Was a bright blue coat, with a rolling collar,
And large gilt buttons,—size of a dollar,—
With tails that the country-folk called "swaller."
He wore a broad-brimmed, bell-crowned hat,
White as the locks on which it sat.

Never had such a sight been seen
For forty years on the village green,
Since old John Burns was a country beau,
And went to the "quiltings" long ago.

Close at his elbows all that day,
Veterans of the Peninsula,
Sunburnt and bearded, charged away;
And striplings, downy of lip and chin,—
Clerks that the Home-Guard mustered in,—
Glanced, as they passed, at the hat he wore,
Then at the rifle his right hand bore;
And hailed him, from out their youthful lore,
With scraps of a slangy repertoire:
"How are you, White Hat?" "Put her through!"
"Your head's level!" and "Bully for you!"
Called him "Daddy,"—begged he'd disclose
The name of the tailor who made his clothes,
And what was the value he set on those;
While Burns, unmindful of jeer or scoff,
Stood there picking the rebels off,—
With his long brown rifle, and bell-crowned hat,
And the swallow-tails they were laughing at.

'Twas but a moment, for that respect
Which clothes all courage their voices checked;
And something the wildest could understand
Spake in the old man's strong right hand,
And his corded throat, and the lurking frown
Of his eyebrows under his old bell-crown;
Until, as they gazed, there crept an awe
Through the ranks in whispers, and some men saw,
In the antique vestments and long white hair,
The Past of the Nation in battle there;
And some of the soldiers since declare
That the gleam of his old white hat afar,

Like the crested plume of the brave Navarre,
That day was their oriflamme of war.

So raged the battle. You know the rest:
How the rebels, beaten and backward pressed,
Broke at the final charge and ran.
At which John Burns—a practical man—
Shouldered his rifle, unbent his brows,
And then went back to his bees and cows.
That is the story of old John Burns;
This is the moral the reader learns:
In fighting the battle, the question's whether
You'll show a hat that's white, or a feather!

BRET HARTE

THE HIGH TIDE AT GETTYSBURG

July 3, 1863

A CLOUD possessed the hollow field,
The gathering battle's smoky shield:
    Athwart the gloom the lightning flashed,
    And through the cloud some horsemen dashed,
And from the heights the thunder pealed.

Then, at the brief command of Lee,
Moved out that matchless infantry,
    With Picket leading grandly down,
    To rush against the roaring crown
Of those dread heights of destiny.

Far heard above the angry guns,
A cry across the tumult runs:

The voice that rang through Shiloh's woods,
And Chickamauga's solitudes:
The fierce South cheering on her sons!

Ah, how the withering tempest blew
Against the front of Pettigrew!
  A Khamsin wind that scorched and singed,
  Like that infernal flame that fringed
The British squares at Waterloo!

A thousand fell where Kemper led;
A thousand died where Garnett bled;
  In blinding flame and strangling smoke,
  The remnant through the batteries broke,
And crossed the works with Armistead.

"Once more in Glory's van with me!"
Virginia cried to Tennessee:
  "We two together, come what may,
  Shall stand upon those works today!"
The reddest day in history.

Brave Tennessee! In reckless way
Virginia heard her comrade say:
  "Close round this rent and riddle rag!"
  What time she set her battle flag
Amid the guns of Doubleday.

But who shall break the guards that wait
Before the awful face of Fate?
  The tattered standards of the South
  Were shriveled at the cannon's mouth,
And all her hopes were desolate.

In vain the Tennesseean set
His breast against the bayonet;
    In vain Virginia charged and raged,
    A tigress in her wrath uncaged,
Till all the hill was red and wet!

Above the bayonets, mixed and crossed,
Men saw a gray, gigantic ghost
    Receding through the battle cloud,
    And heard across the tempest loud
The death cry of a nation lost!

The brave went down! Without disgrace
They leaped to Ruin's red embrace;
    They only heard Fame's thunders wake,
    And saw the dazzling sunburst break
In smiles on Glory's bloody face!

They fell, who lifted up a hand
And bade the sun in heaven to stand;
    They smote and fell, who set the bars
    Against the progress of the stars,
And stayed the march of Motherland!

They stood, who saw the future come
On through the fight's delirium;
    They smote and stood, who held the hope
    Of nations on that slippery slope,
Amid the cheers of Christendom!

God lives! He forged the iron will
That clutched and held that trembling hill!
    God lives and reigns! He built and lent
    The heights for Freedom's battlement,
Where floats her flag in triumph still!

Fold up the banners! Smelt the guns!
Love rules. Her gentler purpose runs.
A mighty mother turns in tears
The pages of her battle years,
Lamenting all her fallen sons!
WILL HENRY THOMPSON

THE CONQUERED BANNER

FURL that Banner, for 't is weary;
Round its staff 't is drooping dreary;
Furl it, fold it—it is best;
For there's not a man to wave it,
And there's not a sword to save it,
And there's not one left to lave it
In the blood which heroes gave it;
And its foes now scorn and brave it;
Furl it, hide it—let it rest!

Take that Banner down! 't is tattered;
Broken is its staff and shattered,
And the valiant hosts are scattered
Over whom it floated high.
Oh, 'tis hard for us to fold it,
Hard to think there's none to hold it,
Hard that those who once unrolled it
Now must furl it with a sigh!

Furl that Banner—furl it sadly;
Once ten thousands hailed it gladly,
And ten thousands wildly, madly
Swore it should forever wave—

Swore that foeman's sword should never
Hearts like theirs entwined dissever,
And that flag should float forever
  O'er their freedom, o'er their grave!

Furl it! for the hands that grasped it,
And the hearts that fondly clasped it,
  Cold and dead are lying low;
And that Banner—it is trailing,
While around it sounds the wailing
  Of its people in their woe;

For, though conquered, they adore it—
Love the cold, dead hands that bore it!
Weep for those who fell before it!
Pardon those who trailed and tore it!
But, oh, wildly they deplore it,
  Now who furl and fold it so!

Furl that Banner! True, 't is gory,
Yet 't is wreathed around with glory,
And 't will live in song and story
  Though its folds are in the dust!
For its fame on brightest pages,
Penned by poets and by sages,
Shall go sounding down the ages—
  Furl its folds though now we must!

Furl that Banner, softly, slowly;
Treat it gently—it is holy,
  For it droops above the dead;
Touch it not—unfold it never;
Let it droop there, furled forever,—
  For its people's hopes are fled.

                 ABRAM J. RYAN

BROTHER JONATHAN'S LAMENT
FOR SISTER CAROLINE

SHE has gone,—she has left us in passion and pride,—
Our stormy-browed sister, so long at our side!
She has torn her own star from our firmament's glow,
And turned on her brother the face of a foe!

O Caroline, Caroline, child of the sun,
We can never forget that our hearts have been one,—
Our foreheads both sprinkled in Liberty's name,
From the fountain of blood with the finger of flame!

You were always too ready to fire at a touch;
But we said: "She is hasty,—she does not mean much."
We have scowled when you uttered some turbulent threat;
But Friendship still whispered: "Forgive and forget."

Has our love all died out? Have its altars grown cold?
Has the curse come at last which the fathers foretold?
Then Nature must teach us the strength of the chain
That her petulant children would sever in vain.

They may fight till the buzzards are gorged with their spoil,—
Till the harvest grows black as it rots in the soil,
Till the wolves and the catamounts troop from their caves,
And the shark tracks the pirate, the lord of the waves:

In vain is the strife! When its fury is past,
Their fortunes must flow in one channel at last,
As the torrents that rush from the mountains of snow
Roll mingled in peace through the valleys below.

Our Union is river, lake, ocean, and sky;
Man breaks not the medal when God cuts the die!
Though darkened with sulphur, though cloven with steel,
The blue arch will brighten, the waters will heal!

O Caroline, Caroline, child of the sun,
There are battles with fate that can never be won!
The star-flowering banner must never be furled,
For its blossoms of light are the hope of the world!

Go, then, our rash sister, afar and aloof,—
Run wild in the sunshine away from our roof;
But when your heart aches and your feet have grown sore,
Remember the pathway that leads to our door!

OLIVER WENDELL HOLMES

APOCALYPSE

Private Arthur Ladd, Sixth Regiment, Massachusetts
Volunteers, First Martyr in the War for Liberty of
1861–5. Slain in Baltimore, April 19, 1861.

STRAIGHT to his heart the bullet crushed;
Down from his breast the red blood gushed,
And over his face a glory rushed.

A sudden spasm shook his frame,
And in his ears there went and came
A sound as of devouring flame,

Which in a moment ceased, and then
The great light clasped his brows again,
So that they shone like Stephen's when

Saul stood apart a little space,
And shook with trembling awe to trace
God's splendors settling o'er his face.

Thus, like a king, erect in pride,
Raising clean hands toward heaven, he cried,
"All hail the Stars and Stripes!" and died.

Died grandly. But before he fell,
(O blessedness ineffable!)
Vision Apocalyptical

Was granted to him, and his eyes,
All radiant with glad surprise,
Looked forward through the centuries,

And saw the seed which sages cast
On the world's soil in cycles past,
Spring up and blossom at the last.

Saw how the souls of men had grown,
And where the scythes of truth had mown
Clear space for Liberty's white throne.

Saw how, by sorrows tried and proved,
The blackening stains had been removed
Forever from the land he loved.

Saw Treason crushed, and Freedom crowned,
And clamorous fury gagged and bound,
Gasping its life upon the ground.

Saw how, across his Country's slopes
Walked swarming troops of cheerful hopes,
Which evermore to broader scopes

Increased, with power that comprehends
The world's weal in its own, and bends
Self-needs to large unselfish ends.

Saw how, throughout the vast extents
Of earth's most populous continents
She dropped such rare-hearted affluence,

That from beyond the utmost seas
The wondering people thronged to seize
Her proffered pure benignities.

Saw how, of all her trebled host
Of widening empires, none might boast
Whose love were best, or strength were most,

Because they grew so equal there
Beneath the flag which, debonair,
Waved joyous in the cleansed air.

With far off vision, gazing clear
Beyond this gloomy atmosphere
Which shuts us in with doubt and fear,

He, marking how her high increase
Ran, greatening in perpetual lease
Through balmy years of odorous peace—

Greeted in one transcendent cry
Of intense passionate ecstasy,
The sight which thrilled him utterly,

Saluting, with most proud disdain
Of murder and of mortal pain,
The vision which shall be again!

So, lifted with prophetic pride,
Raised conquering hands toward heaven and cried,
"All hail the Stars and Stripes!" and died.

RICHARD REALF

REQUIEM

FOR ONE SLAIN IN BATTLE

BREATHE, trumpets, breathe
  Slow notes of saddest wailing,—
Sadly responsive peal, ye muffled drums;
Comrades, with downcast eyes
    And banners trailing,
    Attend him home,—
The youthful warrior comes.

Upon his shield,
  Upon his shield returning,
Borne from the field of honor
  Where he fell;
Glory and grief, together clasped
  In mourning,
His fame, his fate
  With sobs exulting tell.

Wrap round his breast
  The flag his breast defended,—
His country's flag,
  In battle's front unrolled:
For it he died;
  On earth forever ended
His brave young life
  Lives in each sacred fold.

With proud fond tears,
  By tinge of shame untainted,
Bear him, and lay him
  Gently in his grave:
Above the hero write,—
  The young, half-sainted,—
His country asked his life,
  His life he gave!

GEORGE LUNT

THE BLUE AND THE GRAY

BY THE FLOW of the inland river,
  Whence the fleets of iron have fled,
Where the blades of the grave grass quiver,
  Asleep are the ranks of the dead;—
    Under the sod and the dew,
      Waiting the judgment day;—
    Under the one, the Blue;
      Under the other, the Gray.

These in the robings of glory,
  Those in the gloom of defeat,
All with the battle blood gory,
  In the dusk of eternity meet;—
    Under the sod and the dew,
      Waiting the judgment day;—
    Under the laurel, the Blue;
      Under the willow, the Gray.

From the silence of sorrowful hours
  The desolate mourners go,
Lovingly laden with flowers
  Alike for the friend and the foe,—

Under the sod and the dew,
  Waiting the judgment day;—
Under the roses, the Blue;
  Under the lilies, the Gray.

So with an equal splendor
  The morning sun rays fall,
With a touch, impartially tender,
  On the blossoms blooming for all;—
    Under the sod and the dew,
      Waiting the judgment day;—
    'Broidered with gold, the Blue;
      Mellowed with gold, the Gray.

So, when the summer calleth,
  On forest and field of grain
With an equal murmur falleth
  The cooling drip of the rain;—
    Under the sod and the dew,
      Waiting the judgment day;—
    Wet with the rain, the Blue;
      Wet with the rain, the Gray.

Sadly, but not with upbraiding,
  The generous deed was done;
In the storm of the years that are fading,
  No braver battle was won;—
    Under the sod and the dew,
      Waiting the judgment day;—
    Under the blossoms, the Blue;
      Under the garlands, the Gray.

No more shall the war cry sever,
  Or the winding rivers be red;
They banish our anger forever
  When they laurel the graves of our dead!

Under the sod and the dew,
   Waiting the judgment day;—
Love and tears for the Blue,
   Tears and love for the Gray.

FRANCIS MILES FINCH

THE EAGLE'S SONG

THE lioness whelped, and the sturdy cub
Was seized by an eagle and carried up,
And homed for a while in an eagle's nest,
And slept for a while on an eagle's breast;
And the eagle taught it the eagle's song:
"To be stanch, and valiant, and free, and strong!"

The lion whelp sprang from the eyrie nest,
From the lofty crag where the queen birds rest;
He fought the King on the spreading plain,
And drove him back o'er the foaming main.
He held the land as a thrifty chief,
And reared his cattle, and reaped his sheaf
Nor sought the help of a foreign hand
Yet welcomed all to his own free land!

Two were the sons that the country bore
To the Northern lakes and the Southern shore;
And Chivalry dwelt with the Southern son,
And Industry lived with the Northern one.
Tears for the time when they broke and fought!
Tears was the price of the union wrought!
And the land was red in a sea of blood,
Where brother for brother had swelled the flood!

And now that the two are one again,
Behold on their shield the word "Refrain!"

And the lion cubs twain sing the eagle's song:
"To be stanch, and valiant, and free, and strong!"
For the eagle's beak, and the lion's paw,
And the lion's fangs, and the eagle's claw,
And the eagle's swoop, and the lion's might,
And the lion's leap, and the eagle's sight,
Shall guard the flag with the word "Refrain!"
Now that the two are one again!

RICHARD MANSFIELD

LAUS DEO!

On hearing the bells ring on the passage of the constitutional amendment abolishing slavery.

It is done!
Clang of bell and roar of gun
Send the tidings up and down.
How the belfries rock and reel!
How the great guns, peal on peal,
Fling the joy from town to town!

Ring, O bells!
Every stroke exulting tells
Of the burial hour of crime.
Loud and long, that all may hear,
Ring for every listening ear
Of Eternity and Time!

Let us kneel:
God's own voice is in that peal,
And this spot is holy ground.
Lord, forgive us! What are we,
That our eyes this glory see,
That our ears have heard the sound!

For the Lord
On the whirlwind is abroad;
In the earthquake He has spoken;
He has smitten with His thunder
The iron walls asunder,
And the gates of brass are broken!

Loud and long
Lift the old exulting song;
Sing with Miriam by the sea,
He has cast the mighty down;
Horse and rider sink and drown;
"He hath triumphed gloriously!"

Did we dare,
In our agony of prayer,
Ask for more than He has done?
When was ever His right hand
Over any time or land
Stretched as now beneath the sun?

How they pale,
Ancient myth and song and tale,
In this wonder of our days,
When the cruel rod of war
Blossoms white with righteous law,
And the wrath of man is praise!

Blotted out!
All within and all about
Shall a fresher life begin;
Freer breathe the universe
As it rolls its heavy curse
On the dead and buried sin!

It is done!
In the circuit of the sun
Shall the sound thereof go forth.
It shall bid the sad rejoice,
It shall give the dumb a voice,
It shall belt with joy the earth!

Ring and swing,
Bells of joy! On morning's wing
Send the song of praise abroad!
With a sound of broken chains
Tell the nations that He reigns,
Who alone is Lord and God!

JOHN GREENLEAF WHITTIER

"BLOW, BUGLES, BLOW"

BLOW, bugles, blow, soft and sweet and low,
Sing a good-night song for them who bravely faced the foe;
Sing a song of truce to pain,
Where they sleep nor wake again,
'Neath the sunshine or the rain—
Blow, bugles, blow.

Wave, banners, wave, above each hero's grave,
Fold them, O thou stainless flag that they died to save;
All thy stars with glory bright,
Bore they on through Treason's night,
Through the darkness to the light—
Wave, banners, wave.

Fall, blossoms, fall, over one and all,
They who heard their country's cry and answered to the call;

'Mid the shock of shot and shell,
Where they bled and where they fell,
They who fought so long and well—
Fall, blossoms, fall.

Sigh, breezes, sigh, so gently wandering by,
Bend above them tenderly, blue of summer sky;
All their weary marches done,
All their battles fought and won,
Friend and lover, sire and son—
Sigh, breezes, sigh.

JOHN S. McGROARTY

ROLL-CALL

"CORPORAL GREEN!" the Orderly cried;
"Here!" was the answer loud and clear,
From the lips of a soldier standing near,—
And "Here!" was the word the next replied.

"Cyrus Drew!"—then a silence fell;
This time no answer followed the call;
Only his rear-man had seen him fall:
Killed or wounded—he could not tell.

There they stood in the failing light,
These men of battle, with grave, dark looks,
As plain to be read as open books,
While slowly gathered the shades of night.

The fern on the hill-sides was splashed with blood,
And down in the corn, where the poppies grew,
Were redder stains than the poppies knew,
And crimson-dyed was the river's flood.

For the foe had crossed from the other side,
  That day, in the face of a murderous fire
  That swept them down in its terrible ire;
And their life-blood went to color the tide.

"Herbert Cline!"—At the call there came
  Two stalwart soldiers into the line,
  Bearing between them this Herbert Cline,
Wounded and bleeding, to answer his name.

"Ezra Kerr!"—and a voice answered "Here!"
  "Hiram Kerr!"—but no man replied.
  They were brothers, these two; the sad wind sighed,
And a shudder crept through the cornfield near.

"Ephraim Deane!"—then a soldier spoke:
  "Deane carried our regiment's colors," he said,
  "When our ensign was shot; I left him dead
Just after the enemy wavered and broke.

"Close to the roadside his body lies;
  I paused a moment and gave him to drink;
  He murmured his mother's name, I think,
And Death came with it and closed his eyes."

'Twas a victory,—yes; but it cost us dear:
  For that company's roll, when called at night,
  Of a hundred men who went into the fight,
Numbered but twenty that answered *"Here!"*
                    NATHANIEL GRAHAM SHEPHERD

DIRGE

For One Who Fell in Battle

Room for a Soldier! lay him in the clover;
He loved the fields, and they shall be his cover;
Make his mound with hers who called him once her lover:
  Where the rain may rain upon it,
  Where the sun may shine upon it,
  Where the lamb hath lain upon it,
  And the bee will dine upon it.

Bear him to no dismal tomb under city churches;
Take him to the fragrant fields, by the silver birches,
Where the whippoorwill shall mourn, where the oriole perches:
  Make his mound with sunshine on it,
  Where the bee will dine upon it,
  Where the lamb hath lain upon it,
  And the rain will rain upon it.

Busy as the busy bee, his rest should be the clover;
Gentle as the lamb was he, and the fern should be his cover;
Fern and rosemary shall grow my soldier's pillow over:
  Where the rain may rain upon it,
  Where the sun may shine upon it,
  Where the lamb hath lain upon it,
  And the bee will dine upon it.

Sunshine in his heart, the rain would come full often
Out of those tender eyes which evermore did soften;
He never could look cold, till we saw him in his coffin:

Make his mound with sunshine on it,
Where the wind may sigh upon it,
Where the moon may stream upon it,
And Memory shall dream upon it.

"Captain or Colonel,"—whatever invocation
Suit our hymn the best, no matter for thy station,—
On thy grave the rain shall fall from the eyes of a mighty nation!
Long as the sun doth shine upon it
Shall grow the goodly pine upon it,
Long as the stars do gleam upon it
Shall Memory come to dream upon it.

THOMAS WILLIAM PARSONS

THE BIVOUAC OF THE DEAD

The MUFFLED drum's sad roll has beat
The soldier's last tattoo!
No more on life's parade shall meet
The brave and fallen few.
On Fame's eternal camping ground
Their silent tents are spread,
And glory guards with solemn round
The bivouac of the dead.

No rumor of the foe's advance
Now swells upon the wind,
Nor troubled thought of midnight haunts,
Of loved ones left behind;
No vision of the morrow's strife
The warrior's dreams alarms,
No braying horn or screaming fife
At dawn to call to arms.

Their shivered swords are red with rust,
　　Their plumèd heads are bowed,
Their haughty banner, trailed in dust,
　　Is now their martial shroud—
And plenteous funeral tears have washed
　　The red stains from each brow,
And the proud forms by battle gashed
　　Are free from anguish now.

The neighing troop, the flashing blade,
　　The bugle's stirring blast,
The charge,—the dreadful cannonade,
　　The din and shout, are passed;
Nor war's wild notes, nor glory's peal
　　Shall thrill with fierce delight
Those breasts that nevermore shall feel
　　The rapture of the fight.

Like the fierce Northern hurricane
　　That sweeps the great plateau,
Flushed with the triumph yet to gain,
　　Come down the serried foe,
Who heard the thunder of the fray
　　Break o'er the field beneath,
Knew the watchword of the day
　　Was "Victory or death!"

Rest on, embalmed and sainted dead,
　　Dear is the blood you gave—
No impious footstep here shall tread
　　The herbage of your grave.
Nor shall your glory be forgot
　　While Fame her record keeps,
Or honor points the hallowed spot
　　Where valor proudly sleeps.

Yon marble minstrel's voiceless stone
  In deathless song shall tell,
When many a vanquished year hath flown,
  The story how you fell.
Nor wreck nor change, nor winter's blight,
  Nor time's remorseless doom,
Can dim one ray of holy light
  That gilds your glorious tomb.
                              THEODORE O'HARA

DIRGE FOR A SOLDIER

September 1, 1862

CLOSE his eyes; his work is done!
  What to him is friend or foeman,
Rise of moon, or set of sun,
  Hand of man, or kiss of woman?
    Lay him low, lay him low,
    In the clover or the snow!
    What cares he? he cannot know:
    Lay him low!

As man may, he fought his fight,
  Proved his truth by his endeavor;
Let him sleep in solemn night,
  Sleep forever and forever.
    Lay him low, lay him low,
    In the clover or the snow!
    What care he? he cannot know:
    Lay him low!

Fold him in his country's stars,
  Roll the drum and fire the volley!

What to him are all our wars,
　What but death-bemocking folly?
　Lay him low, lay him low,
　In the clover or the snow!
.　What care he? he cannot know:
　　Lay him low!

Leave him to God's watching eye;
　Trust him to the hand that made him.
Mortal love weeps idly by:
　God alone has power to aid him.
　Lay him low, lay him low,
　In the clover or the snow!
　What care he? he cannot know:
　　Lay him low!

GEORGE HENRY BOKER

PATRIOTISM ABROAD

By
ROBERT CHARLES WINTHROP

THE PATRIOT TRAVELLER IN FOREIGN LANDS

IT IS, without all question, my friends, one of the best influences of
a sojourn in foreign lands, upon a heart which is not insensible to
the influences of patriotism, that one forgets for a time, or remembers only with disgust and loathing, the contentions and controversies which so often alienate and embitter us at home. There is
no room on that little map of his country which every patriot bears
abroad with him, photographed on his heart,—there is no room
on that magical miniature map for territorial divisions or sectional
boundaries. Large enough to reflect and reproduce the image and
outlines of the whole Union, it repels all impression of the petty

topographical features which belong to science and the schools. Still more does it repel the miserable seams and scratches by which sectional politicians have sought to illustrate their odious distinctions and comparisons. And so, the patriot traveller in foreign lands, with that chart impressed in lines of light and love on his memory, looks back on his country only as a whole. He learns to love it more than ever as a whole. He accustoms himself to think kindly of it, and to speak kindly of it, as a whole; and he comes home ready to defend it as a whole, alike from the invasion of hostile armies or the assaults of slanderous pens and tongues. He grasps the hand of an American abroad as the hand of a brother, without stopping to inquire whether he hails from Massachusetts or from South Carolina, from Maine or Louisiana, from Vermont or Virginia. It is enough that his passport bears the same broad seal, the same national emblem, with his own. And every time his own passport is inspected, every time he enters a new dominion or crosses a new frontier, every time he is delayed at a custom-house, or questioned by a policeman, or challenged by a sentinel,—every time he is perplexed by a new language, or puzzled by a new variety of coinage or currency,—he thanks his God with fresh fervency, that through all the length and breadth of that land beyond the swelling floods, which he is privileged and proud to call his own land, there is a common language, a common currency, a common Constitution, common laws and liberties, a common inheritance of glory from the past, and, if it be only true to itself, a common destiny of glory for the future!

JOHN BROWN

To the Hon. D. R. Tilden

THE GREAT BULK of mankind estimate each other's actions and motives by the measure of success or otherwise that attends them through life. By that rule, I have been one of the worst and one of the best of men. I do not claim to have been one of the latter, and I leave it to an impartial tribunal to decide whether the world has been the worse or the better for my living or dying in it. My present great anxiety is to get as near in readiness for a different field of action as I well can, since being in a good measure relieved from the fear that my poor broken-hearted wife and children would come to immediate want. May God reward a thousandfold all the kind efforts made in their behalf! I have enjoyed a remarkable cheerfulness and composure of mind ever since my confinement; and it is a great comfort to feel assured that I am permitted to die for a cause,—not merely to pay the debt of nature, as all must. I feel myself to be most unworthy of so great distinction. The particular manner of dying assigned to me gives me but very little uneasiness. I wish I had the time and the ability to give you, my dear friend, some little idea of what is daily, and I might almost say hourly, passing within my prison walls; and could my friends but witness only a few of these scenes, just as they occur, I think they would feel very well reconciled to my being here, just what I am, and just as I am. My whole life before had not afforded me one half the opportunity to plead for the right. In this, also, I find much to reconcile me to both my present condition and my immediate prospect. I may be very insane; and I am so, if insane at all. But if that be so, insanity is like a very pleasant dream to me. I am not in the least degree conscious of my ravings, of my fears, or of any terrible visions whatever; but fancy myself entirely composed, and that my sleep, in particular, is as sweet as that of a healthy, joyous little infant. I pray God that He will grant me a continuance of the same calm but delightful dream, until I come to know of those realities which eyes have not seen and which ears have not heard. I have scarce realized that I am in prison or in irons at all. I certainly think I was never more cheerful in my life.

CHARLESTOWN, 28 November, 1859.

From SPEECH ON THE SLAVERY QUESTION

By
John C. Calhoun

IT IS TIME, Senators, that there should be an open and manly avowal on all sides, as to what is intended to be done. If the question is not now settled, it is uncertain whether it ever can hereafter be; and we, as the representatives of the States of this Union, regarded as governments, should come to a distinct understanding as to our respective views, in order to ascertain whether the great questions at issue can be settled or not. If you, who represent the stronger portion, cannot agree to settle them on the broad principle of justice and duty, say so; and let the States we both represent agree to separate and part in peace. If you are unwilling we should part in peace, tell us so; and we shall know what to do, when you reduce the question of submission or resistance. If you remain silent, you will compel us to infer by your acts what you intend. In that case, California will become the test question. If you admit her, under all the difficulties that oppose her admission, you compel us to infer that you intend to exclude us from the whole of the acquired territories, with the intention of destroying, irretrievably, the equilibrium between the two sections. We would be blind not to perceive in that case, that your real objects are power and aggrandizement, and infatuated not to act accordingly.

I have now, Senators, done my duty in expressing my opinions fully, freely, and candidly, on this solemn occasion. In doing so, I have been governed by the motives which have governed me in all the stages of the agitation of the slavery question since its commencement. I have exerted myself, during the whole period, to arrest it, with the intention of saving the Union, if it could be done; and if it could not, to save the section where it has pleased Providence to cast my lot, and which I sincerely believe has justice and the constitution on its side. Having faithfully done my duty to the best of my ability, both to the Union and my section, throughout this agitation, I shall have the consolation, let what will come, that I am free from all responsibility.

From INAUGURAL ADDRESS OF JEFFERSON DAVIS

February 22, 1862

THE TYRANNY of an unbridled majority, the most odious and least responsible form of despotism, has denied us both the right and remedy. Therefore we are in arms to renew such sacrifices as our fathers made to the holy cause of constitutional liberty. At the darkest hour of our struggle the provisional gives place to the permanent government. After a series of successes and victories, which covered our arms with glory, we have recently met with serious disasters. But in the heart of a people resolved to be free, these disasters tend but to stimulate to increased resistance.

To show ourselves worthy of the inheritance bequeathed to us by the patriots of the Revolution, we must emulate that heroic devotion which made reverse to them but the crucible in which their patriotism was refined.

With confidence in the wisdom and virtue of those who will share with me the responsibility, and aid me in the conduct of public affairs; securely relying on the patriotism and courage of the people, of which the present war has furnished so many examples, I deeply feel the weight of the responsibilities I now, with unaffected diffidence, am about to assume; and, fully realizing the inequality of human power to guide and to sustain, my hope is reverently fixed on Him whose favor is ever vouchsafed to the cause which is just. With humble gratitude and adoration, acknowledging the Providence which has so visibly protected the Confederacy during its brief but eventful career, to Thee, O God! I trustingly commit myself, and prayerfully invoke thy blessing on my country and its cause.

ABOLITION

By
WILLIAM LLOYD GARRISON

ABOLITIONISM is not a hobby, got up for personal or associated aggrandisement; it is not a political ruse; it is not a spasm of sympathy, which lasts but for a moment, leaving the system weak and worn; it is not a fever of enthusiasm; it is not the fruit of fanaticism; it is not a spirit of faction. It is of heaven, not of men. It lives in the heart as a vital principle. It is an essential part of Christianity, and aside from it there can be no humanity. Its scope is not confined to the slave population of the United States, but embraces mankind. Opposition cannot weary it, force cannot put it down, fire cannot consume it.

CIVIL WAR

By
LUCY LARCOM

SABBATH, *April 14, 1861.* This day broke upon our country in gloom; for the sounds of war came up to us from the South,—war between brethren; civil war; well may "all faces gather blackness." And yet the gloom we feel ought to be the result of sorrow for the erring, for the violators of national unity, for those who are in black rebellion against truth, freedom, and peace. The rebels have struck the first blow, and what ruin they are pulling down on their heads may be guessed though not yet fully foretold; but it is plain to see that a dark prospect is before them, since they have no high principle at the heart of their cause.

It will be no pleasure to any American to remember that he lived in this revolution, when brother lifted his hand against brother;

and the fear is, that we shall forget that we are brethren still, though some are so unreasonable and wander so far from the true principles of national prosperity. Though the clouds of this morning have cleared away into brightness, it seems as if we could feel the thunder of those deadly echoes passing to and from Fort Sumter. But there is a right, and God always defends it. War is not according to His wish; though it seems one of the permitted evils yet. He will scatter those who delight in it, and it is not too much to hope and expect that He will uphold the government which has so long been trying to avert bloodshed.

April 21. The conflict is deepening; but thanks to God, there is no wavering, no division, now, at the North! All are united, as one man; and from a peaceful, unwarlike people, we are transformed into an army, ready for the battle at a moment's warning.

The few days I have passed in Boston this week are the only days in which I ever carried my heart into a crowd, or hung around a company of soldiers with anything like pleasure. But I felt a soldier-spirit rising within me, when I saw the men of my native town armed and going to risk their lives for their country's sake; and the dear old flag of our Union is a thousand times more dear than ever before. The streets of Boston were almost canopied with the stars and stripes, and the merchants festooned their shops with the richest goods of the national colors.

And now there are rumors of mobs attacking our troops, of bridges burnt, and arsenals exploded, and many lives lost. The floodgates of war are opened, and when the tide of blood will cease none can tell.

LEE'S FAREWELL TO HIS ARMY

April 10, 1865

Headquarters, Army of Northern Virginia,
April 10, 1865.

AFTER FOUR YEARS of arduous service, marked by unsurpassed courage and fortitude, the Army of Northern Virginia has been compelled to yield to overwhelming numbers and resources. I need not tell the survivors of so many hard-fought battles, who have remained steadfast to the last, that I have consented to this result from no distrust of them; but, feeling that valour and devotion could accomplish nothing that could compensate for the loss that would have attended the continuation of the contest, I have determined to avoid the useless sacrifice of those whose past services have endeared them to their countrymen. By the terms of the agreement, officers and men can return to their homes and remain there until exchanged. You will take with you the satisfaction that proceeds from the consciousness of duty faithfully performed; and I earnestly pray that a merciful God will extend to you His blessing and protection. With an increasing admiration of your constancy and devotion to your country, and a grateful remembrance of your kind and generous consideration of myself, I bid you an affectionate farewell.

R. E. Lee, General

APPOMATTOX

BY
GENERAL ULYSSES S. GRANT

I HAD KNOWN General Lee in the old army, and had served with him in the Mexican War; but did not suppose, owing to the difference in our age and rank, that he would remember me; while I would more naturally remember him distinctly, because he was the chief of staff of General Scott in the Mexican War.

When I left camp that morning I had not expected so soon the result that was then taking place, and consequently was in rough garb. I was without a sword, as I usually was when on horseback on the field, and wore a soldier's blouse for a coat, with the shoulder straps of my rank to indicate to the army who I was. When I went into the house I found General Lee. We greeted each other, and after shaking hands took our seats. I had my staff with me, a good portion of whom were in the room during the whole of the interview.

What General Lee's feelings were I do not know. As he was a man of much dignity, with an impassible face, it was impossible to say whether he felt inwardly glad that the end had finally come, or felt sad over the result, and was too manly to show it. Whatever his feelings, they were entirely concealed from my observation; but my own feelings, which had been quite jubilant on the receipt of his letter, were sad and depressed. I felt like anything rather than rejoicing at the downfall of a foe who had fought so long and valiantly. . . .

MESSAGE TO HIS SOLDIERS

April 10, 1865

By
GENERAL ROBERT E. LEE

WITH ALL my devotion to the Union and the feeling of loyalty and duty of an American citizen, I have not been able to make up my mind to raise my hand against my relatives, my children, my home. I have therefore resigned my commission in the Army, and save in defense of my native State, with the sincere hope that my poor services may never be needed, I hope I may never be called on to draw my sword. I know you will blame me; but you must think as kindly of me as you can, and believe that I have endeavoured to do what I thought right.

To show you the feeling and struggle it has cost me, I send you a copy of my letter of resignation. I have no time for more. May God guard and protect you and yours, and shower upon you everlasting blessings, is the prayer of your devoted brother.

BEGINNING THE MARCH TO THE SEA

By
WILLIAM TECUMSEH SHERMAN

ABOUT 7 A. M. of November 16th we rode out of Atlanta by the Decatur road, filled by the marching troops and wagons of the Fourteenth Corps; and reaching the hill, just outside of the old rebel works, we naturally paused to look back upon the scenes of our past battles. We stood upon the very ground whereon was fought the bloody battle of July 22d, and could see the copse of wood where McPherson fell. Behind us lay Atlanta, smouldering and in ruins, the black smoke rising high in air, and hanging like a pall over the ruined city. Away off in the distance, on the McDonough road, was the rear of Howard's column, the gun-barrels glistening in the sun, the white-topped wagons stretching away to the south; and right before us the Fourteenth Corps, marching steadily and rapidly, with a cheery look and swinging pace, that made light of the thousand miles that lay between us and Richmond. Some band, by accident, struck up the anthem of "John Brown's soul goes marching on"; the men caught up the strain, and never before or since have I heard the chorus of "Glory, glory, hallelujah!" done with more spirit, or in better harmony of time and place.

Then we turned our horses' heads to the east; Atlanta was soon lost behind the screen of trees, and became a thing of the past.

Around it clings many a thought of desperate battle, of hope and fear, that now seem like the memory of a dream; and I have never seen the place since. The day was extremely beautiful, clear sunlight, with bracing air, and an unusual feeling of exhilaration seemed to pervade all minds—a feeling of something to come, vague and undefined, still full of venture and intense interest. Even the common soldiers caught the inspiration, and many a group called out to me as I worked my way past them, "Uncle Billy, I guess Grant is waiting for us at Richmond!" Indeed, the general sentiment was that we were marching for Richmond, and that there we should end the war, but how and when they seemed to care not; nor did they measure the distance, or count the cost in life, or bother their brains about the great rivers to be crossed, and the food required for man and beast, that had to be gathered by the way. There was a "devil-may-care" feeling pervading officers and men, that made me feel the full load of responsibility, for success would be accepted as a matter of course, whereas, should we fail, this "march" would be adjudged the wild adventure of a crazy fool.

SLAVERY

By
William H. Seward

Whoever will study the character of the earliest immigrants to this country will find that they were all alike unquiet under ecclesiastical and civil abridgment of their rights, he will find the same indomitable love of liberty among the Episcopalian adventurers on the Roanoke, the Puritans, who, in the fear of God, established their congregation upon the rock of Plymouth, the Quakers on the Schuylkill, the Catholics on the Susquehannah, the Netherlanders on the Hudson, the Germans on the Lehigh, and the Swedes and Finns at Cape Henlopen. He will be ready to say, that God in his providence, seems to have collected from the nations of Europe, men of sturdy limbs, free minds and bold hearts, to lay broad and deep the foundations of a state, which for the benefit of the human race, was to prove, under the most propitious circumstances, the experiment of a popular and representative government. More elevated, more enlightened, and no less ardent devotion to liberty, distinguished the actors in the heroic struggle by which the colonial relation to Great Britain was severed. Degenerate descendants of such ancestors should we indeed be, did we not value above all other blessings the boon of liberty—above all other distinctions, that of self-government. . . .

THE END OF WAR

By

WILLIAM LLOYD GARRISON

From his Speech at the Thirty-Second Anniversary
Meeting of the American Anti-Slavery Society,
9 May, 1865.

I REJOICE to stand here no longer as an isolated Abolitionist, to be looked at as though I had seven heads and ten horns; and that, as a drop is lost in the ocean, my abolitionism has ceased to be distinctive. The guns of the American Anti-Slavery Society, thank God! are spiked, because slavery is abolished. I promised, years ago, that if the people would abolish the "peculiar institution," I, for one, would be ready for the abolition of the American Anti-Slavery Society; and now that they have done it, what need of any more anti-slavery agitation? We are one people, united in sentiment as against slavery; hence, our work no longer being peculiar as Abolitionists, let us mingle with the millions of our fellow-countrymen, join with them, as they will join with us, in putting into the grave of slavery everything that has sprung out of slavery.

Whatever of complexional prejudice, whatever of proscription, as against those whose skins are not colored like our own, whatever of injustice toward that race, now exists, must be buried in the same common grave. Man is man, and we must recognize him wherever he appears on our soil. We have opened our vast country to all the world besides—to aliens, to strangers and foreigners, to the most besotted and ignorant of mankind; we take them into our arms of brotherly love, and we say, "You shall be citizens here; you shall find freedom here; you shall have all the rights of human nature guaranteed to you here." Shall we say less to those who are native-born; who have made our soil gory with their blood, and who have received nothing hitherto at our hands but injustice and cruelty; and who, in our hour of peril and despair, forgave us all that we had done against them, and came to our rescue? It is through their aid, and by the blessing of God, the nation is saved. We have not saved it ourselves. Two hundred thousand stalwart men, transformed from chattels into freemen, have thrown themselves into the scale, and rebellion, slavery, and treason have kicked the beam. . . .

My friends, I will not detain you longer. I thank God that the day has arrived when we can blend like kindred drops into one, and look to the future for the Divine blessing upon our whole country and people. Though the South is at present a desolation, and the North is still wailing for her lost, yet there is in store for us, because we have resolved to put away the evil thing from among us, abiding peace and abounding prosperity. I rejoice that I have been permitted to see this day. My country! may the windows of heaven be opened, and may such blessings be poured down upon thee that there shall not be room to receive them!

LINCOLN

SOLILOQUY OF LINCOLN BEFORE MANASSAS

From *John Brown's Body*

THEY come to me and talk about God's will
In righteous deputations and platoons,
Day after day, laymen and ministers.
They write me Prayers From Twenty Million Souls
Defining me God's will and Horace Greeley's.
God's will is General This and Senator That,
God's will is those poor colored fellows' will,
It is the will of the Chicago churches,
It is this man's and his worst enemy's.
But all of them are sure they know God's will.
I am the only man who does not know it.

And, yet, if it is probable that God
Should, and so very clearly, state His will
To others, on a point of my own duty,
It might be thought He would reveal it me
Directly, more especially as I
So earnestly desire to know His will.

The will of God prevails. No doubt, no doubt—
Yet, in great contests, each side claims to act
In strict accordance with the will of God.
Both may, one must be wrong.
                              God could have saved

This Union or destroyed it without war
If He so wished. And yet this war began,
And, once begun, goes on, though He could give
Victory, at any time, to either side.
It is unfathomable. Yet I know
This, and this only. While I live and breathe,
I mean to save the Union if I can,
And by whatever means my hands can find
Under the Constitution.

                              If God reads
The hearts of men as clearly as He must
To be Himself, then He can read in mine
And has, for twenty years, the old, scarred wish
That the last slave should be forever free
Here, in this country.

                    I do not go back
From that scarred wish and have not.

                                   But I put
The Union, first and last, before the slave.
If freeing slaves will bring the Union back
Then I will free them; if by freeing some
And leaving some enslaved I help my cause,
I will do that—but should such freedom mean
The wreckage of the Union that I serve
I would not free a slave.

                    O Will of God,
I am a patient man, and I can wait
Like an old gunflint buried in the ground
While the slow years pile up like moldering leaves
Above me, underneath the rake of Time,
And turn, in time, to the dark, fruitful mold
That smells of Sangamon apples, till at last
There's no sleep left there, and the steel event
Descends to strike the live coal out of me
And light the powder that was always there.

                              STEPHEN VINCENT BENÉT

WHEN LILACS LAST IN THE DOORYARD BLOOM'D

Memories of President Lincoln

I

WHEN lilacs last in the dooryard bloom'd,
And the great star early droop'd in the western sky in the night,
I mourn'd, and yet shall mourn with ever-returning spring.

Ever-returning spring, trinity sure to me you bring,
Lilac blooming perennial and drooping star in the west,
And thought of him I love.

II

O powerful western fallen star!
O shades of night—O moody, tearful night!
O great star disappear'd—O the black murk that hides the star!
O cruel hands that hold me powerless—O helpless soul of me!
O harsh surrounding cloud that will not free my soul.

III

In the dooryard fronting an old farm-house near the white-wash'd
    palings,
Stands the lilac-bush tall-growing with heart-shaped leaves of rich
    green,
With many a pointed blossom rising delicate, with the perfume
    strong I love,
With every leaf a miracle—and from this bush in the dooryard,
With delicate-color'd blossoms and heart-shaped leaves of rich
    green,
A sprig with its flower I break.

IV

In the swamp in secluded recesses,
A shy and hidden bird is warbling a song.
Solitary the thrush,
The hermit withdrawn to himself, avoiding the settlements,
Sings by himself a song.

Song of the bleeding throat,
Death's outlet song of life, (for well dear brother I know,
If thou wast not granted to sing thou would'st surely die.)

V

Over the breast of the spring, the land, amid cities,
Amid lanes and through old woods, where lately the violets peep'd
    from the ground, spotting the gray débris,
Amid the grass in the fields each side of the lanes passing the end-
    less grass,
Passing the yellow-spear'd wheat, every grain from its shroud in
    the dark-brown fields uprisen,
Passing the apple-tree blows of white and pink in the orchards,
Carrying a corpse to where it shall rest in the grave,
Night and day journeys a coffin.

VI

Coffin that passes through lanes and streets,
Through day and night with the great cloud darkening the land,
With the pomp of the inloop'd flags with the cities draped in black,
With the show of the States themselves as of crape-veil'd women
    standing,
With processions long and winding and the flambeaus of the night,
With the countless torches lit, with the silent sea of faces and the
    unbared heads

With the waiting depot, the arriving coffin, and the somber faces,
With dirges through the night, with the thousand voices rising
    strong and solemn,
With all the mournful voices of the dirges pour'd around the coffin,
The dim-lit churches and the shuddering organs—where amid
    these you journey,
With the tolling tolling bells' perpetual clang,
Here, coffin that slowly passes,
I give you my sprig of lilac.

VII

(Nor for you, for one alone,
Blossoms and branches green to coffins all I bring,
For fresh as the morning, thus would I chant a song for you O sane
    and sacred death.

All over bouquets of roses,
O death, I cover you over with roses and early lilies,
But mostly and now the lilac that blooms the first,
Copious I break, I break the sprigs from the bushes,
With loaded arms I come, pouring for you,
For you and the coffins all of you O death.)

VIII

O western orb sailing the heaven,
Now I know what you must have meant as a month since I walk'd,
As I walk'd in silence the transparent shadowy night,
As I saw you had something to tell as you bent to me night after
    night,
As you droop'd from the sky low down as if to my side, (while the
    other stars all look'd on,)
As we wander'd together the solemn night, (for something I know
    not what kept me from sleep,)
As the night advanced, and I saw on the rim of the west how full
    you were of woe,

As I stood on the rising ground in the breeze in the cool trans-
    parent night,
As I watch'd where you pass'd and was lost in the netherward
    black of the night,
As my soul in its trouble dissatisfied sank, as where you sad orb,
Concluded, dropt in the night, and was gone.

IX

Sing on there in the swamp,   .
O singer bashful and tender, I hear your notes, I hear your call,
I hear, I come presently, I understand you,
But a moment I linger, for the lustrous star has detain'd me,
The star my departing comrade holds and detains me.

X

O how shall I warble myself for the dead one there I loved?
And how shall I deck my song for the large sweet soul that has
    gone?
And what shall my perfume be for the grave of him I love?

Sea-winds blown from east and west,
Blown from the Eastern sea and blown from the Western sea, till
    there on the prairies meeting,
These and with these and the breath of my chant,
I'll perfume the grave of him I love.

XI

O what shall I hang on the chamber walls?
And what shall the pictures be that I hang on the walls,
To adorn the burial-house of him I love?

Pictures of growing spring and farms and homes,
With the Fourth-month eve at sundown, and the gray smoke lucid
    and bright,

With floods of the yellow gold of the gorgeous, indolent, sinking
    sun, burning, expanding the air,
With the fresh sweet herbage under foot, and the pale green leaves
    of the trees prolific,
In the distance the flowing glaze, the breast of the river, with a
    wind-dapple here and there,
With ranging hills on the banks, with many a line against the sky,
    and shadows,
And the city at hand with dwellings so dense, and stacks of
    chimneys,
And all the scenes of life and the workshops, and the workmen
    homeward returning.

XII

Lo, body and soul—this land,
My own Manhattan with spires, and the sparkling and hurrying
    tides, and the ships,
The varied and ample land, the South and the North in the light,
    Ohio's shores and flashing Missouri,
And ever the far-spreading prairies cover'd with grass and corn.

Lo, the most excellent sun so calm and haughty,
The violet and purple morn with just-felt breezes,
The gentle soft-born measureless light,
The miracle spreading bathing all, the fulfill'd noon,
The coming eve delicious, the welcome night and the stars,
Over my cities shining all, enveloping man and land.

XIII

Sing on, sing on you gray-brown bird,
Sing from the swamps, the recesses, pour your chant from the
    bushes,
Limitless out of the dusk, out of the cedars and pines.

Sing on dearest brother, warble your reedy song,
Loud human song, with voice of uttermost woe.

O liquid and free and tender!
O wild and loose to my soul—O wondrous singer!
You only I hear—yet the star holds me, (but will soon depart,)
Yet the lilac with mastering odor holds me.

XIV

Now while I sat in the day and look'd forth,
In the close of the day with its light and the fields of spring, and
    the farmers preparing their crops,
In the large unconscious scenery of my land with its lakes and
    forests,
In the heavenly aërial beauty, (after the perturb'd winds and the
    storms,)
Under the arching heavens of the afternoon swift passing, and the
    voices of children and women.

The many-moving sea-tides, and I saw the ships how they sail'd,
And the summer approaching with richness, and the fields all busy
    with labor,
And the infinite separate houses, how they all went on, each with
    its meals and minutia of daily usages,
And the streets how their throbbings throbb'd, and the cities pent
    —lo, then and there,
Falling upon them all and among them all, enveloping me with
    the rest,
Appear'd the cloud, appear'd the long black trail,
And I knew death, its thought, and the sacred knowledge of death.
Then with the knowledge of death as walking one side of me,
And the thought of death close-walking the other side of me,
And I in the middle as with companions, and as holding the hands
    of companions,
I fled forth to the hiding receiving night that talks not,

Down to the shores of the water, the path by the swamp in the
    dimness,
To the solemn shadowy cedars and ghostly pines so still.

And the singer so shy to the rest receiv'd me,
The gray-brown bird I know receiv'd us comrades three,
And he sang the carol of death, and a verse for him I love.

From deep secluded recesses,
From the fragrant cedars and the ghostly pines so still,
Came the carol of the bird.

And the charm of the carol rapt me,
As I held as if by their hands my comrades in the night,
And the voice of my spirit tallied the song of the bird.

Come lovely and soothing death,
Undulate round the world, serenely arriving, arriving,
In the day, in the night, to all, to each,
Sooner or later delicate death.

Prais'd be the fathomless universe,
For life and joy, and for objects and knowledge curious,
And for love, sweet love—but praise! praise! praise!
For the sure-enwinding arms of cool-enfolding death.
Dark mother always gliding near with soft feet,
Have none chanted for thee a chant of fullest welcome?
Then I chant it for thee, I glorify thee above all,
I bring thee a song that when thou must indeed come, come un-
*   falteringly.*

Approach strong deliveress,
When it is so, when thou hast taken them I joyously sing the dead,
Lost in the loving floating ocean of thee,
Laved in the flood of thy bliss O death.
From me to thee glad serenades,

Dances for thee I propose saluting thee, adornments and feastings
  for thee,
And the sights of the open landscape and the high-spread sky are
  fitting,
And life and the fields, and the huge and thoughtful night.

The night in silence under many a star,
The ocean shore and the husky whispering wave whose voice I
  know,
And the soul turning to thee O vast and well-veil'd death,
And the body gratefully nestling close to thee.

Over the tree-tops I float thee a song,
Over the rising and sinking waves, over the myriad fields and the
  prairies wide,
Over the dense-pack'd cities all and the teeming wharves and
  ways,
I float this carol with joy, with joy to thee O death.

xv

To the tally of my soul,
Loud and strong kept up the gray-brown bird,
With pure deliberate notes spreading filling the night.

Loud in the pines and cedars dim,
Clear in the freshness moist and the swamp-perfume,
And I with my comrades there in the night.

While my sight that was bound in my eyes unclosed,
As to long panoramas of visions.

And I saw askant the armies,
I saw as in noiseless dreams hundreds of battle-flags,
Borne through the smoke of the battles and pierc'd with missiles
  I saw them,
And carried hither and yon through the smoke, and torn and
  bloody,

And at last but a few shreds left on the staffs, (and all in silence,)
And the staffs all splinter'd and broken.

I saw battle-corpses, myriads of them,
And the white skeletons of young men, I saw them,
I saw the débris and débris of all the slain soldiers of the war,
But I saw they were not as was thought,
They themselves were fully at rest, they suffer'd not,
The living remain'd and suffer'd, the mother suffer'd,
And the wife and the child and the musing comrade suffer'd,
And the armies that remain'd suffer'd.

XVI

Passing the visions, passing the night,
Passing, unloosing the hold of my comrades' hands,
Passing the song of the hermit bird and the tallying song of my
    soul,
Victorious song, death's outlet song, yet varying ever-altering song,
As low and wailing, yet clear the notes, rising and falling, flooding
    the night,
Sadly sinking and fainting, as warning and warning, and yet again
    bursting with joy,
Covering the earth and filling the spread of the heaven,
As that powerful psalm in the night I heard from recesses,
Passing, I leave thee lilac with heart-shaped leaves,
I leave thee there in the door-yard, blooming, returning with
    spring.

I cease from my song for thee,
From my gaze on thee in the west, fronting the west, communing
    with thee,
O comrade lustrous with silver face in the night.

Yet each to keep and all, retrievements out of the night,
The song, the wondrous chant of the gray-brown bird,
And the tallying chant, the echo arous'd in my soul,

With the lustrous and drooping star with the countenance full
   of woe,
With the holders holding my hand nearing the call of the bird,
Comrades mine and I in the midst, and their memory ever to
   keep, for the dead I loved so well,
For the sweetest, wisest soul of all my days and lands—and this
   for his dear sake,
Lilac and star and bird twined with the chant of my soul,
There in the fragrant pines and the cedars dusk and dim.

WALT WHITMAN

THE SNARLERS

WHEN the mighty Maccabean led the armies of the Lord,
And the cohorts of Nicanor feared the red Judean sword,
Though he bore a people's sorrows, though he periled life and
   fame,
Like the shrilling of the locust rose the bitter cry of blame,
With the murmur and the clamor and the hiss and hoot and
   groan
Of the narrow clan that fancy all hearts evil, save their own:
"Ah! he fought upon the Sabbath!—broke the law of hearth and
   home!
Down with Judas Maccabeus! who would sell the land to Rome!
So they left that noble leader in their envy and their pride,
And he fell, for them, in battle. He was happy that he died.

Seven years the Great Virginian faced the legions of the king,
Braving, with his ragged heroes, warfare's rage and winter's
   sting,—
Strong in peril, calm in triumph, lion-hearted through despair,
Till the cloud of conflict lifted and a new-born flag was there.
Through the smoke of field and bivouac, yea, when armèd strife
   was done

And he toiled to weld a nation of the realms his sword had won,
Came the cry of hate and malice fostered by the poisoned pen:
"Dotard! traitor! false usurper!" brawled the breed of little men.
Peace! the Cañon of the Ages echoes not the ass's bray.
While his name resounds forever, his defamers—who were they?

Noble, wise, and simple-hearted, rock against a hundred jars,
Lincoln wrought with constant purpose to unite the sundered
    Stars.
Who may guess his burning anguish that his hand, which sought
    to heal,
First must wound what most he cherished—search the land with
    flame and steel!
Ever when his need was sorest, loud the spiteful cry uprose;
Fiercely, bitterly they chorused, feignèd friends and open foes,
Every action misconstruing, every motive splashing back,
Every mouth its venom spewing, "Butcher! tyrant!" yelped the
    pack,
Till the murderous bullet smote him and he died as martyrs die;
And a nation's wail of mourning gave those dastard throats the lie.

Think! ye shrill and frequent carpers, jealous of the public weal,
Truly, may not they who govern love their land with equal zeal?
May not those who work in silence build in fact a noble dream?
Free your hearts of cant and rancor! Purge your souls of self-
    esteem!
Delve no more in petty errors till your eyes are dim with dust!
View with broader, clearer vision; seek to fathom, learn to trust.
Hail! true souls that, uncomplaining, take the truth of foe and
    friend,
Fearless front the hidden danger! Ye shall triumph at the end.
For the men that do are deathless, spite of scoff and sneer and
    curse,
While the snarlers are forgotten,—or remembered, which is worse.

                                        ARTHUR GUITERMAN

LINCOLN, THE MAN OF THE PEOPLE

When the Norn Mother saw the Whirlwind Hour
Greatening and darkening as it hurried on,
She left the Heaven of Heroes and came down
To make a man to meet the mortal need.
She took the tried clay of the common road—
Clay warm yet with the ancient heat of Earth,
Dashed through it all a strain of prophecy;
Tempered the heap with thrill of human tears;
Then mixed a laughter with the serious stuff.
Into the shape she breathed a flame to light
That tender, tragic, ever-changing face.
Here was a man to hold against the world,
A man to match the mountains and the sea.

The color of the ground was in him, the red earth;
The smell and smack of elemental things:
The rectitude and patience of the cliff;
The good-will of the rain that loves all leaves;
The friendly welcome of the wayside well;
The courage of the bird that dares the sea;
The gladness of the wind that shakes the corn;
The mercy of the snow that hides all scars;
The secrecy of streams that make their way
Beneath the mountain to the rifted rock;
The undelaying justice of the light
That gives as freely to the shrinking flower
As to the great oak flaring to the wind—
To the grave's low hill as to the Matterhorn
That shoulders out the sky.

Sprung from the West,
The strength of virgin forests braced his mind,

The hush of spacious prairies stilled his soul.
Up from log cabin to the Capitol,
One fire was on his spirit, one resolve—
To send the keen ax to the root of wrong,
Clearing a free way for the feet of God.
And evermore he burned to do his deed
With the fine stroke and gesture of a king:
He built the rail-pile as he built the State,
Pouring his splendid strength through every blow,
The conscience of him testing every stroke,
To make his deed the measure of a man.

So came the Captain with the thinking heart;
And when the judgment thunders split the house,
Wrenching the rafters from their ancient rest,
He held the ridgepole up, and spiked again
The rafters of the Home. He held his place—
Held the long purpose like a growing tree—
Held on through blame and faltered not at praise.
And when he fell in whirlwind, he went down
As when a lordly cedar, green with boughs,
Goes down with a great shout upon the hills,
And leaves a lonesome place against the sky.

EDWIN MARKHAM

GOD SAVE OUR PRESIDENT

ALL hail! Unfurl the Stripes and Stars!
   The banner of the free!
Ten times ten thousand patriots greet
   The shrine of Liberty!
Come, with one heart, one hope, one aim,
   An undivided band,
To elevate, with solemn rites,
   The ruler of our land!

Not to invest a potentate
  With robes of majesty,—
Not to confer a kingly crown,
  Nor bend a subject knee.
We bow beneath no sceptred sway,
  Obey no royal nod:—
Columbia's sons, erect and free,
  Kneel only to their God!

Our ruler boasts no titled rank,
  No ancient, princely line,—
No regal right to sovereignty,
  Ancestral and divine.
A patriot,—at his country's call,
  Responding to her voice;
One of the people,—he becomes
  A sovereign by our choice!

And now, before the mighty pile
  We've reared to Liberty,
He swears to cherish and defend
  The charter of the free!
God of our country! seal his oath
  With Thy supreme assent.
God save the Union of the States!
  God save our President!
                    FRANCIS DeHAES JANVIER

THE MASTER

Supposed to have been written not long after the Civil War

A FLYING word from here and there
Had sown the name at which we sneered,
But soon the name was everywhere,
To be reviled and then revered:

A presence to be loved and feared,
We cannot hide it, or deny
That we, the gentlemen who jeered,
May be forgotten by and by.

He came when days were perilous
And hearts of men were sore beguiled;
And having made his note of us,
He pondered and was reconciled.
Was ever master yet so mild
As he, and so untamable?
We doubted, even when he smiled,
Not knowing what he knew so well

He knew that undeceiving fate
Would shame us whom he served unsought;
He knew that he must wince and wait—
The jest of those for whom he fought;
He knew devoutly what he thought
Of us and of our ridicule;
He knew that we must all be taught
Like little children in a school.

We gave a glamor to the task
That he encountered and saw through,
But little of us did he ask,
And little did we ever do.
And what appears if we review
The season when we railed and chaffed?
It is the face of one who knew
That we were learning while we laughed.

The face that in our vision feels
Again the venom that we flung,
Transfigured to the world reveals
The vigilance to which we clung.

Shrewd, hallowed, harassed, and among
The mysteries that are untold,
The face we see was never young
Nor could it wholly have been old.

For he, to whom we had applied
Our shopman's test of age and worth,
Was elemental when he died,
As he was ancient at his birth:
The saddest among kings of earth,
Bowed with a galling crown, this man
Met rancor with a cryptic mirth,
Laconic—and Olympian.

The love, the grandeur, and the fame,
Are bounded by the world alone;
The calm, the smoldering, and the flame
Of awful patience were his own:
With him they are forever flown
Past all our fond self-shadowings,
Wherewith we cumber the Unknown
As with inept, Icarian wings.

For we were not as other men:
'Twas ours to soar and his to see:
But we are coming down again,
And we shall come down pleasantly;
Nor shall we longer disagree
On what it is to be sublime,
But flourish in our perigee
And have one Titan at a time.

EDWIN ARLINGTON ROBINSON

ABRAHAM LINCOLN

Written by the editor of London *Punch,* as that
journal's apology and atonement.

You lay a wreath on murdered Lincoln's bier,
  You, who, with mocking pencil, wont to trace,
Broad for the self-complaisant British sneer,
  His length of shambling limb, his furrowed face,

His gaunt, gnarled hands, his unkempt, bristling hair,
  His garb uncouth, his bearing ill at ease,
His lack of all we prize as debonair,
  Of power or will to shine, of art to please;

You, whose smart pen backed up the pencil's laugh,
  Judging each step as though the way were plain;
Reckless, so it could point its paragraph
  Of chief's perplexity, or people's pain,—

Beside this corpse, that bears for winding-sheet
  The Stars and Stripes he lived to rear anew,
Between the mourners at his head and feet,
  Say, scurrile jester, is there room for *you?*

Yes, he had lived to shame me from my sneer,
  To lame my pencil, and confute my pen;
To make me own this hind of Princes peer,
  This rail-splitter a true-born king of men.

My shallow judgment I had learned to rue,
  Noting how to occasion's height he rose,
How his quaint wit made home-truth seem more true,
  How, iron-like, his temper grew by blows;

How humble, yet how hopeful, he could be;
  How, in good fortune and in ill, the same;
Nor bitter in success, nor boastful he,
  Thirsty for gold, nor feverish for fame.

He went about his work—such work as few
  Ever had laid on head and heart and hand—
As one who knows, where there's a task to do,
  Man's honest will must Heaven's good grace command;

Who trusts the strength will with the burden grow,
  That God makes instruments to work His will,
If but that will we can arrive to know,
  Nor tamper with the weights of good and ill.

So he went forth to battle, on the side
  That he felt clear was Liberty's and Right's,
As in his peasant boyhood he had plied
  His warfare with rude Nature's thwarting mights,—

The uncleared forest, the unbroken soil,
  The iron bark that turns the lumberer's ax,
The rapid that o'erbears the boatman's toil,
  The prairie, hiding the mazed wanderer's tracks,

The ambushed Indian, and the prowling bear,—
  Such were the needs that helped his youth to train:
Rough culture—but such trees large fruit may bear,
  If but their stocks be of right girth and grain.

So he grew up, a destined work to do,
  And lived to do it: four long-suffering years'
Ill-fate, ill-feeling, ill-report, lived through,
  And then he heard the hisses change to cheers,

The taunts to tribute, the abuse to praise,
  And took both with the same unwavering mood;
Till, as he came on light, from darkling days,
  And seemed to touch the goal from where he stood,

A felon hand, between the goal and him,
  Reached from behind his back, a trigger pressed—
And those perplexed and patient eyes were dim,
  Those gaunt, long-laboring limbs were laid to rest.

The words of mercy were upon his lips,
  Forgiveness in his heart and on his pen,
When this vile murderer brought swift eclipse
  To thoughts of peace on earth, good will to men.

The Old World and the New, from sea to sea,
  Utter one voice of sympathy and shame.
Sore heart, so stopped when it at last beat high!
  Sad life, cut short just as its triumph came!

A deed accursed! Strokes have been struck before
  By the assassin's hand, whereof men doubt
If more of horror or disgrace they bore;
  But thy foul crime, like Cain's, stands darkly out,

Vile hand, that brandest murder on a strife,
  Whate'er its grounds, stoutly and nobly striven,
And with the martyr's crown, crownest a life
  With much to praise, little to be forgiven.
                      TOM TAYLOR

ABRAHAM LINCOLN

OH, SLOW to smite and swift to spare,
    Gentle and merciful and just!
Who, in the fear of God, didst bear
    The sword of power, a nation's trust!

In sorrow by thy bier we stand,
    Amid the awe that hushes all,
And speak the anguish of a land
    That shook with horror at thy fall.

Thy task is done; the bond are free:
    We bear thee to an honored grave,
Whose proudest monument shall be
    The broken fetters of the slave.

Pure was thy life; its bloody close
    Hath placed thee with the sons of light,
Among the noble host of those
    Who perished in the cause of Right.
              WILLIAM CULLEN BRYANT

LINCOLN

I

LIKE a gaunt, scraggly pine
Which lifts its head above the mournful sandhills;
And patiently, through dull years of bitter silence,
Untended and uncared for, begins to grow.

Ungainly, laboring, huge,
The wind of the north has twisted and gnarled its branches;
Yet in the heat of midsummer days, when thunder-clouds ring
  the horizon,
A nation of men shall rest beneath its shade.

And it shall protect them all,
Hold everyone safe there, watching aloof in silence;
Until at last one mad stray bolt from the zenith
Shall strike it in an instant down to earth.

II

There was a darkness in this man; an immense and hollow dark-
  ness,
Of which we may not speak, nor share with him, nor enter;
A darkness through which strong roots stretched downwards into
  the earth
Towards old things;
Towards the herdman-kings who walked the earth and spoke
  with God,
Towards the wanderers who sought for they knew not what, and
  found their goal at last;
Towards the men who waited, only waited patiently when all
  seemed lost,
Many bitter winters of defeat;
Down to the granite of patience
These roots swept, knotted fibrous roots, prying, piercing, seeking,
And drew from the living rock and the living waters about it
The red sap to carry upwards to the sun.

Not proud, but humble,
Only to serve and pass on, to endure to the end through service;
For the ax is laid at the root of the trees, and all that bring not
  forth good fruit
Shall be cut down on the day to come and cast into the fire.

III

There is silence abroad in the land today,
And in the hearts of men, a deep and anxious silence;
And, because we are still at last, those bronze lips slowly open,
Those hollow and weary eyes take on a gleam of light.

Slowly a patient, firm-syllabled voice cuts through the endless
    silence
Like laboring oxen that drag a plow through the chaos of rude
    clay-fields:
"I went forward as the light goes forward in early spring,
But there were also many things which I left behind.

"Tombs that were quiet;
One, of a mother, whose brief light went out in the darkness,
One, of a loved one, the snow on whose grave is long falling,
One, only of a child, but it was mine.

"Have you forgot your graves? Go, question them in anguish,
Listen long to their unstirred lips. From your hostages to silence,
Learn there is no life without death, no dawn without sun-setting,
No victory but to Him who has given all."

IV

The clamor of cannon dies down, the furnace-mouth of the battle
    is silent.
The midwinter sun dips and descends, the earth takes on afresh
    its bright colors.
But he whom we mocked and obeyed not, he whom we scorned
    and mistrusted,
He has descended, like a god, to his rest.

Over the uproar of cities,
Over the million intricate threads of life wavering and crossing,

In the midst of problems we know not, tangling, perplexing,
    ensnaring,
Rises one white tomb alone.
Beam over it, stars.
Wrap it round, stripes—stripes red for the pain that he bore for
    you—
Enfold it forever, O flag, rent, soiled, but repaired through your
    anguish;
Long as you keep him there safe, the nations shall bow to your
    law.

Strew over him flowers:
Blue forget-me-nots from the north, and the bright pink arbutus
From the east, and from the west rich orange blossoms,
But from the heart of the land take the passion-flower;

Rayed, violet, dim,
With the nails that pierced, the cross that he bore and the circlet,
And beside it there lay also one lonely snow-white magnolia,
Bitter for remembrance of the healing which has passed.

                                    JOHN GOULD FLETCHER

O CAPTAIN! MY CAPTAIN!

O CAPTAIN! my Captain! our fearful trip is done,
The ship has weather'd every rack, the prize we sought is won.
  The port is near, the bells I hear, the people all exulting,
  While follow eyes the steady keel, the vessel grim and daring;

                But O heart! heart! heart!
                  O the bleeding drops of red,
                Where on the deck my Captain lies,
                  Fallen cold and dead.

O Captain! my Captain! rise up and hear the bells;
Rise up—for you the flag is flung—for you the bugle trills,

For you bouquets and ribbon'd wreaths—for you the shores
    a-crowding,
For you they call, the swaying mass, their eager faces turning;

Here, Captain! dear father!
    This arm beneath your head!
It is some dream that on the deck,
    You've fallen cold and dead.

My Captain does not answer, his lips are pale and still,
My father does not feel my arm, he has no pulse nor will,
    The ship is anchor'd safe and sound, its voyage closed and done,
From fearful trip the victor ship comes in with object won;

Exult, O shores! and ring, O bells!
    But I with mournful tread,
Walk the deck my Captain lies,
    Fallen cold and dead.

                                    WALT WHITMAN

ANNE RUTLEDGE

OUT OF ME unworthy and unknown
The vibrations of deathless music:
"With malice toward none, with charity for all."
Out of me the forgiveness of millions toward millions,
And the beneficent face of a nation
Shining with justice and truth.
I am Anne Rutledge who sleep beneath these weeds,
Beloved in life of Abraham Lincoln,
Wedded to him, not through union,
But through separation.
Bloom forever, O Republic,
From the dust of my bosom!

                                    EDGAR LEE MASTERS

From SPRINGFIELD SPEECH

By
ABRAHAM LINCOLN

June 16, 1858

Speech delivered at Springfield, Illinois, at the close of
the Republican State Convention by which Mr. Lincoln had been named as their candidate for United
States Senator.

Mr. President and Gentlemen of the Convention: If we could
first know where we are, and whither we are tending, we could
better judge what to do, and how to do it. We are now far into
the fifth year since a policy was initiated with the avowed object
and confident promise of putting an end to slavery agitation.
Under the operation of that policy, that agitation has not only
not ceased, but has constantly augmented. In my opinion, it will
not cease until a crisis shall have been reached and passed. "A
house divided against itself cannot stand." I believe this government cannot endure permanently half slave and half free. I do
not expect the Union to be dissolved—I do not expect the house
to fall—but I do expect it will cease to be divided. It will become
all one thing, or all the other. Either the opponents of slavery
will arrest the further spread of it, and place it where the public
mind shall rest in the belief that it is in the course of ultimate
extinction; or its advocates will push it forward till it shall become
alike lawful in all the States, old as well as new, North as well
as South.

LETTER TO LINCOLN FROM HORACE GREELEY URGING EMANCIPATION

August 19, 1862

To Abraham Lincoln, President of the United States:

DEAR SIR: I do not intrude to tell you—for you must know already—that a great proportion of those who triumphed in your election, and of all who desire the unqualified suppression of the rebellion now desolating our country, are sorely disappointed and deeply pained by the policy you seem to be pursuing with regard to the slaves of rebels. I write only to set succinctly and unmistakably before you what we require, what we think we have a right to expect, and of what we complain.

.   .   .   .

VIII. On the face of this wide earth, Mr. President, there is not one disinterested, determined, intelligent champion of the Union cause who does not feel that all attempts to put down the rebellion and at the same time uphold its inciting cause are preposterous and futile—that the rebellion, if crushed out to-morrow, would be renewed within a year if Slavery were left in full vigor— that army officers who remain to this day devoted to Slavery can at best be but half-way loyal to the Union—and that every hour of deference to Slavery is an hour of added and deepened peril to the Union. I appeal to the testimony of your ambassadors in Europe. It is freely at your service, not at mine. Ask them to tell you candidly whether the seeming subserviency of your policy to the slaveholding, slavery-upholding interest, is not the perplexity, the despair of statesmen of all parties, and be admonished by the general answer!

IX. I close as I began with the statement that what an immense majority of the loyal millions of your countrymen require of you is a frank, declared, unqualified, ungrudging execution of the laws of the land, more especially of the Confiscation Act. That act gives freedom to the slaves of rebels coming within our lines, or whom those lines may at any time inclose—we ask you to render it due obedience by publicly requiring all your subordinates to recognize and obey it. The rebels are everywhere using the late anti-negro riots in the North, as they have long used your officers' treatment of negroes in the South, to convince the slaves that they have nothing to hope from a Union success—that we mean in that case to sell them into a bitter bondage to defray the cost of the war. Let them impress this as a truth on the great mass of their ignorant and credulous bondmen, and the Union will never be restored—never. We cannot conquer ten millions of people united in solid phalanx against us, powerfully aided by Northern sympathizers and European allies. We must have scouts, guides, spies, cooks, teamsters, diggers, and choppers from the blacks of the South, whether we allow them to fight for us or not, or we shall be baffled and repelled. As one of the millions who would gladly have avoided this struggle at any sacrifice but that of principle and honor, but who now feel that the triumph of the Union is indispensable not only to the existence of our country but to the well-being of mankind, I entreat you to render a hearty and unequivocal obedience to the law of the land.

Yours,

HORACE GREELEY

ABRAHAM LINCOLN'S LETTER
TO HORACE GREELEY

Executive Mansion,
Washington, August 22, 1862.

Hon. Horace Greeley:

DEAR SIR: I have just read yours of the nineteenth, addressed to myself through the New-York *Tribune*. If there be in it any statements or assumptions of fact which I may know to be erroneous, I do not now and here controvert them. If there be in it any inferences which I may believe to be falsely drawn, I do not now and here argue against them. If there be perceptible in it an impatient and dictatorial tone, I waive it in deference to an old friend, whose heart I have always supposed to be right.

As to the policy I "seem to be pursuing," as you say, I have not meant to leave any one in doubt.

I would save the Union. I would save it the shortest way under the Constitution. The sooner the National authority can be restored, the nearer the Union will be "the Union as it was." If there be those who would not save the Union unless they could at the same time *save* Slavery, I do not agree with them. If there be those who would not save the Union unless they could at the same time *destroy* Slavery, I do not agree with them. My paramount object in this struggle *is* to save the Union, and is *not* either to save or destroy Slavery. If I could save the Union without freeing *any* slave, I would do it; and if I could save it by freeing *all* the slaves, I would do it; and if I could do it by freeing some and leaving others alone, I would also do that. What I do about Slavery and the colored race, I do because I believe it helps to save this Union; and what I forbear, I forbear because I do *not* believe it would help to save the Union. I shall do *less* whenever I shall believe what I am doing hurts the cause, and I shall do *more* whenever I shall believe doing more will help the cause. I shall try to correct errors when shown to be errors; and I shall adopt new views so fast as they shall appear to be true views. I have here stated my purpose according to my view of *official* duty, and I intend no modification of my oft-expressed *personal* wish that all men, everywhere, could be free.   Yours,

A. LINCOLN

EMANCIPATION PROCLAMATION

January 1, 1863

BY THE PRESIDENT OF THE UNITED STATES OF AMERICA:

A Proclamation

WHEREAS, on the twenty-second day of September, in the year of our Lord one thousand eight hundred and sixty-two, a proclamation was issued by the President of the United States, containing, among other things, the following, to wit:

"That on the first day of January, in the year of our Lord one thousand eight hundred and sixty-three, all persons held as slaves within any State, or designated part of a State, the people whereof shall then be in rebellion against the United States, shall be then, thenceforward, and forever free; and the Executive Government of the United States, including the military and naval authority thereof, will recognize and maintain the freedom of such persons, and will do no act or acts to repress such persons, or any of them, in any efforts they may make for their actual freedom.

"That the Executive will, on the first day of January aforesaid, by proclamation, designate the States and parts of States, if any, in which the people thereof respectively shall then be in rebellion against the United States; and the fact that any State, or the people thereof, shall on that day be in good faith represented in the Congress of the United States by members chosen thereto at elections wherein a majority of the qualified voters of such State shall have participated, shall in the absence of strong counter-vailing testimony be deemed conclusive evidence that such State and the people thereof are not then in rebellion against the United States."

Now, therefore, I, Abraham Lincoln, President of the United States, by virtue of the power in me vested as commander-in-chief of the army and navy of the United States, in time of actual armed rebellion against the authority and government of the United States, and as a fit and necessary war measure for suppressing said rebellion, do, on this first day of January, in the year of our Lord one thousand eight hundred and sixty-three, and in accordance with my purpose so to do, publicly proclaimed for the full period of 100 days from the day first above mentioned, order and designate as the States and parts of States wherein the people thereof, respectively, are this day in rebellion against the United States, the following, to wit:

Arkansas, Texas, Louisiana (except the parishes of St. Bernard, Plaquemines, Jefferson, St. John, St. Charles, St. James, Ascension, Assumption, Terre Bonne, Lafourche, St. Mary, St. Martin, and Orleans, including the city of New Orleans), Mississippi, Alabama, Florida, Georgia, South Carolina, North Carolina, and Virginia (except the forty-eight counties designated as West Virginia, and also the counties of Berkeley, Accomac, Northampton, Elizabeth City, York, Princess Ann, and Norfolk, including the cities of Norfolk and Portsmouth), and which excepted parts are for the present left precisely as if this proclamation were not issued.

And by virtue of the power and for the purpose aforesaid, I do order and declare that all persons held as slaves within said designated States and parts of States are, and henceforward shall be, free; and that the Executive Government of the United States, including the military and naval authorities thereof, will recognize and maintain the freedom of said persons.

And I hereby enjoin upon the people so declared to be free to abstain from all violence, unless in necessary self-defence; and I recommend to them that, in all cases when allowed, they labor faithfully for reasonable wages.

And I further declare and make known that such persons of suitable condition will be received into the armed service of the United States to garrison forts, positions, stations, and other places, and to man vessels of all sorts in said service.

And upon this act, sincerely believed to be an act of justice, warranted by the Constitution upon military necessity, I invoke the considerate judgment of mankind and the gracious favor of Almighty God.

In witness whereof, I have hereunto set my hand, and caused the seal of the United States to be affixed.

Done at the city of Washington, this first day of January, in the year of our Lord one thousand eight hundred and [L. S.] sixty-three, and of the independence of the United States of America the eighty-seventh.

ABRAHAM LINCOLN

By the President: WILLIAM H. SEWARD, Secretary of State.

THE GETTYSBURG ADDRESS

By
ABRAHAM LINCOLN

November 19, 1863

FOUR score and seven years ago our fathers brought forth on this continent, a new nation, conceived in Liberty, and dedicated to the proposition that all men are created equal.

Now we are engaged in a great civil war, testing whether that nation or any nation so conceived and so dedicated, can long endure. We are met on a great battle-field of that war. We have come to dedicate a portion of that field, as a final resting place for those who here gave their lives that that nation might live. It is altogether fitting and proper that we should do this.

But, in a larger sense, we can not dedicate—we can not conse-crate—we can not hallow—this ground. The brave men, living and dead, who struggled here, have consecrated it, far above our poor power to add or detract. The world will little note, nor long remember what we say here, but it can never forget what they did here. It is for us the living, rather, to be dedicated here to the unfinished work which they who fought here have thus far so nobly advanced. It is rather for us to be here dedicated to the great task remaining before us—that from these honored dead we take increased devotion to that cause for which they gave the last full measure of devotion—that we here highly resolve that these dead shall not have died in vain—that this nation, under God, shall have a new birth of freedom—and that government of the people, by the people, for the people, shall not perish from the earth.

LINCOLN'S LETTER TO MRS. BIXBY

EXECUTIVE MANSION, WASHINGTON
November 21, 1864.

MRS. BIXBY, BOSTON, MASSACHUSETTS.

DEAR MADAM: I have been shown in the files of the War Department a statement of the Adjutant-General of Massachusetts that you are the mother of five sons who have died gloriously on the field of battle. I feel how weak and fruitless must be any words of mine which should attempt to beguile you from the grief of a loss so overwhelming. But I cannot refrain from tendering to you the consolation that may be found in the thanks of the Republic they died to save. I pray that our heavenly Father may assuage the anguish of your bereavement, and leave you only the cherished memory of the loved and lost, and the solemn pride that must be yours to have laid so costly a sacrifice upon the altar of freedom.

Yours very sincerely and respectfully,

ABRAHAM LINCOLN

From LINCOLN'S SECOND INAUGURAL ADDRESS

March 4, 1865

THE ALMIGHTY has His own purposes. "Woe unto the world because of offenses; for it must needs be that offenses come, but woe to that man by whom the offense cometh." If we shall suppose that American slavery is one of those offenses which, in the providence of God, must needs come, but which, having continued through His appointed time, He now wills to remove, and that He gives to both North and South this terrible war as the woe due to those by whom the offense came, shall we discern therein any departure from those divine attributes which the believers in a living God always ascribe to Him? Fondly do we hope, fervently do we pray, that this mighty scourge of war may speedily pass away. Yet, if God wills that it continue until all the wealth piled by the bondsman's two hundred and fifty years of unrequited toil shall be sunk, and until every drop of blood drawn with the lash shall be paid by another drawn with the sword, as was said three thousand years ago, so still it must be said, "The judgments of the Lord are true and righteous altogether."

With malice toward none, with charity for all, with firmness in the right as God gives us to see the right, let us strive on to finish the work we are in, to bind up the nation's wounds, to care for him who shall have borne the battle and for his widow and his orphan, to do all which may achieve and cherish a just and lasting peace among ourselves and with all nations.

ABRAHAM LINCOLN

By
JAMES RUSSELL LOWELL

IT IS by presence of mind in untried emergencies that the native metal of a man is tested; it is by the sagacity to see, and the fearless honesty to admit, whatever of truth there may be in an adverse opinion, in order more convincingly to expose the fallacy that lurks behind it, that a reasoner at length gains for his mere statement of a fact the force of argument; it is by a wise forecast which allows hostile combinations to go so far as by the inevitable reaction to become elements of his own power, that a politician proves his genius for state-craft; and especially it is by so gently guiding public sentiment that he seems to follow it, by so yielding doubtful points that he can be firm without seeming obstinate in essential ones, and thus gain the advantages of compromise without the weakness of concession; by so instinctively comprehending the temper and prejudices of a people as to make them gradually conscious of the superior wisdom of his freedom from temper and prejudice,—it is by qualities such as these that a magistrate shows himself worthy to be chief in a commonwealth of freemen. And it is for qualities such as these that we firmly believe History will rank Mr. Lincoln among the most prudent of statesmen and the most successful of rulers. If we wish to appreciate him, we have only to conceive the inevitable chaos in which we should now be weltering, had a weak man or an unwise one been chosen in his stead.

COMMENT AT LINCOLN FUNERAL SERVICE, CONCORD, MASS.

April 10, 1865

By
Ralph Waldo Emerson

He (Lincoln) is the true history of the American people in his time. . . . Step by step he walked before them; slow with their slowness, quickening his march to theirs, the true representative of this continent; an entirely public man, father of his country, the pulse of twenty millions throbbing in his heart, the thought of their minds articulated by his tongue.

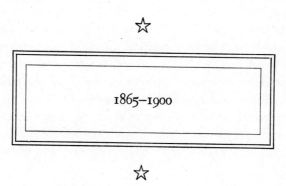

1865–1900

ODE RECITED AT THE HARVARD
COMMEMORATION

July 21, 1865

I

WEAK-WINGED is song,
Nor aims at that clear-ethered height
Whither the brave deed climbs for light:
    We seem to do them wrong,
Bringing our robin's-leaf to deck their hearse
Who in warm life-blood wrote their nobler verse,
Our trivial song to honor those who come
With ears attuned to strenuous trump and drum,
And shaped in squadron-strophes their desire,
Live battle-odes whose lines were steel and fire:
    Yet sometimes feathered words are strong
A gracious memory to buoy up and save
From Lethe's dreamless ooze, the common grave
    Of the unventurous throng.

II

To-day our Reverend Mother welcomes back
    Her wisest Scholars, those who understood
The deeper teaching of her mystic tome,
    And offered their fresh lives to make it good:
        No lore of Greece or Rome,
No science peddling with the names of things,
Or reading stars to find inglorious fates,
    Can lift our life with wings

363

Far from Death's idle gulf that for the many waits,
     And lengthen out our dates
With that clear fame whose memory sings
In manly hearts to come, and nerves them and dilates:
Nor such thy teaching, Mother of us all!
          Not such the trumpet-call
          Of thy diviner mood,
          That could thy sons entice
From happy homes and toils, the fruitful nest
Of those half-virtues which the world calls best,
          Into War's tumult rude;
          But rather far that stern device
The sponsors chose that round thy cradle stood
     In the dim, unventured wood,
     The VERITAS that lurks beneath
     The letter's unprolific sheath,
   Life of whate'er makes life worth living,
Seed-grain of high emprise, immortal food,
     One heavenly thing whereof earth hath the giving.

III

Many loved Truth, and lavished life's best oil
   Amid the dust of books to find her,
Content at last, for guerdon of their toil,
   With the cast mantle she hath left behind her.
     Many in sad faith sought for her,
     Many with crossed hands sighed for her;
     But these, our brothers, fought for her,
     At life's dear peril wrought for her,
     So loved her that they died for her,
     Tasting the raptured fleetness
     Of her divine completeness:
     Their higher instinct knew
Those love her best who to themselves are true,
And what they dare to dream of, dare to do;

They followed her and found her
Where all may hope to find,
Not in the ashes of the burnt-out mind,
But beautiful, with danger's sweetness round her.
Where faith made whole with deed
Breathes its awakening breath
Into the lifeless creed,
They saw her plumed and mailed,
With sweet, stern face unveiled,
And all-repaying eyes, look proud on them in death.

IV

Our slender life runs rippling by, and glides
Into the silent hollow of the past;
What is there that abides
To make the next age better for the last?
Is earth too poor to give us
Something to live for here that shall outlive us?
Some more substantial boon
Than such as flows and ebbs with Fortune's fickle moon?
The little that we see
From doubt is never free;
The little that we do
Is but half-nobly true;
With our laborious hiving
What men call treasure, and the gods call dross,
Life seems a jest of Fate's contriving,
Only secure in every one's conniving,
A long account of nothings paid with loss,
Where we poor puppets, jerked by unseen wires,
After our little hour of strut and rave,
With all our pasteboard passions and desires,
Loves, hates, ambitions, and immortal fires,
Are tossed pell-mell together in the grave.
But stay! no age was e'er degenerate,

Unless men held it at too cheap a rate,
For in our likeness still we shape our fate.
   Ah, there is something here
Unfathomed by the cynic's sneer,
Something that gives our feeble light
A high immunity from Night,
Something that leaps life's narrow bars
To claim its birthright with the hosts of heaven;
  A seed of sunshine that can leaven
Our earthy dulness with the beams of stars
    And glorify our clay
With light from fountains elder than the Day;
  A conscience more divine than we,
  A gladness fed with secret tears,
  A vexing, forward-reaching sense
  Of some more noble permanence;
    A light across the sea,
Which haunts the soul and will not let it be,
Still beaconing from the heights of undegenerate years.

v

    Whither leads the path
    To ampler fates that leads?
    Not down through flowery meads,
    To reap an aftermath
  Of youth's vainglorious weeds,
  But up the steep, amid the wrath
And shock of deadly-hostile creeds,
  Where the world's best hope and stay
By battle's flashes gropes a desperate way,
And every turf the fierce foot clings to bleeds.
  Peace hath her not ignoble wreath,
  Ere yet the sharp, decisive word
Light the black lips of cannon, and the sword
    Dreams in its easeful sheath;

But some day the live coal behind the thought,
  Whether from Baäl's stone obscene,
  Or from the shrine serene
  Of God's pure altar brought,
Bursts up in flame; the war of tongue and pen
Learns with what deadly purpose it was fraught,
And, helpless in the fiery passion caught,
Shakes all the pillared state with shock of men:
Some day the soft Ideal that we wooed
Confronts us fiercely, foe-beset, pursued,
And cries reproachful: "Was it, then, my praise,
And not myself was loved? Prove now thy truth;
I claim of thee the promise of thy youth;
Give me thy life, or cower in empty phrase,
The victim of thy genius, not its mate!"
  Life may be given in many ways,
  And loyalty to Truth be sealed
As bravely in the closet as the field,
  So bountiful is Fate;
  But then to stand beside her,
  When craven churls deride her,
To front a lie in arms and not to yield,
  This shows, methinks, God's plan
  And measure of a stalwart man,
  Limbed like the old heroic breeds,
  Who stands self-poised on manhood's solid earth,
  Not forced to frame excuses for his birth,
Fed from within with all the strength he needs.

VI

Such was he, our Martyr-Chief,
  Whom late the Nation he had led,
  With ashes on her head,
Wept with the passion of an angry grief:
Forgive me, if from present things I turn

To speak what in my heart will beat and burn,
And hang my wreath on his world-honored urn.
 Nature, they say, doth dote,
 And cannot make a man
 Save on some worn-out plan,
 Repeating us by rote:
For him her Old-World moulds aside she threw,
 And, choosing sweet clay from the breast
 Of the unexhausted West,
With stuff untainted shaped a hero new,
Wise, steadfast in the strength of God, and true.
 How beautiful to see
Once more a shepherd of mankind indeed,
Who loved his charge, but never loved to lead;
One whose meek flock the people joyed to be,
 Not lured by any cheat of birth,
 But by his clear-grained human worth,
And brave old wisdom of sincerity!
 They knew that outward grace is dust;
 They could not choose but trust
In that sure-footed mind's unfaltering skill,
 And supple-tempered will
That bent like perfect steel to spring again and thrust.
 His was no lonely mountain-peak of mind
 Thrusting to thin air o'er our cloudy bars,
 A sea-mark now, now lost in vapors blind;
 Broad prairie rather, genial, level-lined,
 Fruitful and friendly for all human kind,
Yet also nigh to heaven and loved of loftiest stars,
  Nothing of Europe here,
Or, then, of Europe fronting mornward still,
 Ere any names of Serf and Peer
 Could Nature's equal scheme deface
 And thwart her genial will;
 Here was a type of the true elder race,

And one of Plutarch's men talked with us face to face.
    I praise him not; it were too late;
And some innative weakness there must be
In him who condescends to victory
Such as the Present gives, and cannot wait,
    Safe in himself as in a fate.
      So always firmly he:
      He knew to bide his time,
      And can his fame abide,
Still patient in his simple faith sublime,
      Till the wise years decide.
  Great captains, with their guns and drums,
    Disturb our judgment for the hour,
      But at last silence comes;
These all are gone, and, standing like a tower,
Our children shall behold his fame,
    The kindly-earnest, brave, foreseeing man,
Sagacious, patient, dreading praise, not blame,
  New birth of our new soil, the first American.

VII

  Long as man's hope insatiate can discern
    Or only guess some more inspiring goal
    Outside of Self, enduring as the pole,
Along whose course the flying axles burn
Of spirits bravely-pitched, earth's manlier brood;
    Long as below we cannot find
The meed that stills the inexorable mind;
So long this faith to some ideal Good,
Under whatever mortal names it masks,
Freedom, Law, Country, this ethereal mood
That thanks the Fates for their severer tasks,
    Feeling its challenged pulses leap,
    While others skulk in subterfuges cheap,

And, set in Danger's van, has all the boon it asks,
  Shall win man's praise and woman's love,
  Shall be a wisdom that we set above
All other skills and gifts to culture dear,
  A virtue round whose forehead we inwreathe
  Laurels that with a living passion breathe
When other crowns grow, while we twine them, sear.
  What brings us thronging these high rites to pay,
And seal these hours the noblest of our year,
  Save that our brothers found this better way?

VIII

  We sit here in the Promised Land
  That flows with Freedom's honey and milk;
  But 't was they won it, sword in hand,
Making the nettle danger soft for us as silk.
  We welcome back our bravest and our best;—
  Ah me! not all! some come not with the rest,
Who went forth brave and bright as any here!
I strive to mix some gladness with my strain,
      But the sad strings complain,
      And will not please the ear:
I sweep them for a pæan, but they wane
      Again and yet again
Into a dirge, and die away, in pain.
In these brave ranks I only see the gaps,
Thinking of dear ones whom the dumb turf wraps,
Dark to the triumph which they died to gain:
  Fitlier may others greet the living,
  For me the past is unforgiving;
    I with uncovered head
    Salute the sacred dead,
Who went, and who return not.—Say not so!
'T is not the grapes of Canaan that repay,
But the high faith that failed not by the way;

Virtue treads paths that end not in the grave;
No ban of endless night exiles the brave;
      And to the saner mind
We rather seem the dead that stayed behind.
Blow, trumpets, all your exultations blow!
For never shall their aureoled presence lack;
I see them muster in a gleaming row,
With ever-youthful brows that nobler show;
We find in our dull road their shining track;
      In every nobler mood
We feel the orient of their spirit glow,
Part of our life's unalterable good,
Of all our saintlier aspiration;
      They come transfigured back,
Secure from change in their high-hearted ways,
Beautiful evermore, and with the rays
Of morn on their white Shields of Expectation!

IX

      But is there hope to save
  Even this ethereal essence from the grave?
  What ever 'scaped Oblivion's subtle wrong
Save a few clarion names, or golden threads of song?
      Before my musing eye
   The mighty ones of old sweep by,
Disvoicèd now and insubstantial things,
As noisy once as we; poor ghosts of kings,
Shadows of empire wholly gone to dust,
And many races, nameless long ago,
To darkness driven by that imperious gust
Of ever-rushing Time that here doth blow:
O visionary world, condition strange,
  Where naught abiding is but only Change,
Where the deep-bolted stars themselves still shift and range!
  Shall we to more continuance make pretence?

Renown builds tombs; a life-estate is Wit;
    And, bit by bit,
The cunning years steal all from us but woe;
  Leaves are we, whose decays no harvest sow.
      But, when we vanish hence,
Shall they lie forceless in the dark below,
Save to make green their little length of sods,
Or deepen pansies for a year or two,
Who now to us are shining-sweet as gods?
Was dying all they had the skill to do?
That were not fruitless: but the Soul resents
Such short-lived service, as if blind events
Ruled without her, or earth could so endure;
She claims a more divine investiture
Of longer tenure than Fame's airy rents;
Whate'er she touches doth her nature share;
Her inspiration haunts the ennobled air,
    Gives eyes to mountains blind,
Ears to the deaf earth, voices to the wind,
And her clear trump sings succor everywhere
By lonely bivouacs to the wakeful mind;
For soul inherits all that soul could dare:
    Yea, Manhood hath a wider span
And larger privilege of life than man.
The single deed, the private sacrifice,
So radiant now through proudly-hidden tears,
Is covered up erelong from mortal eyes
With thoughtless drift of the deciduous years;
But that high privilege that makes all men peers,
That leap of heart whereby a people rise
    Up to a noble anger's height,
And, flamed on by the Fates, not shrink, but grow more bright,
  That swift validity in noble veins,
  Of choosing danger and disdaining shame,
    Of being set on flame
  By the pure fire that flies all contact base,

But wraps its chosen with angelic might,
  These are imperishable gains,
 Sure as the sun, medicinal as light,
  These hold great futures in their lusty reins
And certify to earth a new imperial race.

x

   Who now shall sneer?
  Who dare again to say we trace
  Our lines to a plebeian race?
    Roundhead and Cavalier!
Dumb are those names erewhile in battle loud;
Dream-footed as the shadow of a cloud,
   They flit across the ear:
That is best blood that hath most iron in 't.
To edge resolve with, pouring without stint
   For what makes manhood dear.
   Tell us not of Plantagenets,
Hapsburgs, and Guelfs, whose thin bloods crawl
Down from some victor in a border-brawl!
   How poor their outworn coronets,
Matched with one leaf of that plain civic wreath
Our brave for honor's blazon shall bequeath,
  Through whose desert a rescued Nation sets
Her heel on treason, and the trumpet hears
Shout victory, tingling Europe's sullen ears
  With vain resentments and more vain regrets!

xi

  Not in anger, not in pride,
  Pure from passion's mixture rude
  Ever to base earth allied,
  But with far-heard gratitude,
  Still with heart and voice renewed,
 To heroes living and dear martyrs dead,

The strain should close that consecrates our brave.
  Lift the heart and lift the head!
    Lofty be its mood and grave,
    Not without a martial ring,
    Not without a prouder tread
    And a peal of exultation:
    Little right has he to sing
    Through whose heart in such an hour
    Beats no march of conscious power,
    Sweeps no tumult of elation!
    'T is no Man we celebrate,
    By his country's victories great,
A hero half, and half the whim of Fate,
    But the pith and marrow of a Nation
    Drawing force from all her men,
    Highest, humblest, weakest, all,
    For her time of need, and then
    Pulsing it again through them,
  Till the basest can no longer cower,
  Feeling his soul spring up divinely tall,
  Touched but in passing by her mantle-hem.
  Come back, then, noble pride, for 't is her dower!
    How could poet ever tower,
    If his passions, hopes, and fears,
    If his triumphs and his tears,
    Kept not measure with his people?
Boom, cannon, boom to all the winds and waves!
Clash out, glad bells, from every rocking steeple!
Banners, advance with triumph, bend your staves!
    And from every mountain-peak,
    Let beacon-fire to answering beacon speak,
    Katahdin tell Monadnock, Whiteface he,
And so leap on in light from sea to sea,
      Till the glad news be sent
      Across a kindling continent,

Making earth feel more firm and air breathe braver:
"Be proud! for she is saved, and all have helped to save her!
    She that lifts up the manhood of the poor,
    She of the open soul and open door,
    With room about her hearth for all mankind!
    The fire is dreadful in her eyes no more;
    From her bold front the helm she doth unbind,
    Sends all her handmaid armies back to spin,
    And bids her navies, that so lately hurled
    Their crashing battle, hold their thunders in,
    Swimming like birds of calm along the unharmful shore.
    No challenge sends she to the elder world,
    That looked askance and hated; a light scorn
    Plays o'er her mouth, as round her mighty knees
    She calls her children back, and waits the morn
Of nobler day, enthroned between her subject seas."

XII

Bow down, dear Land, for thou hast found release!
    Thy God, in these distempered days,
    Hath taught thee the sure wisdom of His ways,
And through thine enemies hath wrought thy peace!
    Bow down in prayer and praise!
No poorest in thy borders but may now
Lift to the juster skies a man's enfranchised brow.
O Beautiful! my Country! ours once more!
Smoothing thy gold of war-dishevelled hair
O'er such sweet brows as never other wore,
    And letting thy set lips,
    Freed from wrath's pale eclipse,
The rosy edges of their smile lay bare,
What words divine of lover or of poet
Could tell our love and make thee know it,

Among the Nations bright beyond compare?
What were our lives without thee?
What all our lives to save thee?
We reck not what we gave thee;
We will not dare to doubt thee,
But ask whatever else, and we will dare!

JAMES RUSSELL LOWELL

CUSTER'S LAST CHARGE

DEAD! Is it possible? He, the bold rider,
  Custer, our hero, the first in the fight,
Charming the bullets of yore to fly wider,
  Far from our battle-king's ringlets of light!
Dead, our young chieftain, and dead, all forsaken!
  No one to tell us the way of his fall!
Slain in the desert, and never to waken,
  Never, not even to victory's call!

Proud for his fame that last day that he met them!
  All the night long he had been on their track,
Scorning their traps and the men that had set them,
  Wild for a charge that should never give back.
There on the hilltop he halted and saw them,—
  Lodges all loosened and ready to fly;
Hurrying scouts with the tidings to awe them,
  Told of his coming before he was nigh.

All the wide valley was full of their forces,
  Gathered to cover the lodges' retreat!—
Warriors running in haste to their horses,
  Thousands of enemies close to his feet!
Down in the valleys the ages had hollowed,
  There lay the Sitting Bull's camp for a prey!
Numbers! What recked he? What recked those who followed—
  Men who had fought ten to one ere that day?

Out swept the squadrons, the fated three hundred,
   Into the battle-line steady and full;
Then down the hillside exultingly thundered,
   Into the hordes of the old Sitting Bull!
Wild Ogalallah, Arapahoe, Cheyenne,
   Wild Horse's braves, and the rest of their crew,
Shrank from that charge like a herd from a lion,—
   Then closed around, the grim horde of wild Sioux!

Right to their centre he charged, and then facing—
   Hark to those yells! and around them, O see!
Over the hilltops the Indians come racing,
   Coming as fast as the waves of the sea!
Red was the circle of fire around them;
   No hope of victory, no ray of light,
Shot through that terrible black cloud without them,
   Brooding in death over Custer's last fight.

Then did he blench? Did he die like a craven,
   Begging those torturing fiends for his life?
Was there a soldier who carried the Seven
   Flinched like a coward or fled from the strife?
No, by the blood of our Custer, no quailing!
   There in the midst of the Indians they close,
Hemmed in by thousands, but ever assailing,
   Fighting like tigers, all 'bayed amid foes!

Thicker and thicker the bullets came singing;
   Down go the horses and riders and all;
Swiftly the warriors round them were ringing,
   Circling like buzzards awaiting their fall.
See the wild steeds of the mountain and prairie,
   Savage eyes gleaming from forests of mane;
Quivering lances with pennons so airy,
   War-painted warriors charging amain.

Backward, again and again, they were driven,
  Shrinking to close with the lost little band;
Never a cap that had worn the bright Seven
  Bowed till its wearer was dead on the strand.
Closer and closer the death circle growing,
  Ever the leader's voice, clarion clear,
Rang out his words of encouragement glowing,
  "We can but die once, boys,—we'll sell our lives dear!"

Dearly they sold them like Berserkers raging,
  Facing the death that encircled them round;
Death's bitter pangs by their vengeance assuaging,
  Marking their tracks by their dead on the ground.
Comrades, our children shall yet tell their story,—
  Custer's last charge on the old Sitting Bull;
And ages shall swear that the cup of his glory
  Needed but that death to render it full.

                                    FREDERICK WHITTAKER

AN ODE IN TIME OF HESITATION

Written after seeing at Boston the statue of Robert
Gould Shaw killed while storming Fort Wagner,
July 18, 1863, at the head of the first enlisted Negro
Regiment, the Fifty-fourth Massachusetts.

I

BEFORE the living bronze Saint-Gaudens made
Most fit to thrill the passer's heart with awe,
And set here in the city's talk and trade
To the good memory of Robert Shaw,
This bright March morn I stand
And hear the distant spring come up the land;
Knowing that what I hear is not unheard

Of this boy soldier and his negro band,
For all their gaze is fixed so stern ahead,
For all the fatal rhythm of their tread.
The land they died to save from death and shame
Trembles and waits, hearing the spring's great name,
And by her pangs these resolute ghosts are stirred.

II

Through street and mall the tides of people go
Heedless; the trees upon the Common show
No hint of green; but to my listening heart
The still earth doth impart
Assurance of her jubilant emprise,
And it is clear to my long-searching eyes
That love at last has might upon the skies.
The ice is runnelled on the little pond;
A telltale patter drips from off the trees;
The air is touched with southland spiceries,
As if but yesterday it tossed the frond
Of pendent mosses where the live oaks grow
Beyond Virginia and the Carolines,
Or had its will among the fruits and vines
Or aromatic isles asleep beyond
Florida and the Gulf of Mexico.

III

Soon shall the Cape Ann children laugh in glee,
Spying the arbutus, spring's dear recluse;
Hill lads at dawn shall hearken the wild goose
Go honking northward over Tennessee;
West from Oswego to Sault Saint-Marie,
And on to where the Pictured Rocks are hung,
And yonder where, gigantic, wilful, young,
Chicago sitteth at the northwest gates,

With restless violent hands and casual tongue
Moulding her mighty fates,
The Lakes shall robe them in ethereal sheen;
And like a larger sea, the vital green
Of springing wheat shall vastly be outflung
Over Dakota and the prairie states.
By desert people immemorial
On Arizonan mesas shall be done
Dim rites unto the thunder and the sun;
Nor shall the primal gods lack sacrifice
More splendid, when the white Sierras call
Unto the Rockies straightway to arise
And dance before the unveiled ark of the year,
Clashing their windy cedars as for shawms,
Unrolling rivers clear
For flutter of broad phylacteries;
While Shasta signals to Alaskan seas
That watch old sluggish glaciers downward creep
To fling their icebergs thundering from the steep,
And Mariposa through the purple calms
Gazes at far Hawaii crowned with palms
Where East and West are met,—
A rich seal on the ocean's bosom set
To say that East and West are twain,
With different loss and gain:
The Lord hath sundered them; let them be sundered yet.

IV

Alas! what sounds are these that come
Sullenly over the Pacific seas,—
Sounds of ignoble battle, striking dumb
The season's half-awakened ecstasies?
Must I be humble, then,
Now when my heart hath need of pride?
Wild love falls on me from these sculptured men;

By loving much the land for which they died
I would be justified.
My spirit was away on pinions wide
To soothe in praise of her its passionate mood
And ease it of its ache of gratitude.
Too sorely heavy is the debt they lay
On me and the companions of my day.
I would remember now
My country's goodliness, make sweet her name.
Alas! what shade art thou
Of sorrow or of blame
Liftest the lyric leafage from her brow,
And pointest a slow finger at her shame?

v

Lies! lies! It cannot be! The wars we wage
Are noble, and our battles still are won
By justice for us, ere we lift the gage.
We have not sold our loftiest heritage.
The proud republic hath not stooped to cheat
And scramble in the market-place of war;
Her forehead weareth yet its solemn star.
Here is her witness: this, her perfect son,
This delicate and proud New England soul
Who leads despised men, with just-unshackled feet,
Up the large ways where death and glory meet,
To show all peoples that our shame is done,
That once more we are clean and spirit-whole.

VI

Crouched in the sea fog on the moaning sand
All night he lay, speaking some simple word
From hour to hour to the slow minds that heard,
Holding each poor life gently in his hand

And breathing on the base rejected clay
Till each dark face shone mystical and grand
Against the breaking day;
And lo, the shard the potter cast away
Was grown a fiery chalice, crystal-fine,
Fulfilled of the divine
Great wine of battle wrath by God's ring-finger stirred.
Then upward, where the shadowy bastion loomed
Huge on the mountain in the wet sea light,
Whence now, and now, infernal flowerage bloomed,
Bloomed, burst, and scattered down its deadly seed,
They swept, and died like freemen on the height,
Like freemen, and like men of noble breed;
And when the battle fell away at night
By hasty and contemptuous hands were thrust
Obscurely in a common grave with him
The fair-haired keeper of their love and trust.
Now limb doth mingle with dissolvèd limb
In nature's busy old democracy
To flush the mountain laurel when she blows
Sweet by the southern sea,
And heart with crumbled heart climbs in the rose:—
The untaught hearts with the high heart that knew
This mountain fortress for no earthly hold
Of temporal quarrel, but the bastion old
Of spiritual wrong,
Built by an unjust nation sheer and strong,
Expugnable but by a nation's rue
And bowing down before that equal shrine
By all men held divine,
Whereof his band and he were the most holy sign.

VII

O bitter, bitter shade!
Wilt thou not put the scorn

And instant tragic question from thine eyes?
Do thy dark brows yet crave
That swift and angry stave—
Unmeet for this desirous morn—
That I have striven, striven to evade?
Gazing on him, must I not deem they err
Whose careless lips in street and shop aver
As common tidings, deeds to make his cheek
Flush from the bronze, and his dead throat to speak?
Surely some elder singer would arise,
Whose harp hath leave to threaten and to mourn
Above this people when they go astray.
Is Whitman, the strong spirit, overworn?
Has Whittier put his yearning wrath away?
I will not and I dare not yet believe!
Though furtively the sunlight seems to grieve,
And the spring-laden breeze
Out of the gladdening west is sinister
With sounds of nameless battle overseas;
Though when we turn and question in suspense
If these things be indeed after these ways,
And what things are to follow after these,
Our fluent men of place and consequence
Fumble and fill their mouths with hollow phrase,
Or for the end-all of deep arguments
Intone their dull commercial liturgies—
I dare not yet believe! My ears are shut!
I will not hear the thin satiric praise
And muffled laughter of our enemies,
Bidding us never sheathe our valiant sword
Till we have changed our birthright for a gourd
Of wild pulse stolen from a barbarian's hut;
Showing how wise it is to cast away
The symbols of our spiritual sway,
That so our hands with better ease
May wield the driver's whip and grasp the jailer's keys.

VIII

Was it for this our fathers kept the law?
This crown shall crown their struggle and their ruth?
Are we the eagle nation Milton saw
Mewing its mighty youth,
Soon to possess the mountain winds of truth,
And we a swift familiar of the sun
Where aye before God's face His trumpets run?
Or have we but the talons and the maw,
And for the abject likeness of our heart
Shall some less lordly bird be set apart?—
Some gross-billed wader where the swamps are fat?
Some gorger in the sun? Some prowler with the bat?

IX

Ah no!
We have not fallen so.
We are our fathers' sons: let those who lead us know!
'T was only yesterday sick Cuba's cry
Came up the tropic wind, "Now help us, for we die!"
Then Alabama heard,
And rising, pale, to Maine and Idaho
Shouted a burning word;
Proud state with proud impassioned state conferred,
And at the lifting of a hand sprang forth,
East, west, and south, and north,
Beautiful armies. Oh, by the sweet blood and young
Shed on the awful hill slope at San Juan,
By the unforgotten names of eager boys
Who might have tasted girls' love and been stung
With the old mystic joys
And starry griefs, now the spring nights come on,
But that the heart of youth is generous,—
We charge you, ye who lead us,

Breathe on their chivalry no hint of stain!
Turn not their new-world victories to gain!
One least leaf plucked for chaffer from the bays
Of their dear praise,
One jot of their pure conquest put to hire,
The implacable republic will require;
With clamor, in the glare and gaze of noon,
Or subtly, coming as a thief at night,
But surely, very surely, slow or soon
That insult deep we deeply will require.
Tempt not our weakness, our cupidity!
For save we let the island men go free,
Those baffled and dislaurelled ghosts
Will curse us from the lamentable coasts
Where walk the frustrate dead.
The cup of trembling shall be drainèd quite,
Eaten the sour bread of astonishment,
With ashes of the hearth shall be made white
Our hair, and wailing shall be in the tent:
Then on your guiltier head
Shall our intolerable self-disdain
Wreak suddenly its anger and its pain;
For manifest in that disastrous light
We shall discern the right
And do it, tardily.—O ye who lead,
Take heed!
Blindness we may forgive, but baseness we will smite.
                          WILLIAM VAUGHN MOODY

THE FIGHTING RACE

"READ OUT the names!" and Burke sat back,
    And Kelly drooped his head,
While Shea—they called him Scholar Jack—
    Went down the list of the dead.

Officers, seamen, gunners, marines,
   The crews of the gig and yawl,
The bearded man and the lad in his teens,
   Carpenters, coal passers—all.
Then, knocking the ashes from out his pipe,
   Said Burke in an offhand way:
"We're all in that dead man's list, by cripe!
   Kelly and Burke and Shea."
"Well, here's to the Maine, and I'm sorry for Spain,"
   Said Kelly and Burke and Shea.

"Wherever there's Kellys there's trouble," said Burke.
   "Wherever fighting's the game,
Or a spice of danger in grown man's work,"
   Said Kelly, "you'll find my name."
"And do we fall short," said Burke, getting mad,
   "When it's touch and go for life?"
Said Shea, "It's thirty-odd years, bedad,
   Since I charged to drum and fife
Up Marye's Heights, and my old canteen
   Stopped a rebel ball on its way;
There were blossoms of blood on our sprigs of green—
   Kelly and Burke and Shea—
And the dead didn't brag." "Well, here's to the flag!"
   Said Kelly and Burke and Shea.

"I wish 'twas in Ireland, for there's the place,"
   Said Burke, "that we'd die by right,
In the cradle of our soldier race,
   After one good stand-up fight.
My grandfather fell on Vinegar Hill,
   And fighting was not his trade;
But his rusty pike's in the cabin still,
   With Hessian blood on the blade."
"Aye, aye," said Kelly, "the pikes were great
   When the word was 'clear the way!'

We were thick on the roll in ninety-eight—
   Kelly and Burke and Shea."
"Well, here's to the pike and the sword and the like!"
   Said Kelly and Burke and Shea.

And Shea, the scholar, with rising joy,
   Said, "We were at Ramillies;
We left our bones at Fontenoy
   And up in the Pyrenees;
Before Dunkirk, on Landen's plain,
   Cremona, Lille, and Ghent;
We're all over Austria, France and Spain,
   Wherever they pitched a tent.
We've died for England from Waterloo
   To Egypt and Dargai;
And still there's enough for a corps or crew,
   Kelly and Burke and Shea."
"Well, here's to good honest fighting blood!"
   Said Kelly and Burke and Shea.

"Oh, the fighting races don't die out,
   If they seldom die in bed,
For love is first in their hearts, no doubt,"
   Said Burke; then Kelly said:
"When Michael, the Irish Archangel, stands,
   The Angel with the sword,
And the battle dead from a hundred lands
   Are ranged in one big horde,
Our line, that for Gabriel's trumpet waits,
   Will stretch three deep that day,
From Jehoshaphat to the Golden Gates—
   Kelly and Burke and Shea."
"Well, here's thank God for the race and the sod!"
   Said Kelly and Burke and Shea.

JOSEPH I. C. CLARKE

ON A SOLDIER FALLEN IN THE PHILIPPINES

STREETS of the roaring town,
Hush for him, hush, be still!
He comes, who was stricken down
Doing the word of our will.
Hush! Let him have his state.
Give him his soldier's crown.
The grists of trade can wait
Their grinding at the mill,
But he cannot wait for his honor, now the trumpet has been blown.
Wreathe pride now for his granite brow, lay love on his breast of
stone.

Toll! Let the great bells toll
Till the clashing air is dim,
Did we wrong this parted soul?
We will make it up to him.
Toll! Let him never guess
What work we set him to.
Laurel, laurel, yes;
He did what we bade him do.
Praise, and never a whispered hint but the fight he fought was
good;
Never a word that the blood on his sword was his country's own
heart's blood.

A flag for the soldier's bier
Who dies that his land may live;
Oh, banners, banners here,
That he doubt not nor misgive!
That he heed not from the tomb
The evil days draw near

When the nation, robed in gloom,
With its faithless past shall strive.
Let him never dream that his bullet's scream went wide of its
island mark,
Home to the heart of his sinning land where she stumbled and
sinned in the dark.

WILLIAM VAUGHN MOODY

UNMANIFEST DESTINY

To WHAT new fates, my country, far
And unforseen of foe or friend,
Beneath what unexpected star
Compelled to what unchosen end,

Across the sea that knows no beach,
The Admiral of Nations guides
Thy blind obedient keels to reach
The harbor where thy future rides!

The guns that spoke at Lexington
Knew not that God was planning then
The trumpet word of Jefferson
To bugle forth the rights of men.

To them that wept and cursed Bull Run,
What was it but despair and shame?
Who saw behind the cloud the sun?
Who knew that God was in the flame?

Had not defeat upon defeat,
Disaster on disaster come,
The slave's emancipated feet
Had never marched behind the drum.

There is a Hand that bends our deeds
   To mightier issues than we planned:
Each son that triumphs, each that bleeds,
   My country, serves Its dark command.

I do not know beneath what sky
   Nor on what seas shall be thy fate:
I only know it shall be high,
   I only know it shall be great.

                              RICHARD HOVEY

GOD, GIVE US MEN!

GOD, GIVE US MEN! A time like this demands
Strong minds, great hearts, true faith and ready hands;
   Men whom the lust of office does not kill;
Men whom the spoils of office cannot buy;
   Men who possess opinions and a will;
Men who have honor; men who will not lie;
Men who can stand before a demagogue
   And damn his treacherous flatteries without winking!
Tall men, sun-crowned, who live above the fog
   In public duty and in private thinking;
For while the rabble, with their thumb-worn creeds,
Their large professions and their little deeds,
Mingle in selfish strife, lo! Freedom weeps,
Wrong rules the land and waiting Justice sleeps.

                         JOSIAH GILBERT HOLLAND

THE MEN BEHIND THE GUNS

A CHEER and salute for the Admiral, and here's to the Captain
   bold,
And never forget the Commodore's debt when the deeds of might
   are told!

They stand to the deck through the battle's wreck when the great
    shells roar and screech—
And never they fear when the foe is near to practise what they
    preach:
But off with your hat and three times three for Columbia's true-
    blue sons,
The men below who batter the foe—the men behind the guns!

Oh, light and merry of heart are they when they swing into port
    once more,
When, with more than enough of the "green-backed stuff," they
    start for their leave-o'-shore;
And you'd think, perhaps, that the blue-bloused chaps who loll
    along the street
Are a tender bit, with salt on it, for some fierce "mustache" to
    eat—
Some warrior bold, with straps of gold, who dazzles and fairly
    stuns
The modest worth of the sailor boys—the lads who serve the guns.

But say not a word till the shot is heard that tells the fight is on,
Till the long, deep roar grows more and more from the ships of
    "Yank" and "Don,"
Till over the deep the tempests sweep of fire and bursting shell,
And the very air is a mad Despair in the throes of a living hell;
Then down, deep down, in the mighty ship, unseen by the midday
    suns,
You'll find the chaps who are giving the raps—the men behind the
    guns!

Oh, well they know how the cyclones blow that they loose from
    their cloud of death,
And they know is heard the thunder-word their fierce ten-incher
    saith!
The steel decks rock with the lightning shock, and shake with
    the great recoil,

And the sea grows red with the blood of the dead and reaches for
    his spoil—
But not till the foe has gone below or turns his prow and runs,
Shall the voice of peace bring sweet release to the men behind the
    guns!

JOHN JEROME ROONEY

BATTLE-SONG OF THE OREGON

THE billowy headlands swiftly fly
   The crested path I keep,
My ribboned smoke stains many a sky,
   My embers dye the deep;
A continent has hardly space—
   Mid-ocean little more,
Wherein to trace my eager race
   While clang the alarums of war.

I come, the warship Oregon,
   My wake a whitening world,
My cannon shotted, thundering on
   With battle-flags unfurled.
My land knows no successful foe—
   Behold, to sink or save,
From stoker's flame to gunner's aim
   The race that rules the wave!

A nation's prayers my bulwark are
   Though ne'er so wild the sea;
Flow time or tide, come storm or star,
   Throbs my machinery.
Lands Spain has lost forever peer
   From every lengthening coast,
Till rings the cheer that proves me near
   The flag of Columbia's host.

Defiantly I have held my way
  From the vigorous shore where Drake
Dreamed a New Albion in the day
  He left New Spain a-quake;
His shining course retraced, I fight
  The self-same foe he fought,
All earth to light with signs of might
  Which God our Captain wrought.

Made mad, from Santiago's mouth
  Spain's ships-of-battle dart:
My bulk comes broadening from the south
  A hurricane at heart;
Its desperate armories blaze and boom,
  Its ardent engines beat;
And fiery doom finds root and bloom
  Aboard of the Spanish fleet. . . .

The hundredweight of the Golden Hind
  With me are ponderous tons,
The ordnance great her deck that lined
  Would feed my ravening guns,
Her spacious reach in months and years
  I've shrunk to nights and days;
Yet in my ears are ringing cheers
  Sir Frank himself would raise;

For conquereth not mine engines' breath
  Nor sides steel-clad and strong,
Nor bulk, nor rifles red with death:
  To Spain, too, these belong;
What made that old Armada break
  This newer victory won:
Jehovah spake by the Sons of Drake
  At each incessant gun.

I come, the warship Oregon,
　My wake a whitening world,
My cannon shotted, thundering on
　With battle-flags unfurled.
My land knows no successful foe—
　Behold, to sink or save,
From stoker's flame to gunner's aim
　The race that rules the wave!

WALLACE RICE

CENTENNIAL HYMN

I

OUR fathers' God! from out whose hand
The centuries fall like grains of sand,
We meet to-day, united, free,
And loyal to our land and Thee,
To thank Thee for the era done,
And trust Thee for the opening one.

II

Here, where of old, by Thy design,
The fathers spake that word of Thine
Whose echo is the glad refrain
Of rended bolt and falling chain,
To grace our festal time, from all
The zones of earth our guests we call.

III

Be with us while the New World greets
The Old World thronging all its streets,
Unveiling all the triumphs won

By art or toil beneath the sun;
And unto common good ordain
This rivalship of hand and brain.

IV

Thou, who hast here in concord furled
The war flags of a gathered world,
Beneath our Western skies fulfil
The Orient's mission of good-will,
And, freighted with love's Golden Fleece,
Send back its Argonauts of peace.

V

For art and labor met in truce,
For beauty made the bride of use,
We thank Thee; but, withal, we crave
The austere virtues strong to save,
The honor proof to place or gold,
The manhood never bought nor sold!

VI

Oh make Thou us, through centuries long,
In peace secure, in justice strong;
Around our gift of freedom draw
The safeguards of Thy righteous law:
And, cast in some diviner mould,
Let the new cycle shame the old!
                    JOHN GREENLEAF WHITTIER

THE LAST RESERVATION

SULLEN and dark, in the September day,
     On the bank of the river
They waited the boat that would bear them away
     From their poor homes forever.

For progress strides on, and the order had gone
     To these wards of the nation,
"Give us land and more room," was the cry, "and move on
     To the next reservation."

With her babe, she looked back at the home 'neath the trees
     From which they were driven,
Where the smoke of the last camp fire, borne on the breeze,
     Rose slowly toward heaven.

Behind her, fair fields, and the forest and glade,
     The home of her nation;
Around her, the gleam of the bayonet and blade
     Of civilization.

Clasping close to her bosom the small dusky form,
     With tender caressing,
She bent down, on the cheek of her babe soft and warm
     A mother's kiss pressing.

There's a splash in the river—the column moves on,
     Close-guarded and narrow,
With hardly more note of the two that are gone
     Than the fall of a sparrow.

Only an Indian! Wretched, obscure,
     To refinement a stranger,
And a babe, that was born, in a wigwam as poor
     And rude as a manger.

Moved on—to make room for the growth in the West
 Of a brave Christian nation,
Moved on—and, thank God, forever at rest
 In the last reservation.

WALTER LEARNED

THE KLONDIKE

NEVER mind the day we left, or the way the women clung to us;
All we need now is the last way they looked at us.
Never mind the twelve men there amid the cheering—
Twelve men or one man, 't will soon be all the same;
For this is what we know: we are five men together,
Five left o' twelve men to find the golden river.

Far we came to find it out, but the place was here for all of us;
Far, far we came, and here we have the last of us.
We that were the front men, we that would be early,
We that had the faith, and the triumph in our eyes:
We that had the wrong road, twelve men together,—
Singing when the devil sang to find the golden river.

Say the gleam was not for us, but never say we doubted it;
Say the wrong road was right before we followed it.
We that were the front men, fit for all forage,—
Say that while we dwindle we are front men still;
For this is what we know to-night: we're starving here together—
Starving on the wrong road to find the golden river.

Wrong, we say, but wait a little: hear him in the corner there;
He knows more than we, and he'll tell us if we listen there—
He that fought the snow-sleep less than all the others
Stays awhile yet, and he knows where he stays:
Foot and hand a frozen clout, brain a freezing feather,
Still he's here to talk with us and to the golden river.

"Flow," he says, "and flow along, but you cannot flow away from
    us;
All the world's ice will never keep you far from us;
Every man that heeds your call takes the way that leads him—
The one way that's his way, and lives his own life:
Starve or laugh, the game goes on, and on goes the river;
Gold or no, they go their way—twelve men together.

"Twelve," he says, "who sold their shame for a lure you call too
    fair for them—
You that laugh and flow to the same word that urges them:
Twelve who left the old town shining in the sunset,
Left the weary street and the small safe days:
Twelve who knew but one way out, wide the way or narrow:
Twelve who took the frozen chance and laid their lives on yellow.

"Flow by night and flow by day, nor ever once be seen by them;
Flow, freeze, and flow, till time shall hide the bones of them:
Laugh and wash their names away, leave them all forgotten,
Leave the old town to crumble where it sleeps;
Leave it there as they have left it, shining in the valley,—
Leave the town to crumble down and let the women marry.

"Twelve of us or five," he says, "we know the night is on us now:
Five while we last, and we may as well be thinking now:
Thinking each his own thought, knowing, when the light comes,
Five left or none left, the game will not be lost.
Crouch or sleep, we go the way, the last way together:
Five or none, the game goes on, and on goes the river.

"For after all that we have done and all that we have failed to do,
Life will be life and the world will have its work to do:
Every man who follows us will heed in his own fashion
The calling and the warning and the friends who do not know:
Each will hold an icy knife to punish his heart's lover,
And each will go the frozen way to find the golden river."

There you hear him, all he says, and the last we'll ever get from
    him.
Now he wants to sleep, and that will be the best for him.
Let him have his own way—no, you needn't shake him—
Your own turn will come, so let the man sleep.
For this is what we know: we are stalled here together—
Hands and feet and hearts of us, to find the golden river.

And there's a quicker way than sleep? . . . Never mind the looks
    of him:
All he needs now is a finger on the eyes of him.
You there on the left hand, reach a little over—
Shut the stars away, or he'll see them all night:
He'll see them all night and he'll see them all to-morrow,
Crawling down the frozen sky, cold and hard and yellow.

Won't you move an inch or two—to keep the stars away from him?
—No, he won't move, and there's no need of asking him.
Never mind the twelve men, never mind the women;
Three while we last, we'll let them all go;
And we'll hold our thoughts north while we starve here together,
Looking each his own way to find the golden river.

                       EDWIN ARLINGTON ROBINSON

COLUMBIA

By
BENJAMIN HARRISON

COLUMBIA should have been the name of the western hemisphere
—the republic half of the world—the hemisphere without a king
on the ground—the world where God sent the trodden spirits of
men to be revived; to find, where all things were primitive,—men's
primitive rights.

OUR COUNTRY

By
BENJAMIN HARRISON

HAVE you not learned that not stocks or bonds or stately houses, or products of mill or field are our country? It is a spiritual thought that is in our minds.

A MESSAGE TO GARCIA

By
ELBERT HUBBARD

IN ALL this Cuban business there is one man stands out on the horizon of my memory like Mars at perihelion. When war broke out between Spain and the United States it was very necessary to communicate quickly with the leader of the insurgents. Garcia was somewhere in the mountain fastnesses of Cuba—no one knew where. No mail or telegraph message could reach him. The President must secure his coöperation, and quickly.

What to do!

Some one said to the President, "There's a fellow by the name of Rowan will find Garcia for you, if anybody can."

Rowan was sent for and given a letter to be delivered to Garcia. How "the fellow by the name of Rowan" took the letter, sealed it up in an oilskin pouch, strapped it over his heart, in four days landed by night off the coast of Cuba from an open boat, disappeared into the jungle, and in three weeks came out on the other side of the island, having traversed a hostile country on foot, and delivered his letter to Garcia—are things I have no special desire to tell in detail now. The point I wish to make is this: McKinley gave Rowan a letter to be delivered to Garcia; Rowan took the letter and did not ask, "Where is he at?" By the Eternal! there is a man whose form should be cast in deathless bronze and the statue placed in every college in the land. It is not book-learning young men need, nor instruction about this or that, but a stiffening of the vertebræ that will cause them to be loyal to a trust, to act promptly, concentrate their energies: do the thing—"Carry a message to Garcia."

General Garcia is dead now, but there are other Garcias. No man who has endeavored to carry out an enterprise wherein many hands were needed, but has been well-nigh appalled at times by the imbecility of the average man—the inability or unwillingness to concentrate on a thing and do it.

Slipshod assistance, foolish inattention, dowdy indifference, and half-hearted work seem the rule; and no man succeeds unless, by hook or crook or threat, he forces or bribes other men to assist him; or mayhap, God in His goodness performs a miracle, and sends him an Angel of Light for an assistant.

ON A CERTAIN CONDESCENSION IN FOREIGNERS

By
James Russell Lowell

Till after our Civil War it never seemed to enter the head of any foreigner, especially of any Englishman, that an American had what could be called a country, except as a place to eat, sleep, and trade in. Then it seemed to strike them suddenly. "By Jove, you know, fellahs don't fight like that for a shop-till!" No, I rather think not. To Americans America is something more than a promise and an expectation. It has a past and traditions of its own. A descent from men who sacrificed everything and came hither, not to better their fortunes, but to plant their idea in virgin soil, should be a good pedigree. There was never colony save this that went forth, not to seek gold, but God. Is it not as well to have sprung from such as these as from some burly beggar who came over with Wilhelmus Conquestor, unless, indeed, a line grown better as it runs farther away from stalwart ancestors? And for our history, it is dry enough, no doubt, in the books, but, for all that, is of a kind that tells in the blood.

THE POLITICAL LIFE OF AMERICA

By
CARL SCHURZ

. . . EVERY glance into the political life of America strengthens my convictions that the aim of a revolution can be nothing else than to make room for the will of the people—in other words, to break every authority which has its organization in the life of the state, and, as far as is possible, to overturn the barriers to individual liberty. The will of the people will have its fling and indulge in all kinds of foolishness—but that is its way; if you want to show it the way and then give it liberty of action, it will, nevertheless, commit its own follies. Each one of these follies clears away something, while the wisest thing that is done for the people accomplishes nothing until the popular judgment has progressed far enough to be able to do it for itself. Until then, conditions must stand à force de l'autorité, or they will totter. But if they exist by the force of authority, then democracy is in a bad way. Here in America you can every day see how slightly a people needs to be governed. In fact, the thing that is not named in Europe without a shudder, anarchy, exists here in full bloom. Here are governments but no rulers—governors, but they are clerks. . . . It is only here that you realize how superfluous governments are in many affairs in which, in Europe, they are considered entirely indispensable, and how the possibility of doing something inspires a desire to do it.

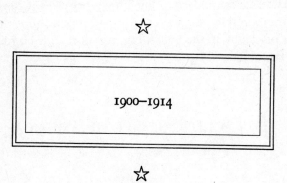

★

1900–1914

★

HYMN OF THE WEST

World's Fair, St. Louis, Mo., 1904

O THOU, whose glorious orbs on high
  Engird the earth with splendor round,
From out Thy secret place draw nigh
  The courts and temples of this ground;
    Eternal Light,
    Fill with Thy might
These domes that in Thy purpose grew,
And lift a nation's heart anew!

Illumine Thou each pathway here,
  To show the marvels God hath wrought!
Since first Thy people's chief and seer
  Looked up with that prophetic thought,
    Bade Time unroll
    The fateful scroll,
And empire unto Freedom gave
From cloudland height to tropic wave.

Poured through the gateways of the North
  Thy mighty rivers join their tide,
And, on the wings of morn sent forth,
  Their mists the far-off peaks divide.
    By Thee unsealed,
    The mountains yield
Ores that the wealth of Ophir shame,
And gems enwrought of seven-hued flame.

Lo, through what years the soil hath lain,
 At Thine own time to give increase—
The greater and the lesser grain,
 The ripening boll, the myriad fleece!
  Thy creatures graze
  Appointed ways;
League after league across the land
The ceaseless herds obey Thy hand.

Thou, whose high archways shine most clear
 Above the plenteous Western plain,
Thine ancient tribes from round the sphere
 To breathe its quickening air are fain:
  And smiles the sun
  To see made one
Their brood throughout Earth's greenest space,
Land of the new and lordlier race!
    EDMUND CLARENCE STEDMAN

BLOOD IS THICKER THAN WATER

EBBED and flowed the muddy Pei-Ho by the gulf of Pechili,
 Near its waters swung the yellow dragon-flag;
Past the batteries of China, looking westward we could see
 Lazy junks along the lazy river lag;
Villagers in near-by Ta-Kou toiled beneath their humble star,
 On the flats the ugly mud fort lay and dreamed;
While the Powhatan swung slowly at her station by the bar,
 While the Toey-Wan with Tattnall onward steamed.

Lazy East and lazy river, fort of mud in lazy June,
 English gunboats through the waters slowly fare,
With the dragon-flag scarce moving in the lazy afternoon
 O'er the mud-heap storing venom in the glare.

We were on our way to Peking, to the Son of Heaven's throne,
  White with peace was all our mission to his court,
Peaceful, too, the English vessels on the turbid stream bestrown
  Seeking passage up the Pei-Ho past the fort.

By the bar lay half the English, while the rest, with gallant Hope,
  Wrestled with the slipping ebb-tide up the stream;
They had cleared the Chinese irons, reached the double chain and
    rope,
  Where the ugly mud fort scowled upon their beam—
Boom! the heavens split asunder with the thunder of the fight
  As the hateful dragon made its faith a mock;
Every cannon spat its perfidy, each casemate blazed its spite,
  Crashing down upon the English, shock on shock.

In his courage Rason perished, brave McKenna fought and fell;
  Scores were dying as they'd lived, like valiant men;
And the meteor flag that upward prayed to Heaven from that hell,
  Wept below for those who ne'er should weep again.
Far away the English launches near the Powhatan swung slow,
  All despairing, useless, out of reach of war,
Knew their comrades in the battle, felt them reel beneath the blow,
  Lying helpless 'gainst the ebb-tide by the bar.

On the Toey-Wan stood Tattnall, Stephen Trenchard by his side—
  "Old Man" Tattnall, he who dared at Vera Cruz,—
Saw here, crippled by the cannon; saw there, throttled by the tide,
  Men of English blood and speech—could he refuse?
I'll be damned, says he to Trenchard, *if old Tattnall's standing by,*
  Seeing white men butchered here by such a foe.
Where's my barge? No side-arms, mind you! See those English
    fight and die—
  Blood is thicker, sir, than water. Let us go.

Quick we man the boat, and quicker plunge into that devil's brew—
  "An official call," and Tattnall went in state.

Trenchard's hurt, our flag in ribbons, and the rocking barge shot
    through,
  Hart, our coxswain, dies beneath the Chinese hate;
But the cheers those English give us as we gain their Admiral's
    ship
  Make the shattered boat and weary arms seem light—
Then the rare smile from "Old" Tattnall, and Hope's hearty word
    and grip,
  Lying wounded, bleeding, brave in hell's despite.

Tattnall nods, and we go forward, find a gun no longer fought—
  What is peace to us when all its crew lie dead?
One bright English lad brings powder and a wounded man the
    shot,
  And we scotch that Chinese dragon, tail and head.
Hands are shaken, faith is plighted, sounds our Captain's cheery
    call,
  In a British boat we speed us fast and far;
And the Toey-Wan and Tattnall down the ebb-tide slide and fall
  To the launches lying moaning by the bar.

Eager for an English vengeance, battle-light on every face,
  See the Clustered Stars lead on the Triple Cross!
Cheering, swinging into action, valiant Hope takes heart of grace
  From the cannon's cloudy roar, the lanyards' toss.
How they fought, those fighting English! How they cheered the
    Toey-Wan,
  Cheered our sailors, cheered "Old" Tattnall, grim and gray!
And their cheers ring down the ages as they rang beneath the sun
  O'er those bubbling, troubled waters far away.

Ebbs and flows the muddy Pei-Ho by the gulf of Pechili,
  Idly floats beside the stream the dragon-flag;
Past the batteries of China, looking westward still you see
  Lazy junks along the lazy river lag.

Let the long, long years drip slowly on that lost and ancient land,
  Ever dear one scene to hearts of gallant men;
There's a hand-clasp and a heart-throb, there's a word we under-
    stand:
  Blood is thicker, sir, than water, now as then.

WALLACE RICE

ON THE BUILDING OF SPRINGFIELD

LET not our town be large, remembering
That little Athens was the Muses' home,
That Oxford rules the heart of London still,
That Florence gave the Renaissance to Rome.

Record it for the grandson of your son—
A city is not builded in a day:
Our little town cannot complete her soul
Till countless generations pass away.

Now let each child be joined as to a church
To her perpetual hopes, each man ordained:
Let every street be made a reverent aisle
Where Music grows and Beauty is unchained.

Let Science and Machinery and Trade
Be slaves of her, and make her all in all,
Building against our blatant, restless time
An unseen, skilful, medieval wall.

Let every citizen be rich toward God,
Let Christ, the beggar, teach divinity.
Let no man rule who holds his money dear.
Let this, our city, be our luxury.

We should build parks that students from afar
Would choose to starve in, rather than go home,
Fair little squares, with Phidian ornament,
Food for the spirit, milk and honeycomb.

Songs shall be sung by us in that good day,
Songs we have written, blood within the rhyme,
Beating as when Old England still was glad,—
The purple, rich Elizabethan time.

. . . .

Say, is my prophecy too fair and far?
I only know, unless her faith be high,
The soul of this, our Nineveh, is doomed,
Our little Babylon will surely die.

Some city on the breast of Illinois
No wiser and no better at the start
By faith shall rise redeemed, by faith shall rise
Bearing the western glory in her heart.

The genius of the Maple, Elm and Oak,
The secret hidden in each grain of corn,
The glory that the prairie angels sing
At night when sons of Life and Love are born,

Born but to struggle, squalid and alone,
Broken and wandering in their early years.
When will they make our dusty streets their goal,
Within our attics hide their sacred tears?

When will they start our vulgar blood athrill
With living language, words that set us free?
When will they make a path of beauty clear
Between our riches and our liberty?

We must have many Lincoln-hearted men.
A city is not builded in a day.
And they must do their work, and come and go,
While countless generations pass away.

VACHEL LINDSAY

FIRST INAUGURAL ADDRESS

By
GROVER CLEVELAND

IN THE discharge of my official duty I shall endeavor to be guided by a just and proper construction of the Constitution, a careful observance of the distinction between the powers granted to the federal government and those reserved to the States or to the people, and by a cautious appreciation of those functions which by the Constitution and laws have been assigned to the executive branches of the government.

But the man who takes the oath today to preserve, protect and defend the Constitution of the United States only assumes the solemn obligation which every patriotic citizen—on the farm, in the workshop, in the busy marts of trade and everywhere—should share with him. The Constitution which prescribes his oath, my countrymen, is yours; the government you have chosen him to administer for a time is yours; the laws and the entire scheme of our civil rule, from the town meeting to the State capitals and the national capital, is yours. Every voter, as surely as your chief magistrate, under the same high sanction, though in a different sphere, exercises a public trust. Nor is this all. Every citizen owes to the country a vigilant watch and close scrutiny of its public servants and a fair and reasonable estimate of their fidelity and usefulness. Thus is the people's will impressed upon the whole framework of our civil polity—municipal, state and federal; and this is the price of our liberty and the inspiration of our faith in the republic.

GOOD CITIZENSHIP

From Patriotism and Holiday Observance, address
before the Union League Club, Chicago, February
22, 1907.

By

GROVER CLEVELAND

OUR country is infinitely more than a domain affording to those
who dwell upon it immense material advantages and opportunities. In such a country we live. But I love to think of a glorious
nation built upon the will of free men, set apart for the propaga-
tion and cultivation of humanity's best ideal of a free government,
and made ready for the growth and fruitage of the highest aspirations of patriotism. This is the country that lives in us. I indulge in
no mere figure of speech when I say that our nation, the immortal
spirit of our domain, lives in us—in our hearts and minds and con-
sciences. There it must find its nutriment or die. This thought
more than any other presents to our minds the impressiveness and
responsibility of American citizenship. The land we live in seems
to be strong and active. But how fares the land that lives in us?
Are we sure that we are doing all we ought to keep it in vigor and
health? Are we keeping its roots well surrounded by the fertile
soil of loving allegiance, and are we furnishing them the invigor-
ating moisture of unselfish fidelity? Are we as diligent as we ought
to be to protect this precious growth against the poison that must
arise from the decay of harmony and honesty and industry and
frugality; and are we sufficiently watchful against the deadly, bur-
rowing pests of consuming greed and cankerous cupidity? Our
answers to these questions make up the account of our steward-
ship as keepers of a sacred trust.

ON THE McKINLEY ASSASSINATION

By

SENATOR HOAR

Extract from an Address by United States Senator
Hoar at the Republican State Convention, Boston,
October 4, 1901.

WE CAN undoubtedly provide some additional legal safeguards
against the recurrence of this terrible crime. We can, I suppose,
make the preaching, counseling, or advising the killing of or doing
violence to our National officers, high or law, or those of foreign
countries, an offense against our National law, punishable with
severe penalties. We can, if we think fit, make the conspiring to
accomplish this punishable with death, or any overt act or attempt
to accomplish it punishable with death. We may, perhaps, devise
some additional security against the coming into our ports of
criminal persons known to entertain the purposes of carrying out
anarchists' sentiments by overt acts. I dare say that other protec-
tions may be devised.

But we cannot give up free speech or constitutional liberty because of the danger of a recurrence of such crimes. We cannot
abandon free speech or constitutional liberty for fear of Guiteau
or Czolgosz. We may as well desert our habitations in our beautiful fields or on the banks of our rivers and lakes, because science
has discovered that the mosquito carries on his sting a poison fatal
to human life. The restraining of free speech and of the free press,
disagreeable as are their excesses, must come in the main from the
individual's sense of duty, and not by law. There are already some
comforting signs of returning health in this matter. Yellow journal-
ism is already being rebuked by the yellowest of yellow journals.

Let it be understood, as a most important practical lesson for the
State, that while political sentiments and political measures are to

be denounced if they seem dangerous to the State, or contrary to righteousness or justice, or constitutional liberty, with the most unsparing fearlessness, yet the arrogant demand of any man to penetrate the individual soul of his neighbor, and to judge of his motives or personal worth by what seems to be the error of his political opinions, is that presumptuous and arrogant Pharisaism which excited to its sublimest wrath the gentle spirit of the Saviour of mankind. It was the publican and not the Pharisee who went back to his house justified rather than the other. "Judge not that ye be not judged" is the divine command. And the divine penalty is that "with what judgment ye judged ye shall be judged."

You and I are Republicans. You and I are men of the North. Most of us are Protestants in religion. We are men of native birth. Yet, if every Republican were to-day to fall in his place, as William McKinley has fallen, I believe our countrymen of the other party, in spite of what we deem their errors, would take the Republic and bear on the flag to liberty and glory. I believe if every Protestant were to be stricken down by a lightning stroke that our brethren of the Catholic faith would still carry on the Republic in the spirit of a true and liberal freedom. I believe if every man of native birth within our borders were to die this day, the men of foreign birth, who have come here to seek homes and liberty under the shadow of the Republic, would carry on the Republic in God's appointed way. I believe if every man of the North were to die, the new and chastened South, with the virtues it has cherished from the beginning, of love of home and love of State and love of freedom, with its courage and its constancy, would take the country and bear it on to the achievement of its lofty destiny. The anarchist must slay seventy-five million Americans before he can slay the Republic.

Of course, there would be mistakes. Of course, there would be disappointments and grievous errors. Of course, there would be many things for which the lovers of liberty would mourn. But America would survive them all, and the Nation our fathers planted would abide in perennial life.

HIGH OF HEART

By
THEODORE ROOSEVELT

THIS is a new nation, based on a mighty continent, of boundless possibilities. No other nation in the world has such resources. No other nation has ever been so favored. If we dare to rise level to the opportunities offered us, our destiny will be vast beyond the power of imagination. We must master this destiny, and make it our own; and we can thus make it our own only if we, as a vigorous and separate nation, develop a great and wonderful nationality, distinctively different from any other nationality, of either the present or the past. For such a nation all of us can well afford to give up all other allegiances, and high of heart to stand, a mighty and united people, facing a future of glorious promise.

UNITED STATES COLONIAL POLICY

By
ELIHU ROOT

"IN ALL the forms of government and administrative provisions which they are authorized to prescribe, the commission should bear in mind that the government they are establishing is designed not for our satisfaction or for the expression of our political views, but for the happiness, peace and prosperity of the people of the Philippine Islands, and the measures adopted should be made to conform to their customs, their habits and even their prejudices to the fullest extent consistent with the accomplishment of the indispensable requisites of just and effective government."

AMERICAN TRADITION

By
WILLIAM G. SUMNER

THE United States, starting on a new continent, with full chance to select the old-world traditions which they would adopt, have become the representatives and champions in modern times of all the principles of individualism and personal liberty. We have had no neighbors to fear. We have had no necessity for stringent State discipline. Each one of us has been able to pursue happiness in his own way, unhindered by the demands of a State which would have worn out our energies by expenditure simply in order to maintain the State. The State has existed of itself. The one great exception, the Civil War, only illustrates the point more completely per contra. The old Jeffersonian party rose to power and held it, because it conformed to the genius of the country and bore along the true destinies of a nation situated as this one was. It is the glory of the United States, and its calling in history, that it shows what the power of personal liberty is—what self-reliance, energy, enterprise, hard sense men can develop when they have room and liberty and when they are emancipated from the burden of traditions and faiths which are nothing but the accumulated follies and blunders of a hundred generations of "statesmen."

WORLD WAR

ABRAHAM LINCOLN WALKS AT MIDNIGHT

It is portentous, and a thing of state
 That here at midnight, in our little town
A mourning figure walks, and will not rest
 Near the old court-house pacing up and down.

Or by his homestead, or the shadowed yards
 He lingers where his children used to play,
Or through the market, on the well-worn stones
 He stalks until the dawn-stars burn away.

A bronzed, lank man! His suit of ancient black,
 A famous high top-hat and plain worn shawl
Make him the quaint great figure that men love,
 The prairie-lawyer, master of us all.

He cannot sleep upon his hillside now.
 He is among us, as in times before!
And we who toss and lie awake for long
 Breathe deep, and start, to see him pass the door.

His head is bowed. He thinks on men and kings.
 Yea, when the sick world cries, how can he sleep?
Too many peasants fight, they know not why,
 Too many homesteads in black terror weep.

The sins of all the war-lords burn his heart.
 He sees the dreadnaughts scouring every main.
He carries on his shawl-wrapt shoulders now
 The bitterness, the folly and the pain.

He cannot rest until a spirit-dawn
  Shall come;—the shining hope of Europe free;
The league of sober folk, the Workers' Earth
  Bringing long peace to Cornland, Alp and Sea.

It breaks his heart that kings must murder still,
  That all his hours of travail here for men
Seem yet in vain. And who will bring white peace
  That he may sleep upon his hill again?

VACHEL LINDSAY

TO THE UNITED STATES OF AMERICA

BROTHERS in blood! They who this wrong began
To wreck our commonwealth, will rue the day
When first they challenged freemen to the fray,
And with the Briton dared the American.
Now are we pledged to win the Rights of man;
Labor and Justice now shall have their way,
And in a League of Peace—God grant we may—
Transform the earth, not patch up the old plan.

Sure is our hope since he who led your nation
Spake for mankind, and ye arose in awe
Of that high call to work the world's salvation;
Clearing your minds of all estranging blindness
In the vision of Beauty and the Spirit's law,
Freedom and Honor and sweet Loving-kindness.

ROBERT BRIDGES

A BATTLE-PLANE IN FRANCE

MY DRIVER came this morning on the run.
High above his head he waved a paint brush,
And in his other hand were some small cans.

He wore a new coat, a spickity-span coat,
A coat of brownish yellow. It was khaki!
Bronze buttons it had, with an eagle on each—
A fierce beaked eagle!
Very carefully he laid the coat down,
Tenderly, like something precious,
Then he opened the cans, and, as he worked,
He whistled "Yankee Doodle" and "Dixie."
His eyes were all alight with something splendid,
Like the eyes of one who loves greatly.
He sighed just a little as he painted
The insignia of France from my wings.
He has flown far, and high, and well, for France!
Then, smiling, he dashed blood-red stripes on my wings,
Until there were seven,
And white stripes he painted,
And a field of clear dark blue, and many small stars.
Standing erect, he gazed at it awhile, and said:
"Dear God! It's wonderful—that flag!"

O. C. A. CHILD

THERE'S ABOUT TWO MILLION FELLOWS—

THERE's about two million fellows from the North, South, East,
and West
Who scurried up the gangplank of a ship;
They have felt the guy ropes paying and the troopship gently
swaying
As it started on its journey from the country of the blest.
They have washed in hard salt water, bucked the Army transport
grub,
Had a hitch of crow's-nest duty on the way;
Strained their eyes, mistaking whitecaps for a humpback Prussian
sub
Just at twilight when "the danger's great, they say."
When their ship had lost the convoy they were worried just a bit,

And kinda thought the skipper should be canned;
And the sigh of heartfelt feeling almost set the boat to reeling
When each of those two million sighted land.

There's about two million fellows that have landed here in
 France—
They're scattered God and G. H. Q. knows where;
By the cranes where steamers anchor, schooner, tramp, or greasy
 tanker,
There's an O. D. outfit waiting just to make the cargo dance.
They are chopping in the forest, double-timing on the roads,
Putting two ways where a single went before;
In the cabs of sweating engines, pushing, pulling double loads
When the R. T. O.'s in frenzied tones implore.
For it's duty, solid duty with the hustling men behind
From the P. of E.'s on up to No Man's Land;
And there's never chance of shirking when the boys up front are
 working—
Night and day must go the answer to the front line's stern demand.

There's about two million fellows and there's some of them who lie
Where eighty-eights and G. I.'s gently drop;
Where the trucks and trains are jamming and the colonel he is
 damning
Half the earth and in particular the Service of Supply.
They have had a stretch of trenches, beat the Prussian at his best,
Seen their buddies fall like heroes right beside;
But—there's nigh two million fellows from the country of the blest
Who know the cause for which their comrades died,
Who have crossed the sluggish shallows where their little life-
 streams ran
And broadened just a trifle, you will find;
And their vision's cleaner, clearer and they hold just that much
 dearer
The great and glorious land they left behind!

ALBERT JAY COOK

THE LITTLE FLAG ON OUR HOUSE

To G. C. D.

THE little flag on our house
Is floating all the day
Beside the great big Stars and Stripes;
You can almost hear it say
To all the folks in our street,
As the breezes make it dance:
"Look up and see my one blue star—
We've got a boy in France!"

The little flag on our house,
It floats sometimes at night,
And you can see it 'way up there
When the street lamp shines just right.
And sometimes, 'long towards morning,
When the cop comes by, perchance
It signals with its one blue star:
"We've got a boy in France!"

The little flag on our house
Will wave, and wave, and wave
Until our boy comes home again,
Or finds in France his grave.
Nay—tho' its blue star turn to gold,
Because of War's grim chance,
It still shall wave to say: "Thank God!
We've got a boy in France!"

"WILL SEEDY"
(*Wm. Curtis Demorest*)

YANKS

O'LEARY, from Chicago, and a first-class fightin' man,
Born in County Clare or Kerry, where the gentle art began;
Sergeant Dennis P. O'Leary, from somewhere on Archie Road,
Dodgin' shells and smellin' powder while the battle ebbed and
   flowed.

And the captain says: "O'Leary, from your fightin' company
Pick a dozen fightin' Yankees and come skirmishin' with me;
Pick a dozen fightin' devils, and I know it's you who can,"
And O'Leary, he saluted like a first-class fightin' man.

O'Leary's eye was piercin' and O'Leary's voice was clear:
"Dimitri Georgoupoulos!" and Dimitri answered, "Here!"
Then, "Vladimir Slaminsky! Step three paces to the front,
For we're wantin' you to join us in a little Heinie hunt!"

"Garibaldi Ravioli!" Garibaldi was to share;
And, "Ole Axel Kettelson!" and, "Thomas Scalp-the-Bear!"
Who was Choctaw by inheritance, bred in the blood and bones,
But set down in army records by the name of Thomas Jones.

"Van Winkle Schuyler Stuyvesant!" Van Winkle was a bud
From the ancient tree of Stuyvesant and had it in his blood;
"Don Miguel de Colombo!" Don Miguel's next of kin
Were across the Rio Grande when Don Miguel went in.

"Ulysses Grant O'Sheridan!" Ulysses' sire, you see,
Had been at Appomattox near the famous apple tree;
And, "Patrick Michael Casey!" Patrick Michael, you can tell,
Was a fightin' man by nature with three fightin' names as well.

"Joe Wheeler Lee!" And Joseph had a pair of fightin' eyes;
And his grandad was a Johnny, as perhaps you might surmise;
Then, "Robert Bruce MacPherson!" And the Yankee squad was
   done
With, "Isaac Abie Cohen!" once a lightweight champion.

Then O'Leary paced 'em forward and, says he: "You Yanks,
   fall in!"
And he marched 'em to the captain. "Let the skirmishin' begin,"
Says he, "The Yanks are comin', and you beat 'em if you can!"
And saluted like a soldier and a first-class fightin' man!

JAMES W. FOLEY

WHEN JOHNNY COMES MARCHING HOME

When Johnny comes marching home again,
   Hurrah! hurrah!
We'll give him a hearty welcome then,
   Hurrah! hurrah!
The men will cheer, the boys will shout,
The ladies, they will all turn out,
   And we'll all feel gay,
When Johnny comes marching home.

The old church-bell will peal with joy,
   Hurrah! hurrah!
To welcome home our darling boy,
   Hurrah! hurrah!
The village lads and lasses say,
With roses they will strew the way;
   And we'll all feel gay,
When Johnny comes marching home.

Get ready for the jubilee,
   Hurrah! hurrah!
We'll give the hero three times three,
   Hurrah! hurrah!
The laurel-wreath is ready now
To place upon his loyal brow,
   And we'll all feel gay,
When Johnny comes marching home.

Let love and friendship on that day,
   Hurrah! hurrah!
Their choicest treasures then display,
   Hurrah! hurrah!
And let each one perform some part,
To fill with joy the warrior's heart;
   And we'll all feel gay,
When Johnny comes marching home.

PATRICK SARSFIELD GILMORE

THE ROAD TO FRANCE

THANK God our liberating lance
Goes flaming on the way to France!
To France—the trail the Gurkhas found!
To France—old England's rallying ground!
To France—the path the Russians strode!
To France—the Anzac's glory road!
To France—where our Lost Legion ran
To fight and die for God and man!
To France—with every race and breed
That hates Oppression's brutal creed!

   Ah France—how could our hearts forget
   The path by which came Lafayette?
   How could the haze of doubt hang low

Upon the road of Rochambeau?
At last, thank God! At last we see
There is no tribal Liberty!
No beacon lighting just our shores!
No Freedom guarding but our doors!
The flame she kindled for our sires
Burns now in Europe's battle fires!
The soul that led our fathers west
Turns back to free the world's oppressed!

Allies, you have not called in vain;
We share your conflict and your pain.
"Old Glory," through new stains and rents,
Partakes of Freedom's sacraments.
Into that hell his will creates
We drive the foe—his lusts, his hates.
Last come, we will be last to stay,
Till Right has had her crowning day.
Replenish, comrades, from our veins,
The blood the sword of despot drains,
And make our eager sacrifice
Part of the freely-rendered price
You pay to lift humanity—
You pay to make our brothers free!
See, with what proud hearts we advance
        To France!
                    DANIEL HENDERSON

ODE TO A SIDE CAR

OH, IT's hell to sit in a side car when the trucks are crashing by,
With never a spark in the darkness to cheer one's straining eye
Save the flash of a shell when it scatters the mud on the passers-by!
When the road is packed with silent troops, it's a hell of a place
    to die!

The shells are not so bad—they hit you if Fate decrees—
But it's awful to dash along in the dark and feel that you're on the
  "skees"
With a big wet ditch beside you, and the orders they need in your
  hand,
And thousands of tons of whizzing stuff that any moment may
  land
Wrong side up on your stomach while you are finally "canned";
When you know that the P. C. before you is wondering why you
  delay
With the dope from the general commanding for the work of the
  coming day.

Yes, it's hell to ride in a side car in the dark of a drenching rain,
And the only reason I mention it is that again and again and again
One hears that the life of the "gilded staff" is free from care and
  pain!
A good, clean shot in the gizzard or a gob of gas in the chest
May give you a chance for a gilded V and those soft, white hands
  that caress.
But the grinding wheels of a two-ton truck can make you a horrible
  mess!
So when you scoff at the "gilded staff" with its breeches neatly
  pressed,
Remember their nights in the side car! They take their chance with
  the rest.

J. P. H.

ROUGE BOUQUET

IN A WOOD they call the Rouge Bouquet
  There is a new-made grave today,
  Built by never a spade nor pick
  Yet covered with earth ten metres thick.

There lie many fighting men,
    Dead in their youthful prime,
Never to laugh nor love again
    Nor taste the Summertime.
For Death came flying through the air
And stopped his flight at the dugout stair,
Touched his prey and left them there,
    Clay to clay.
He hid their bodies stealthily
In the soil of the land they fought to free
    And fled away.
Now over the grave abrupt and clear
    Three volleys ring;
And perhaps their brave young spirits hear
    The bugle sing:
"Go to sleep!
Go to sleep!
Slumber well where the shell screamed and fell.
Let your rifles rest on the muddy floor,
You will not need them any more.
Danger's past;
Now at last,
Go to sleep!"

There is on earth no worthier grave
To hold the bodies of the brave
Than this place of pain and pride
Where they nobly fought and nobly died.
Never fear but in the skies
Saints and angels stand
Smiling with their holy eyes
    On this new-come band.
St. Michael's sword darts through the air
And touches the aureole on his hair
And he sees them stand saluting there,
    His stalwart sons:

And Patrick, Brigid, Columkill
Rejoice that in the veins of warriors still
  The Gael's blood runs.
And up to Heaven's doorway floats,
  From the wood called Rouge Bouquet,
A delicate cloud of bugle notes
  That softly say:
"Farewell!
Farewell!
Comrades true, born anew, peace to you!
Your souls shall be where the heroes are
And your memory shine like the morning-star.
Brave and dear,
Shield us here.
Farewell!"

                              JOYCE KILMER

THE 1ST DIVISION MARCHES

September 1919

THE last to leave—the first to go—
  So is their laurel wrought;
And now they march back home below
  The skies for which they fought;
The skies of home which shed their blue
  Upon the steel-shod clan,
The same blue steel that swept them through
  Cantigny to Sedan.

Not all of them. Somewhere in France,
  Beyond the mist-hung shore,
Stained crosses mark the last advance
  Of those who come no more;

In Soissons drifts, by Argonne streams,
  Or Cheppy's wooded glen,
Beneath his helmet each one dreams
  That he is home again.

The gaps are filled—each in his place
  Will hear the wild acclaim;
With all the valor of their race,
  They played the crimson game;
But when the first gray shadows creep,
  Send one prayer on before,
Where rust-red rifles guard the sleep
  Of those who come no more.

For those who march will turn to find
  Some ghostly mate in vain;
Some buddy who was left behind
  To face the winter rain;
And spring shall bring "blue days and fair"
  Where star-dust crowns their night;
But they shall neither know nor care
  Who hold Valhalla's height.

GRANTLAND RICE

SONGS ABOVE THE DUST

WHERE rain-wet crosses know the dawn that gleams,
Safe from the crashing shell, the raw steel's thrust,
They face the resurrection of their dreams
Where only songs now live above their dust.

Songs of forgotten valor, where the storm
Of unleashed lightning hurled its dread barrage;
Songs of old shadows that again take form
In grim and silent waiting for the charge.

This is their recompense—the gray wind brings
Lost threnodies still vibrant with their fame,
And from the snow-clad uplands winter sings
Old songs they helped to write in blood and flame.

What mound of earth can keep their voices still?
What pressing coverlet of clay or clod
Can dim the deathless strains by plain or hill
Where Seeger sleeps and Brooke smiles up to God?

Their ghostly music lingers like the breath
Of summer when the harvest has its yield,
Before each knew his "rendezvous with Death,"
In "some far corner of a foreign field."

What hate or greed or cowardice can bar
The eerie, golden echoes that still creep
Where Kilmer waits beyond some flaming star
That lights the holy darkness of his sleep?

They sang their songs heroic with the fire
Of unstained courage through the shell-swept mud,
Up to the barricade of trench and wire
That knew the shining glory of their blood.

Let beauty light the world and hold its sway,
Let life and love drift by, twin souls of time,
Soft arms, and lips of roses, and the play
Of starlight eyes that give the world its rhyme.

Yet there is still a deeper glow that shines,
A deeper thrill that comes with bated breath,
As the faint dawn breaks through on waiting lines
And the blue steel means victory or death.

Shall their songs be forgotten with their dust?
Songs which their valor wrote by hill and glen?
Sing, winds, above their rifles, red with rust!
Blow, bugles, soft and low, blow Taps again!

GRANTLAND RICE

REVEILLÉ

April 6, 1917

WHAT sudden bugle calls us in the night
   And wakes us from a dream that we had shaped;
Flinging us sharply up against a fight
   We thought we had escaped?

It is no easy waking, and we win
   No final peace; our victories are few.
But still imperative forces pull us in
   And sweep us somehow through.

Summoned by a supreme and confident power
   That wakes our sleeping courage like a blow,
We rise, half-shaken, to the challenging hour,
   And answer it—and go. . . .

LOUIS UNTERMEYER

THE NEED OF THE HOUR

FLING forth the triple-colored flag to dare
The bright, untraveled highways of the air.
Blow the undaunted bugles, blow, and yet
Let not the boast betray us to forget.

Lo, there are high adventures for this hour—
Tourneys to test the sinews of our power.
For we must parry—as the years increase—
The hazards of success, the risks of peace!

What do we need to keep the nation whole,
  To guard the pillars of the State? We need
  The fine audacities of honest deed;
The homely old integrities of soul;
The swift temerities that take the part
Of outcast right—the wisdom of the heart;
Brave hopes that Mammon never can detain,
Nor sully with his gainless clutch for gain.

We need the Cromwell fire to make us feel
  The common burden and the public trust
  To be a thing as sacred and august
As the white vigil where the angels kneel.
We need the faith to go a path untrod,
The power to be alone and vote with God.

                                    EDWIN MARKHAM

I HAVE A RENDEZVOUS WITH DEATH

I HAVE A RENDEZVOUS with Death
At some disputed barricade,
When Spring comes back with rustling shade
And apple blossoms fill the air—
I have a rendezvous with Death
When Spring brings back blue days and fair.

It may be he shall take my hand,
And lead me into his dark land,

And close my eyes and quench my breath—
It may be I shall pass him still.
I have a rendezvous with Death
On some scarred slope of battered hill,
When Spring comes round again this year
And the first meadow flowers appear.

God knows 'twere better to be deep
Pillowed in silk and scented down,
Where Love throbs out in blissful sleep,
Pulse nigh to pulse, and breath to breath,
Where hushed awakenings are dear . . .
But I've a rendezvous with Death
At midnight in some flaming town,
When Spring trips north again this year;
And I to my pledged word am true,
I shall not fail that rendezvous.

ALAN SEEGER

IN FLANDERS FIELDS

IN FLANDERS FIELDS the poppies blow
Between the crosses, row on row,
   That mark our place; and in the sky
   The larks, still bravely singing, fly
Scarce heard amid the guns below.

We are the Dead. Short days ago
We lived, felt dawn, saw sunset glow,
   Loved and were loved, and now we lie
   In Flanders fields.

Take up our quarrel with the foe:
To you from failing hands we throw
   The torch; be yours to hold it high.
   If ye break faith with us who die
We shall not sleep, though poppies grow
   In Flanders fields.

JOHN McCRAE

VICTORY BELLS

I HEARD the bells across the trees,
I heard them ride the plunging breeze
Above the roofs from tower and spire,
And they were leaping like a fire,
And they were shining like a stream
With sun to make its music gleam.
Deep tones as though the thunder tolled,
Cool voices thin as tinkling gold,
They shook the spangled autumn down
From out the tree-tops of the town;
They left great furrows in the air
And made a clangor everywhere
As of metallic wings. They flew
Aloft in spirals to the blue
Tall tent of heaven and disappeared.
And others, swift as though they feared
The people might not heed their cry
Went shouting Victory up the sky.
They did not say that war is done,
Only that glory has begun
Like sunrise, and the coming day
Will burn the clouds of war away.
There will be time for dreams again,
And home-coming for weary men.

GRACE HAZARD CONKLING

WAR AGAINST GERMANY

By
WOODROW WILSON

IT IS a war against all nations. American ships have been sunk, American lives taken, in ways which it has stirred us very deeply to learn of, but the ships and people of other neutral and friendly nations have been sunk and overwhelmed in the waters in the same way. There has been no discrimination. The challenge is to all mankind. Each nation must decide for itself how it will meet it. The choice we make for ourselves must be made with a moderation of counsel and a temperateness of judgment befitting our character and our motives as a nation. We must put excited feeling away. Our motive will not be revenged or the victorious assertion of the physical might of the nation, but only the vindication of right, of human right, of which we are only a single champion.

When I addressed the Congress on the twenty-sixth of February last I thought that it would suffice to assert our neutral rights with arms, our right to use the seas against unlawful interference, our right to keep our people safe against unlawful violence. But armed neutrality, it now appears, is impracticable. Because submarines are in effect outlaws when used as the German submarines have been used against merchant shipping, it is impossible to defend ships against their attacks as the law of nations has assumed that merchantmen would defend themselves against privateers or cruisers, visible craft giving chase upon the open sea. It is common prudence in such circumstances, grim necessity indeed, to endeavour to destroy them before they have shown their own intention. They must be dealt with upon sight, if dealt with at all. The German Government denies the right of neutrals to use arms at all within the areas of the sea which it has proscribed, even in the defense of rights which no modern pub-

licist has ever before questioned their right to defend. The intima-
tion is conveyed that the armed guards which we have placed on
our merchant ships will be treated as beyond the pale of law and
subject to be dealt with as pirates would be. Armed neutrality
is ineffectual enough at best; in such circumstances and in the
face of such pretensions it is worse than ineffectual; it is likely only
to produce what it was meant to prevent; it is practically certain
to draw us into the war without either the rights or the effectiveness
of belligerents. There is one choice we cannot make, we are incapable of making: we will not choose the path of submission and
suffer the most sacred rights of our nation and our people to be
ignored or violated. The wrongs against which we now array ourselves are no common wrongs: they cut to the very roots of human
life.

With a profound sense of the solemn and even tragical character
of the step I am taking and of the grave responsibilities which it
involves, but in unhesitating obedience to what I deem my constitutional duty, I advise that the Congress declare the recent
course of the Imperial German Government to be in fact nothing
less than war against the government and people of the United
States; that it formally accept the status of belligerent which has
thus been thrust upon it; and that it take immediate steps not
only to put the country in a more thorough state of defense but
also to exert all its power and employ all its resources to bring
the Government of the German Empire to terms and end the war.

.   .   .   .

We have no quarrel with the German people. We have no feeling towards them but one of sympathy and friendship. It was not
upon their impulse that their government acted in entering this
war. It was not with their previous knowledge or approval. It was
a war determined upon as wars used to be determined upon in the
old, unhappy days when peoples were nowhere consulted by their
rulers and wars were provoked and waged in the interest of
dynasties or of little groups of ambitious men who were accustomed to use their fellow men as pawns and tools. Self-governed

nations do not fill their neighbour states with spies or set the course of intrigue to bring about some critical posture of affairs which will give them an opportunity to strike and make conquest. Such designs can be successfully worked out only under cover and where no one has the right to ask questions. Cunningly contrived plans of deception or aggression, carried, it may be, from generation to generation, can be worked out and kept from the light only within the privacy of courts or behind the carefully guarded confidences of a narrow and privileged class. They are happily impossible where public opinion commands and insists upon full information concerning all the nation's affairs.

"I AM AN AMERICAN"

By
ELIAS LIEBERMAN

THE Great War in Europe made a strong call for the exercise of American patriotism. And why should not Americans be patriotic? If the German believes that his Fatherland is of more value than life itself; if the Englishman thrills at the thought of the British Empire; if the Irishman knows no country as dear as the Emerald Isle; if the Frenchman's living and dying prayer is, *"Vive la France";* if the Chinaman pities everybody born outside the Flowery Kingdom, and the Japanese give their sole devotion to the Land of the Rising Sun—shall not we, in this land of glorious liberty, have some thought and love of country?

At a meeting of school children in Madison Square Garden, New York City, to celebrate the Fourth of July, one boy, a descendant of native Americans, spoke as follows:

"I am an American. My father belongs to the Sons of the Revolution; my mother, to the Colonial Dames. One of my ancestors pitched tea overboard in Boston Harbor; another stood his ground with Warren; another hungered with Washington at Valley Forge.

My forefathers were American in the making: they spoke in her council halls; they died on her battlefields; they commanded her ships; they cleared her forests. Dawns reddened and paled. Stanch hearts of mine beat fast at each new star in the nation's flag. Keen eyes of mine foresaw her greater glory; the sweep of her seas, the plenty of her plains, the man-hives in her billion-wired cities. Every drop of blood in me holds a heritage of patriotism. I am proud of my past. I am an American."

Then a foreign-born boy arose and said:

"I am an American. My father was an atom of dust, my mother was a straw in the wind, to His Serene Majesty. One of my ancestors died in the mines of Siberia; another was crippled for life by twenty blows of the *knout;* another was killed defending his home during the massacres. The history of my ancestors is a trail of blood to the palace-gate of the Great White Czar. But then the dream came—the dream of America. In the light of the Liberty torch the atom of dust became a man and the straw in the wind became a woman for the first time. 'See,' said my father, pointing to the flag that fluttered near, 'that flag of stars and stripes is yours; it is the emblem of the promised land. It means, my son, the hope of humanity. Live for it . . . die for it!' Under the open sky of my new country I swore to do so; and every drop of blood in me will keep that vow. I am proud of my future. I am an American."

CONTEMPORARY AMERICA

AMERICA FOR ME

'TIS FINE to see the Old World, and travel up and down
Among the famous palaces and cities of renown,
To admire the crumbly castles and the statues of the kings,—
But now I think I've had enough of antiquated things.

So it's home again, and home again, America for me!
My heart is turning home again, and there I long to be
In the land of youth and freedom beyond the ocean bars,
Where the air is full of sunlight and the flag is full of stars.

Oh, London is a man's town, there's power in the air;
And Paris is a woman's town, with flowers in her hair;
And it's sweet to dream in Venice, and it's great to study Rome,
But when it comes to living, there is no place like home.

I like the German fir-woods, in green battalions drilled;
I like the gardens of Versailles with flashing fountains filled;
But, oh, to take your hand, my dear, and ramble for a day
In the friendly western woodland where Nature has her way!

I know that Europe's wonderful, yet something seems to lack!
The Past is too much with her, and the people looking back.
But the glory of the Present is to make the Future free,—
We love our land for what she is and what she is to be.

Oh, it's home again, and home again, America for me!
I want a ship that's westward bound to plough the rolling sea,
To the blessed Land of Room Enough beyond the ocean bars,
Where the air is full of sunlight and the flag is full of stars.

HENRY VAN DYKE

THE COMING AMERICAN

BRING ME MEN to match my mountains,
Bring me men to match my plains,
And new eras in their brains.
Bring me men to match my prairies,
Men to match my inland seas,
Men whose thoughts shall pave a highway
Up to ampler destinies,
Pioneers to cleanse thought's marshlands,
   And to cleanse old error's fen;
Bring me men to match my mountains—
   Bring me men!

Bring me men to match my forests,
Strong to fight the storm and beast,
Branching toward the skyey future,
Rooted on the futile past.
Bring me men to match my valleys,
   Tolerant of rain and snow,
Men within whose fruitful purpose
   Time's consummate blooms shall grow,
Men to tame the tigerish instincts
   Of the lair and cave and den,
Cleanse the dragon slime of nature—
   Bring me men!

Bring me men to match my rivers,
   Continent cleansers, flowing free,
Drawn by eternal madness,
   To be mingled with the sea—
Men of oceanic impulse,
   Men whose moral currents sweep

Toward the wide, infolding ocean
    Of an undiscovered deep—
Men who feel the strong pulsation
    Of the central sea, and then
Time their currents by its earth throbs—
    Bring me Men.

SAM WALTER FOSS

AMERICAN LAUGHTER

OH, THE MEN who laughed the American laughter
Whittled their jokes from the tough bull-pines;
They were tall men, sharpened before and after;
They studied the sky for the weather-signs;
They tilted their hats and they smoked long-nines!

Their laughter was ladled in Western flagons
And poured down throats that were parched for more;
This was the laughter of democrat wagons
And homely men at the crossroads store
—It tickled the shawl that a lawyer wore!

It hurt the ears of the dainty and pretty
But they laughed the louder and laughed their fill,
A laughter made for Virginia City,
Springfield, and Natchez-under-the-Hill,
And the river that flows past Hannibal still!

American laughter was lucky laughter,
A coonskin tune by a homespun bard;
It tasted of hams from the smokehouse rafter
And locust trees in the courthouse yard,
And Petroleum Nasby and Artemus Ward!

They laughed at the Mormons and Mike Fink's daughter,
And the corncob tale of Sut Lovingood's dog,
Till the ague fled from the fever-water
And the damps deserted the tree-stump bog,
—They laughed at the tale of the jumping frog!

They laughed at the British, they laughed at Shakers,
At Horace Greeley, and stovepipe hats;
They split their fences and ploughed their acres,
And treed their troubles like mountain-cats;
—They laughed calamity out of the flats!

Now the Boston man, according to rumor,
Said, as he turned in his high-backed bed,
"This doesn't conform to my rules for humor,"
And he settled his nightcap over his head,
—But it shook the earth like the buffalo-tread!

And the corn grew tall and the fields grew wider,
And the land grew sleek with the mirth they sowed;
They laughed the fat meat into the spider,
They laughed the blues from the Wilderness Road,
—They crossed hard times to the Comstock Lode!

KENNETH ALLAN ROBINSON

"SCUM O' THE EARTH"

I

AT THE gate of the West I stand,
On the isle where the nations throng.
We call them "scum o' the earth";

Stay, are we doing you wrong,
Young fellow from Socrates' land?—

You, like a Hermes so lissome and strong
Fresh from the master Praxiteles' hand?
So you're of Spartan birth?
Descended, perhaps, from one of the band—
Deathless in story and song—
Who combed their long hair at Thermopylæ's pass? . . .
Ah, I forget what straits (alas!),
More tragic than theirs, more compassion-worth,
Have doomed you to march in our "immigrant class"
Where you're nothing but "scum o' the earth."

II

You Pole with the child on your knee,
What dower bring you to the land of the free?
Hark! does she croon
The sad little tune
That Chopin once found on his Polish lea
And mounted in gold for you and for me?
Now a ragged young fiddler answers
In wild Czech melody
That Dvořak took whole from the dancers.
And the heavy faces bloom
In the wonderful Slavic way;
The little, dull eyes, the brows a-gloom,
Suddenly dawn like the day.
While, watching these folk and their mystery,
I forget that we,
In our scornful mirth,
Brand them as "polacks"—and "scum o' the earth."

III

Genoese boy of the level brow,
Lad of the lustrous, dreamy eyes
Agaze at Manhattan's pinnacles now

In the first, sweet shock of a hushed surprise;
Within your far-rapt seer's eyes
I catch the glow of the wild surmise
That played on the Santa Maria's prow
In that still gray dawn,
Four centuries gone,
When a world from the wave began to rise.
Oh, who shall foretell what high emprise
Is the goal that gleams
When Italy's dreams
Spread wing and sweep into the skies.
Cæsar dreamed him a world ruled well;
Dante dreamed Heaven out of Hell;
Angelo brought us there to dwell;
And you, are you of a different birth?—
You're only a "dago,"—and "scum o' the earth"!

IV

Stay, are we doing you wrong
Calling you "scum o' the earth,"
Man of the sorrow-bowed head,
Of the features tender yet strong,—
Man of the eyes full of wisdom and mystery
Mingled with patience and dread?
Have not I known you in history,
Sorrow-bowed head?
Were you the poet-king, worth
Treasures of Ophir unpriced?
Were you the prophet, perchance, whose art
Foretold how the rabble would mock
That shepherd of spirits, ere long,
Who should gather the lambs to his heart
And tenderly feed his flock?
Man—lift that sorrow-bowed head. . . .
Behold, the face of the Christ!

The vision dies at its birth.
You're merely a butt for our mirth.
You're a "sheeny"—and therefore despised
And rejected as "scum o' the earth."

V

Countrymen, bend and invoke
Mercy for us blasphemers,
For that we spat on these marvellous folk,
Nations of darers and dreamers,
Scions of singers and seers,
Our peers, and more than our peers.
"Rabble and refuse," we name them
And "scum o' the earth," to shame them.
Mercy for us of the few, young years,
Of the culture so callow and crude,
Of the hands so grasping and rude,
The lips so ready for sneers
At the sons of our ancient more-than-peers.
Mercy for us who dare despise
Men in whose loins our Homer lies;
Mothers of men who shall bring to us
The glory of Titian, the grandeur of Huss;
Children in whose frail arms may rest
Prophets and singers and saints of the West.

Newcomers all from the eastern seas,
Help us incarnate dreams like these.
Forget, and forgive, that we did you wrong.
Help us to father a nation strong
In the comradeship of an equal birth,
In the wealth of the richest bloods of earth.

ROBERT HAVEN SCHAUFFLER

MARE LIBERUM

You dare to say with perjured lips,
  "We fight to make the ocean free?"
You, whose black trail of butchered ships
  Bestrews the bed of every sea
Where German submarines have wrought
Their horrors! Have you never thought,—
  What you call freedom, men call piracy!

Unnumbered ghosts that haunt the wave
  Where you have murdered, cry you down;
And seamen whom you would not save
  Weave now in weed-grown depths a crown
Of shame for your imperious head,—
A dark memorial of the dead,—
  Women and children whom you sent to drown.

Nay, not till thieves are set to guard
  The gold, and corsairs called to keep
O'er peaceful commerce watch and ward,
  And wolves to herd the helpless sheep,
Shall men and women look to thee,
Thou ruthless Old Man of the Sea,
  To safeguard law and freedom on the deep!

In nobler breeds we put our trust:
  The nations in whose sacred lore
The "Ought" stands out above the "Must,"
  And honor rules in peace and war.
With these we hold in soul and heart,
With these we choose our lot and part,
  Till liberty is safe on sea and shore.

                              HENRY VAN DYKE

INVOCATION

AMERICAN muse, whose strong and diverse heart
So many men have tried to understand
But only made it smaller with their art,
Because you are as various as your land,

As mountainous-deep, as flowered with blue rivers,
Thirsty with deserts, buried under snows,
As native as the shape of Navajo quivers,
And native, too, as the sea-voyaged rose.

Swift runner, never captured or subdued,
Seven-branched elk beside the mountain stream,
That half a hundred hunters have pursued
But never matched their bullets with the dream,

Where the great huntsmen failed, I set my sorry
And mortal snare for your immortal quarry.

You are the buffalo-ghost, the broncho-ghost
With dollar-silver in your saddle-horn,
The cowboys riding in from Painted Post,
The Indian arrow in the Indian corn,

And you are the clipped velvet of the lawns
Where Shropshire grows from Massachusetts sods,
The grey Maine rocks—and the war-painted dawns
That break above the Garden of the Gods.

The prairie-schooners crawling toward the ore
And the cheap car, parked by the station-door.

Where the skyscrapers lift their foggy plumes
Of stranded smoke out of a stony mouth
You are that high stone and its arrogant fumes,
And you are ruined gardens in the South

And bleak New England farms, so winter-white
Even their roofs look lonely, and the deep
The middle grainland where the wind of night
Is like all blind earth sighing in her sleep.

A friend, an enemy, a sacred hag
With two tied oceans in her medicine-bag.

They tried to fit you with an English song
And clip your speech into the English tale.
But, even from the first, the words went wrong,
The catbird pecked away the nightingale.

The homesick men begot high-cheekboned things
Whose wit was whittled with a different sound
And Thames and all the rivers of the kings
Ran into Mississippi and were drowned.

They planted England with a stubborn trust.
But the cleft dust was never English dust.

Stepchild of every exile from content
And all the disavouched, hard-bitten pack
Shipped overseas to steal a continent
With neither shirts nor honor to their back.

Pimping grandee and rump-faced regicide,
Apple-cheeked younkers from a windmill-square,
Puritans stubborn as the nails of Pride,
Rakes from Versailles and thieves from County Clare,

The black-robed priests who broke their hearts in vain
To make you God and France or God and Spain.

These were your lovers in your buckskin-youth.
And each one married with a dream so proud
He never knew it could not be the truth
And that he coupled with a girl of cloud.

And now to see you is more difficult yet
Except as an immensity of wheel
Made up of wheels, oiled with inhuman sweat
And glittering with the heat of ladled steel.

All these you are, and each is partly you,
And none is false, and none is wholly true.

So how to see you as you really are,
So how to suck the pure, distillate, stored
Essence of essence from the hidden star
And make it pierce like a riposting sword.

For, as we hunt you down, you must escape
And we pursue a shadow of our own
That can be caught in a magician's cape
But has the flatness of a painted stone.

Never the running stag, the gull at wing,
The pure elixir, the American thing.

.   .   .   .

To strive at last, against an alien proof
And by the changes of an alien moon,
To build again that blue, American roof
Over a half-forgotten battle-tune

And call unsurely, from a haunted ground,
Armies of shadows and the shadow-sound.

STEPHEN VINCENT BENÉT

NEW YORK

THE city is cutting a way,
  The gasmen are hunting a leak;
They're putting down asphalt to-day,
  To change it for stone in a week.

The builders are raising a wall,
  The wreckers are tearing one down,
Enacting the drama of all
  Our changeable, turbulent town.

For here is an edifice meant
  To stand for an eon or more;
And there is a gospeler's tent,
  And there is a furniture-store.

Our suburbs are under the plow,
  Our scaffolds are raw in the sun;
We're drunk and disorderly now,
      BUT—
  'Twill be a great place when it's done!
                    ARTHUR GUITERMAN

THE AMERICAN DREAM

By
JAMES TRUSLOW ADAMS

THE point is that if we are to have a rich and full life in which all
are to share and play their parts, if the American dream is to be a
reality, our communal spiritual and intellectual life must be distinctly higher than elsewhere, where classes and groups have their
separate interests, habits, markets, arts, and lives. If the dream is

not to prove possible of fulfillment, we might as well become stark realists, become once more class-conscious, and struggle as individuals or classes against one another. If it is to come true, those on top, financially, intellectually, or otherwise, have got to devote themselves to the "Great Society," and those who are below in the scale have got to strive to rise, not merely economically, but culturally. We cannot become a great democracy by giving ourselves up as individuals to selfishness, physical comfort, and cheap amusements. The very foundation of the American dream of a better and richer life for all is that all, in varying degrees, shall be capable of wanting to share in it. It can never be wrought into a reality by cheap people or by "keeping up with the Joneses." There is nothing whatever in a fortune merely in itself or in a man merely in himself. It all depends on what is made of each. Lincoln was not great because he was born in a log cabin, but because he got out of it—that is, because he rose above the poverty, ignorance, lack of ambition, shiftlessness of character, contentment with mean things and low aims which kept so many thousands in the huts where they were born.

MY AMERICA

By
John Buchan

The United States is the richest, and, both actually and potentially, the most powerful state on the globe. She has much, I believe, to give to the world; indeed, to her hands is chiefly entrusted the shaping of the future. If democracy in the broadest and truest sense is to survive, it will be mainly because of her guardianship. For, with all her imperfections, she has a clearer view than any other people of the democratic fundamentals.

She starts from the right basis, for she combines a firm grip on the past with a quick sense of present needs and a bold outlook on the future. This she owes to her history; the combination of the British tradition with the necessities of a new land; the New England township and the Virginian manor *plus* the frontier. Much of that tradition was relinquished as irrelevant to her needs, but much remains: a talent for law which is not incompatible with a lawless practice; respect for a certain type of excellence in character which has made her great men uncommonly like our own; a disposition to compromise, but only after a good deal of arguing; an intense dislike of dictation. To these instincts the long frontier struggles added courage in the face of novelties, adaptability, enterprise, a doggedness which was never lumpish, but alert and expectant.

That is the historic basis of America's democracy, and today she is the chief exponent of a creed which I believe on the whole to be the best in this imperfect world. She is the chief exponent for two reasons. The first is her size; she exhibits its technique in large type, so that he who runs may read. More important, she exhibits it in its most intelligible form, so that its constituents are obvious. Democracy has become with many an unpleasing parrot-cry, and, as I have urged elsewhere in this book, it is well to be clear what it means. It is primarily a spiritual testament, from which certain political and economic orders naturally follow. But the essence is the testament; the orders may change while the testament stands. This testament, this ideal of citizenship, she owes to no one teacher. There was a time when I fervently admired Alexander Hamilton and could not away with Jefferson; the latter only began to interest me, I think, after I had seen the University of Virginia, which he created. But I deprecate partisanship in those ultimate matters. The democratic testament derives from Hamilton as well as from Jefferson.

It has two main characteristics. The first is that the ordinary man believes in himself and in his ability, along with his fellows, to govern his country. It is when a people loses its self-confidence that it surrenders its soul to a dictator or an oligarchy. In Mr. Walter Lippmann's tremendous metaphor, it welcomes manacles to prevent its hands shaking. The second is the belief, which is fundamental also in Christianity, of the worth of every human soul

—the worth, not the equality. This is partly an honest emotion, and partly a reasoned principle—that something may be made out of anybody, and that there is something likeable about everybody if you look for it—or, in canonical words, that ultimately there is nothing common or unclean.

The democratic testament is one lesson that America has to teach the world. A second is a new reading of nationalism. Some day and somehow the peoples must discover a way to brigade themselves for peace. Now, there are on the globe only two proven large-scale organisations of social units, the United States and the British Empire. The latter is not for export, and could not be duplicated; its strength depends upon a thousand-year-old monarchy and a store of unformulated traditions. But the United States was the conscious work of men's hands, and a task which has once been performed can be performed again. She is the supreme example of a federation in being, a federation which recognises the rights and individuality of the parts, but accepts the overriding interests of the whole. To achieve this compromise she fought a desperate war. If the world is ever to have prosperity and peace, there must be some kind of federation—I will not say of democracies, but of states which accept the reign of Law. In such a task she seems to me to be the predestined leader. Vigorous as her patriotism is, she has escaped the jealous, barricadoed nationalism of the Old World. Disraeli, so often a prophet in spite of himself, in 1863, at a critical moment of the Civil War, spoke memorable words:

There is a grave misapprehension, both in the ranks of Her Majesty's Government and of Her Majesty's Opposition, as to what constitutes the true meaning of the American democracy. The American democracy is not made up of the scum of the great industrial cities of the United States, nor of an exhausted middle class that speculates in stocks and calls that progress. The American democracy is made up of something far more stable, that may ultimately decide the fate of the two Americas and of 'Europe.'

For forty years I have regarded America not only with a student's interest in a fascinating problem, but with the affection of one to whom she has become almost a second motherland. Among her citizens I count many of my closest friends; I have known all her presidents, save one, since Theodore Roosevelt, and all her ambassadors to the Court of Saint James's since John Hay; for five years I have been her neighbour in Canada. But I am not blind to the grave problems which confront her. Democracy, after all, is a negative thing. It provides a fair field for the Good Life, but it is not in itself the Good Life. In these days when lovers of freedom may have to fight for their cause, the hope is that the ideal of the Good Life, in which alone freedom has any meaning, will acquire a stronger potency. It is the task of civilisation to raise every citizen above want, but in so doing to permit a free development and avoid the slavery of the beehive and the antheap. A humane economic policy must not be allowed to diminish the stature of man's spirit. It is because I believe that in the American people the two impulses are of equal strength that I see her in the vanguard of that slow upward trend, undulant or spiral, which today is our modest definition of progress. Her major prophet is still Whitman. 'Everything comes out of the dirt—everything; everything comes out of the people, everyday people, the people as you find them and leave them; people, people, just people!'

It is only out of the dirt that things grow.

THE FULL-FLEDGED AMERICAN

By
STRUTHERS BURT

WERE I to have a vision of a full-fledged American it would be something like this: A man who, with sufficient knowledge of the past, would walk fairly constantly with the thought that he was blood-brother, if not by actual race then by the equally subtle method of mental vein transfusing into mental vein, of Washington and Lincoln; of Jefferson and Lee, and of all the men like them. Who would walk, because of this, carefully and proudly, and also humbly, lest he fail them. And, with a keen sense of the present and the future, would say to himself: "I am an American and therefore what I do, however small, is of importance."

Never in history have the times been more ripe for a sober discussion, a deep contemplation, of the kind of patriotism I imply. The American citizen is no longer a frontiersman; he can no longer make a million here and lose it there, and go on and make a million somewhere else, and meanwhile let his country take care of itself. The American is no longer a colonial, even in retrospect. Circumstances are forcing him into a deep, straight, independent form of thinking.

Pseudo-patriotism may be the last refuge of a scoundrel, but it is beginning to be apparent that before long, real patriotism, as so often before in history, will be not only the last, and only possible, refuge of the intelligent and far-visioned citizen, but also his sword, his rallying cry, and the emblem of his advance.

STATE OF CONNECTICUT

A PROCLAMATION

By His Excellency
WILBUR L. CROSS, *Governor*

As THE colors of autumn stream down the wind, scarlet in sumach and maple, spun gold in the birches, a splendor of smoldering fire in the oaks along the hill, and the last leaves flutter away, and dusk falls briefly about the worker bringing in from the field a late load of its fruit, and Arcturus is lost to sight and Orion swings upward that great sun upon his shoulder, we are stirred once more to ponder the Infinite Goodness that has set apart for us, in all this moving mystery of creation, a time of living and a home. In such a spirit I appoint Thursday, the twenty-fourth of November, a day of

PUBLIC THANKSGIVING

In such a spirit I call upon the people to acknowledge heartily, in friendly gathering and house of prayer, the increase of the season nearing now its close: the harvest of earth, the yield of patient mind and faithful hand, that have kept us fed and clothed and have made for us a shelter even against the storm. It is right that we whose arc of sky has been darkened by no war hawk, who have been forced by no man to stand and speak when to speak was to choose between death and life, should give thanks also for the further mercies we have enjoyed, beyond desert or any estimation, of Justice, Freedom, Loving-kindness, Peace—resolving, as we prize them, to let no occasion go without some prompting or some effort worthy in a way however humble of those proudest among man's ideals, which burn, though it may be like candles fitfully in our gusty world, with a light so clear we name its source divine.

Given under my hand and seal of the State at the Capitol, in Hartford, this tenth day of November, in the year of our Lord one thousand nine hundred and thirty-eight and of the independence of the United States the one hundred and sixty-third.

WILBUR L. CROSS

By His Excellency's Command:
    C. JOHN SATTI
      Secretary.

FLAG DAY—1940

WHAT's a flag? What's the love of country for which it stands? Maybe it begins with love of the land itself. It is the fog rolling in with the tide at Eastport, or through the Golden Gate and among the towers of San Francisco. It is the sun coming up behind the White Mountains, over the Green, throwing a shining glory on Lake Champlain and above the Adirondacks. It is the storied Mississippi rolling swift and muddy past St. Louis, rolling past Cairo, pouring down past the levees of New Orleans. It is lazy noontide in the pines of Carolina, it is a sea of wheat rippling in Western Kansas, it is the San Francisco peaks far north across the glowing nakedness of Arizona, it is the Grand Canyon and a little stream coming down out of a New England ridge, in which are trout.

It is men at work. It is the storm-tossed fishermen coming into Gloucester and Providence and Astoria. It is the farmer riding his great machine in the dust of harvest, the dairyman going to the barn before sunrise, the lineman mending the broken wire, the miner drilling for the blast. It is the servants of fire in the murky splendor of Pittsburgh, between the Allegheny and the Mononga-hela, the trucks rumbling through the night, the locomotive engineer bringing the train in on time, the pilot in the clouds, the riveter running along the beam a hundred feet in air. It is the clerk in the office, the housewife doing the dishes and sending the children off to school. It is the teacher, doctor and parson tending and helping, body and soul, for small reward.

It is small things remembered, the little corners of the land, the houses, the people that each one loves. We love our country because there was a little tree on a hill, and grass thereon, and a sweet valley below; because the hurdy-gurdy man came along on a sunny morning in a city street; because a beach or a farm or a lane or a house that might not seem much to others were once, for each of us, made magic. It is voices that are remembered only, no longer heard. It is parents, friends, the lazy chat of street and store and office, and the ease of mind that makes life tranquil. It is Summer and Winter, rain and sun and storm. These are flesh of our flesh, bone of our bone, blood of our blood, a lasting part of what we are, each of us and all of us together.

It is stories told. It is the Pilgrims dying in their first dreadful Winter. It is the minute man standing his ground at Concord

Bridge, and dying there. It is the army in rags, sick, freezing, starving at Valley Forge. It is the wagons and the men on foot going westward over Cumberland Gap, floating down the great rivers, rolling over the great plains. It is the settler hacking fiercely at the primeval forest on his new, his own lands. It is Thoreau at Walden Pond, Lincoln at Cooper Union, and Lee riding home from Appomattox. It is corruption and disgrace, answered always by men who would not let the flag lie in the dust, who have stood up in every generation to fight for the old ideals and the old rights, at risk of ruin or of life itself.

It is a great multitude of people on pilgrimage, common and ordinary people, charged with the usual human failings, yet filled with such a hope as never caught the imaginations and the hearts of any nation on earth before. The hope of liberty. The hope of justice. The hope of a land in which a man can stand straight, without fear, without rancor.

The land and the people and the flag—the land a continent, the people of every race, the flag a symbol of what humanity may aspire to when the wars are over and the barriers are down; to these each generation must be dedicated and consecrated anew, to defend with life itself, if need be, but, above all, in friendliness, in hope, in courage, to live for.

N. Y. Times—6-14-40

SELF-EVIDENT TRUTHS

By
BURTON RASCOE

BUT in his heart and mind the American remains very much himself. He may not know why he thinks and feels the way he does, because it is largely a matter of instinct and tradition. The tradition is the American tradition and it stems from the Constitution and the Bill of Rights, none of the makers of which seems to have been any too articulate as to just why he felt and thought the way he did. He just felt and thought that way, that's all. When a Founding Father tried to be articulate about what he felt, he bungled into the highly poetical and not easily verifiable statement: "We hold these truths to be self-evident, and all men are created equal, that they are endowed by their Creator with certain inalienable Rights, that among these are Life, Liberty, and the pursuit of Happiness."

Realists from Lycurgus to Blackstone and from Cambyses to Machiavelli and from Aristotle to Jennings would have laughed (or smiled) at the thought of somebody's trying to adduce proof in substantiation of these "self-evident" Truths. Yet for the American these Truths are, from some imponderable reason, self-evident. That is, they don't need any proof: they just are.

Holding these Truths to be self-evident the American, be he an immigrant who has just got his citizenship papers, or a Mayflower descendant, is largely unaffected by all the vociferous winds of doctrine and does what he feels is his patriotic and social duty without bothering his head about the howling of these winds.

THE DEFENSE OF LIBERTY

By
ROSE WILDER LANE

AMERICANS are still paying the price of individual liberty, which is individual responsibility and insecurity.

These unnoticed Americans are defending the principle on which this republic was founded, the principle that created this country and has, in fact, brought the greatest good to the greatest number. By such courage and endurance, the American principle has been successfully defended, time after time, for more than a century.

We remember the Americans who died in the wars of this country. We build memorials to their memory and lay flowers on their graves. It was the Americans who lived and kept their fighting spirit through the hard and bitter times that followed every surge of prosperity, it was men and women who cared enough for their own personal freedom to take the risks of self-reliance and starve if they could not feed themselves, who created our country, the free country, the richest and the happiest country in the world.

But during that first century, the western world was turning toward democracy. The test of strength comes now, when half of Europe has definitely turned back from democracy to the old stability in which the multitudes, having no authority, have no responsibility, but leave both the power and the burden to their rulers.

THE AMERICAN CHARACTER

By
GEORGE SANTAYANA

AT THE same time, the American is imaginative; for where life is intense, imagination is intense also. Were he not imaginative he would not live so much in the future. But his imagination is practical, and the future it forecasts is immediate; it works with the clearest and least ambiguous terms known to his experience, in terms of number, measure, contrivance, economy, and speed. He is an idealist working on matter. Understanding as he does the material potentialities of things, he is successful in invention, conservative in reform, and quick in emergencies. All his life he jumps into the train after it has started and jumps out before it has stopped; and he never once gets left behind, or breaks a leg. There is an enthusiasm in his sympathetic handling of material forces which goes far to cancel the illiberal character which it might otherwise assume. The good workman hardly distinguishes his artistic intention from the potency in himself and in things which is about to realize that intention. Accordingly his ideals fall into the form of premonitions and prophecies; and his studious prophecies often come true. So do the happy workmanlike ideals of the American. When a poor boy, perhaps, he dreams of an education, or at least a degree; he dreams of growing rich, and he grows rich —only more slowly and modestly, perhaps, than he expected; he dreams of marrying his Rebecca and, even if he marries a Leah instead, he ultimately finds in Leah his Rebecca after all. He dreams of helping to carry on and to accelerate the movement of a vast, seething, progressive society, and he actually does so. Ideals clinging so close to nature are almost sure of fulfilment; the American beams with a certain self-confidence and sense of mastery; he feels that God and nature are working with him.

GERMAN-AMERICANS

By
GEORGE S. KAUFMAN and MOSS HART

IRMA

No, NO, Martin, I cannot tear these people out of my heart, just because now there is a war. I was born in Germany, Martin. I grew up there. So did you. I love this country—yes, but I love Germany too. I cannot help that. It is deep inside of me. My heart breaks enough when I think that these two countries I love must fight each other. But that Karl should go over there, a gun in his hand, and kill those people I grew up with—that I cannot stand.

MARTIN

Don't you think that I am tortured too, Irma? When I wake in the night and hear you crying beside me, don't you think *my* heart breaks? I love Germany too, Irma. Do you think I can forget the little town that we were born in? My mother and father, those boys and girls we went to school with—they must have sons now too, Irma, like our Karl. Do you think I *want* him to go over and kill those people?

IRMA

Then for God's sake, Martin, do not let Karl go! Do not let him go!

MARTIN

No, Irma—Karl *must* go. This country opened its arms to us, reared our children. Everything that we have and everything that we are, we owe to America. Lisa's baby is an American; the children that Karl will have will be Americans, and *I* am an American, Irma. And so are you!

IRMA

(*Brokenly*)
No, no! Don't let him go, Martin. Please! Please!

MARTIN

Irma Liebchen, he must go. This is our country, Irma, and I am proud that we *have* a son to go. We cannot divide our allegiance, Irma—we are either Germans or we are Americans, and I say we are Americans!

COOLIDGE'S FATHER ADMINISTERS THE PRESIDENTIAL OATH

By
Claude M. Fuess

Even those who were present at that dramatic scene differ in their recollection of precisely what happened. The reporters took the message as it was handed to them and made their way to Ludlow to file their stories. Soon the telephone was ready, and Coolidge talked both with his Secretary, "Ted" Clark, and with Mr. Hughes, the Secretary of State, who advised him on the form which the oath should take. Attorney General Daugherty also sent a telegram requesting Coolidge to take the oath immediately. Meanwhile Colonel Coolidge, after some searching, had found a copy of the Constitution of the United States and had read Article II, Section 1, Paragraph 8, which gives the wording of the oath or affirmation, but does not specify by whom it shall be administered. Finally, however, Coolidge reached a decision. "Father," he asked, "are you still a notary?" "Yes, Cal," was the reply. "Then I want you to administer the oath." Colonel Coolidge, who meanwhile had gone out to the kitchen to shave and put on a collar and tie, returned and stood erect with his back to the porch, facing his son across the marble-topped table, which had been cleared except for two oil lamps and the copy of the Bible which had belonged to Coolidge's mother. The Vice President stood directly beneath a framed picture of himself on the wall. Between them was Mrs. Coolidge, and in the background were Dale, Geisser, Fountain, McInerney, Crawford, and L. L. Lane, a railway mailman who had accompanied Dale. Then Colonel Coolidge, adjusting his spectacles and clearing his throat, read the prescribed oath, "I do solemnly swear that I will faithfully execute the office of President of the United States and will, to the best of my ability, preserve, protect, and defend the Constitution of the United States." Calvin Coolidge repeated the words in a firm voice, with his right hand raised, added, "So help me God!" and then, by the glow of the lamps, signed the oath in triplicate. The time was precisely 2.47 A.M. As he laid his pen aside, and his father affixed the seal, he raised his head and glanced at Mrs. Coolidge, who still stood near by. Speaking no word, he nodded, and the two left the room. He was President of the United States.

Colonel John Coolidge, now thoroughly awake, sat up all night, but the President went back to bed for a few hours of rest, and actually, according to his testimony, went to sleep. He had been struck by the fact that never in history before that time had a father administered to his son the qualifying oath of office which made him the chief magistrate of a nation. The scene might well, in its simplicity, have been contrasted with Napoleon's coronation or the elaborate ritual which accompanies the crowning of an English monarch in Westminster Abbey. It was indeed a solemn moment when so much power and obligation fell unexpectedly on the shoulders of a single man. A candidate elected in normal course to the Presidency has ample time in which to adjust himself. Calvin Coolidge had none. Some years later, when the artist, Charles Hopkinson, was painting the President's portrait, he was discouraged by the lack of animation in his face and finally asked, "Mr. Coolidge, what was the first thought that came into your mind when you were told that Mr. Harding was dead and that the Presidency was yours?" Thinking a moment, Mr. Coolidge, without changing his expression in the slightest, said, "I thought I could swing it."

IN THE GREEN MOUNTAIN COUNTRY

By
CLARENCE DAY

HE GOT up at seven as usual, and he and his wife had breakfast together. At half past eight he went to his office in the town. His old friend and partner was already there when he entered. They were both early risers. They spoke with each other for a moment and then he went to his desk.

He was not feeling quite well. He said nothing about it. He had no idea that this was his last day of life.

There were a number of letters and other matters for him to go over and settle. He went to work methodically at them. He disliked to leave things undone. All his life he had attended to his duties, large or small, systematically. He was a sound, seasoned New Englander of sixty, and he had accomplished a lot.

By ten o'clock he had finished. He still wasn't feeling any better.

He said to his secretary, "Mr. Ross, I guess we'll go to the house."

They motored back together through the streets and under the bare, spreading trees, till they came to the beeches and elms that surrounded his home. He had lived in half of a two-family house most of his life, but it had no grounds around it, and when he was fifty-eight he had moved; "so the doggies can have a place to play," he had said.

His wife was out—she had gone down town on foot to do some shopping. He and his secretary went to the library. He toyed with a jigsaw puzzle a moment. They spoke of the partridge hunting they had had in October, and of the hay fever that had bothered him in July—a "pollen attack" he called it. He made little of it. He had been lucky—he had had very few illnesses.

As they sat there talking he said he was thirsty. The cook and maid were at hand, and so was Mr. Ross, but he didn't like to be waited on—he went to the kitchen and got a glass of water himself. He heard the gardener in the cellar and he went down there to say something to him. The gardener was the last man he spoke to. When people asked him later what his employer had said he couldn't remember. He told them that it was something about the house or the grounds, and that it had not seemed important—to him.

Leaving the gardener this man went upstairs to his bedroom. He took off his coat and waistcoat to shave, but sank to the floor. He was dead.

The news spread through the town. Children on their way home from school stopped to look through the gates. A few policemen arrived. When reporters and camera men came the Chief of Police took them aside and asked them not to bother the family. He left one policeman on guard and everyone else went away.

The flag on the schoolhouse had been lowered. Now, on all public buildings, other flags went to half-mast. In town after town, and city after city, the flags fluttered down.

The next day the guns began booming. For thousands of miles throughout the nation, and at its army posts over-seas, at half hour intervals all day long, cannon by cannon they spoke. And when evening came and the bugles had sounded retreat, there were last, long, slow salutes everywhere of forty-eight guns, one for each of the forty-eight States of his country.

The hotel in Northampton was crowded that night. Friends of his had arrived for the funeral, and there were many reporters. The reporters swapped stories of the days before he had retired. One time when he had been suddenly needed, they said, for some national conference, and when nobody knew where he was, he had been found down in the storeroom, fishing a pickle out of a jar with two fingers. He had liked homemade pickles and people had sent him quantities of them, but he never got any at table, they were all kept on shelves in the storeroom, because of the chance that cranks might send jars that were poisoned.

Early in the morning the long special trains came rolling in. The President and his wife, the Vice-President, the Chief Justice, several Cabinet members, and committees of Senators and Congressmen got out of the sleeping cars from Washington and walked through the crowd at the station. Governors of near-by States and other officials arrived in their motors. They went to the Congregational Church and sat in its plain oak pews.

The service was brief. There was no eulogy, no address of any kind. Two hymns were sung, parts of the Bible were read, and the young minister prayed. He rose, and gave the great of the land who stood before him his blessing. They filed slowly out.

The streets emptied as the visitors left. The motors and trains rolled away.

When the town was alone with its own again, six sober-faced policemen lifted the coffin and carried it out to the street. Light rain was falling. Drops glistened on the coffin as it was placed in the hearse. A few motors fell in behind it, and the little procession moved off along the old country roads.

In every village they went through, there were small troops of boy scouts and veterans of the great war, standing at attention in silence as the motors sped by. In the yards of factories and mills, workmen stood in groups, waiting. Men held their hats or caps to their hearts, women folded their hands. Farms and fields on the road had been tidied up, as a mark of respect, and at a place where carpenters were building a house they had cleared away the lumber and chips.

The rain stopped for a while. The mists that had drifted low over the mountains gave place to blue sky. White, straight birch trunks glistened, and ice began to melt in the sunshine. But as they drove on, deeper into the Green Mountain country, black clouds spread and rain fell again, harder. The red tail lights of the cars gleamed on the road in the wintry and dark afternoon.

When the cars reached the end of the journey, the skies lightened palely a moment. The burying ground was outside the village where the dead man was born. Generations of his ancestors had been laid to rest there, in graves on the hillside. The cars climbed the steep road and stopped. The family and a handful of friends got out and stood waiting.

Across the road, in a rocky field, the men and women of the village had gathered. They were not the kind of people to intrude or crowd nearer, and they kept complete silence. The young minister said a few words as the coffin was lowered. A sudden storm of hail pelted down.

The widow, who had tried to smile that morning coming out of the church, could no longer hold back her tears.

The cars left. The bent-shouldered sexton signaled to his helpers. They filled in the grave. Four country militiamen took up their positions on guard. Snow fell that night on the hillside and the slopes of Salt Ash Mountain.

The headstone that now marks the quiet spot bears no inscription but the name, Calvin Coolidge, the dates, and the President's seal.

BASIC AMERICAN IDEALS

THE STAR-SPANGLED BANNER

O! say, can you see, by the dawn's early light,
  What so proudly we hailed at the twilight's last gleaming:
Whose broad stripes and bright stars, through the perilous fight,
  O'er the ramparts we watched were so gallantly streaming,
And the rocket's red glare, the bombs bursting in air,
Gave proof through the night that our flag was still there;

  O! say, does the Star-spangled Banner still wave
  O'er the land of the free and the home of the brave?

On the shore, dimly seen through the mist of the deep,
  Where the foe's haughty host in dread silence reposes,
What is that which the breeze, o'er the towering steep,
  As it fitfully blows, half conceals, half discloses?
Now it catches the gleam of the morning's first beam—
In full glory reflected, now shines on the stream;

  'Tis the Star-spangled Banner, O! long may it wave
  O'er the land of the free and the home of the brave.

And where is the band who so vauntingly swore
  That the havoc of war and the battle's confusion
A home and a country would leave us no more?
  Their blood has washed out their foul footsteps' pollution.
No refuge could save the hireling and slave
From the terror of flight or the gloom of the grave!

  And the Star-spangled Banner in triumph doth wave
  O'er the land of the free and the home of the brave.

O! thus be it ever when freemen shall stand
  Between their loved homes and the foe's desolation;
Bless'd with victory and peace, may our Heaven-rescued land
  Praise the Power that hath made and preserved us a nation.
Then conquer we must, for our cause it is just—
  And this be our motto—"In God is our trust!"

And the Star-spangled Banner in triumph shall wave
O'er the land of the free and the home of the brave.

FRANCIS SCOTT KEY

COLUMBIA

Columbia, Columbia, to glory arise,
The queen of the world, and the child of the skies;
Thy genius commands thee; with rapture behold,
While ages on ages thy splendor unfold,
Thy reign is the last, and the noblest of time,
Most fruitful thy soil, most inviting thy clime;
Let the crimes of the east ne'er encrimson thy name,
Be freedom, and science, and virtue thy fame.

To conquest and slaughter let Europe aspire;
Whelm nations in blood, and wrap cities in fire;
Thy heroes the rights of mankind shall defend,
And triumph pursue them, and glory attend.
A world is thy realm: for a world be thy laws,
Enlarged as thine empire, and just as thy cause;
On Freedom's broad basis, that empire shall rise,
Extend with the main, and dissolve with the skies.

Fair science her gates to thy sons shall unbar,
And the east see the morn hide the beams of her star.

New bards, and new sages, unrivalled shall soar
To fame unextinguished, when time is no more;
To thee, the last refuge of virtue designed,
Shall fly from all nations the best of mankind;
Here, grateful to heaven, with transport shall bring
Their incense, more fragrant than odors of spring,

Nor less shall thy fair ones to glory ascend,
And genius and beauty in harmony blend;
The graces of form shall awake pure desire,
And the charms of the soul ever cherish the fire;
Their sweetness unmingled, their manners refined,
And virtue's bright image, instamped on the mind,
With peace and soft rapture shall teach life to glow,
And light up a smile in the aspect of woe.

Thy fleets to all regions thy power shall display,
The nations admire and the ocean obey;
Each shore to thy glory its tribute unfold,
And the east and the south yield their spices and gold.
As the day-spring unbounded, thy splendor shall flow,
And earth's little kingdoms before thee shall bow;
While the ensigns of union, in triumph unfurled,
Hush the tumult of war and give peace to the world.

Thus, as down a lone valley, with cedars o'erspread,
From war's dread confusion I pensively strayed,
The gloom from the face of fair heaven retired;
The winds ceased to murmur; the thunders expired;
Perfumes as of Eden flowed sweetly along,
And a voice as of angels, enchantingly sung:
"Columbia, Columbia, to glory arise,
The queen of the world, and the child of the skies."

TIMOTHY DWIGHT

HAIL COLUMBIA

HAIL! Columbia, happy land!
Hail! ye heroes, heav'n-born band,
Who fought and bled in freedom's cause,
Who fought and bled in freedom's cause,
And when the storm of war was gone,
Enjoyed the peace your valor won;
Let independence be your boast,
Ever mindful what it cost,
Ever grateful for the prize,
Let its altar reach the skies.

> *Chorus*—Firm, united let us be,
>   Rallying round our liberty,
>   As a band of brothers joined,
>   Peace and safety we shall find.

Immortal patriots, rise once more!
Defend your rights, defend your shore;
Let no rude foe with impious hand,
Let no rude foe with impious hand
Invade the shrine where sacred lies
Of toil and blood the well-earned prize;
While offering peace, sincere and just,
In heav'n we place a manly trust,
That truth and justice may prevail,
And ev'ry scheme of bondage fail.

Sound, sound the trump of fame!
Let Washington's great name
Ring thro' the world with loud applause!
Ring thro' the world with loud applause!

Let ev'ry clime to freedom dear
Listen with a joyful ear;
With equal skill, with steady pow'r,
He governs in the fearful hour
Of horrid war, or guides with ease
The happier time of honest peace.

Behold the chief, who now commands,
Once more to serve his country stands,
The rock on which the storm will beat!
The rock on which the storm will beat!
But armed in virtue, firm and true,
His hopes are fixed on heav'n and you.
When hope was sinking in dismay,
When gloom obscured Columbia's day,
His steady mind, from changes free,
Resolved on death or liberty.

JOSEPH HOPKINSON

NATIONAL HYMN

GOD of our fathers, whose almighty hand
Leads forth in beauty all the starry band
Of shining worlds in splendor through the skies,
Our grateful songs before Thy throne arise.

Thy love divine hath led us in the past,
In this free land by Thee our lot is cast;
Be Thou our ruler, guardian, guide, and stay,
Thy word our law, Thy paths our chosen way.

From war's alarms, from deadly pestilence,
Be Thy strong arm our ever-sure defence;
Thy true religion in our hearts increase,
Thy bounteous goodness nourish us in peace.

Refresh Thy people on their toilsome way,
Lead us from night to never-ending day;
Fill all our lives with love and grace divine,
And glory, laud and praise be ever Thine.

DANIEL C. ROBERTS

AMERICA

MY COUNTRY, 'tis of thee,
Sweet land of liberty,
    Of thee I sing;
Land where my fathers died,
Land of the Pilgrims' pride;
From every mountain side,
    Let freedom ring.

My native country, thee—
Land of the noble free—
    Thy name I love;
I love thy rocks and rills,
Thy woods and templed hills;
My heart with rapture thrills,
    Like that above.

Let music swell the breeze,
And ring from all the trees
    Sweet freedom's song;
Let mortal tongues awake;
Let all that breathe partake;
Let rocks their silence break—
    The sound prolong.

Our father's God, to thee,
Author of liberty,
    To Thee we sing;

Long may our land be bright
With freedom's holy light:
Protect us by Thy might,
   Great God, our King.
      SAMUEL FRANCIS SMITH

AMERICA THE BEAUTIFUL

O BEAUTIFUL for spacious skies,
   For amber waves of grain,
For purple mountain majesties
   Above the fruited plain!
America! America!
   God shed His grace on thee
And crown thy good with brotherhood
   From sea to shining sea!

O beautiful for pilgrim feet,
   Whose stern, impassioned stress
A thoroughfare for freedom beat
   Across the wilderness!
America! America!
   God mend thine every flaw,
Confirm thy soul in self-control,
   Thy liberty in law!

O beautiful for heroes proved
   In liberating strife,
Who more than self their country loved,
   And mercy more than life!
America! America!
   May God thy gold refine,
Till all success be nobleness
   And every gain divine!

O beautiful for patriot dream
   That sees beyond the years
Thine alabaster cities gleam
   Undimmed by human tears!
America! America!
   God shed His grace on thee,
And crown thy good with brotherhood
   From sea to shining sea!

                    KATHARINE LEE BATES

AMERICA

FOR, O America, our country!—land
   Hid in the west through centuries, till men
Through countless tyrannies could understand
   The priceless worth of freedom,—once again
The world was new-created when thy shore
   First knew the Pilgrim keels, that one last test
The race might make of manhood, nor give o'er
   The strife with evil till it proved its best.
Thy true sons stand as torch-bearers, to hold
   A guiding light. Here the last stand is made.
If we fail here, what new Columbus bold,
   Steering brave prow through black seas unafraid,
Finds out a fresh land where man may abide
   And freedom yet be saved? The whole round earth
Has seen the battle fought. Where shall men hide
   From tyranny and wrong, where life have worth,
If here the cause succumb? If greed of gold
   Or lust of power or falsehood triumph here,
The race is lost! A globe dispeopled, cold,
   Rolled down the void a voiceless, lifeless sphere,
Were not so stamped by all which hope debars
   As were this earth, plunging along through space

Conquered by evil, shamed among the stars,
  Bearing a base, enslaved, dishonored race!
Here has the battle its last vantage ground;
  Here all is won, or here must all be lost;
Here freedom's trumpets one last rally sound;
  Here to the breeze its blood-stained flag is tossed.
America, last hope of man and truth,
  Thy name must through all coming ages be
The badge unspeakable of shame and ruth,
  Or glorious pledge that man through truth is free.
This is thy destiny; the choice is thine
  To lead all nations and outshine them all;—
But if thou failest, deeper shame is thine,
  And none shall spare to mock thee in thy fall.

                                    ARLO BATES

"OH MOTHER OF A MIGHTY RACE"

          OH MOTHER of a mighty race,
          Yet lovely in thy youthful grace!
          The elder dames, thy haughty peers,
          Admire and hate thy blooming years.
                  With words of shame
          And taunts of scorn they join thy name.

          For on thy cheeks the glow is spread
          That tints thy morning hills with red;
          Thy step—the wild-deer's rustling feet
          Within thy woods are not more fleet;
                  Thy hopeful eye
          Is bright as thine own sunny sky.

          Ay, let them rail—those haughty ones,
          While safe thou dwellest with thy sons.

They do not know how loved thou art,
How many a fond and fearless heart
        Would rise to throw
Its life between thee and the foe.

They know not, in their hate and pride,
What virtues with thy children bide;
How true, how good, thy graceful maids
Make bright, like flowers, the valley-shades;
        What generous men
Spring, like thine oaks, by hill and glen;—

What cordial welcomes greet the guest
By thy lone rivers of the West;
How faith is kept, and truth revered,
And man is loved, and God is feared,
        In woodland homes,
And where the ocean border foams.

There's freedom at thy gates and rest
For Earth's down-trodden and opprest,
A shelter for the hunted head,
For the starved laborer toil and bread.
        Power, at thy bounds,
Stops and calls back his baffled hounds.

Oh, fair young mother! on thy brow
Shall sit a nobler grace than now.
Deep in the brightness of the skies
The thronging years in glory rise,
        And, as they fleet,
Drop strength and riches at thy feet.

Thine eye, with every coming hour,
Shall brighten, and thy form shall tower;

And when thy sisters, elder born,
Would brand thy name with words of scorn,
   Before thine eye,
Upon their lips the taunt shall die.
WILLIAM CULLEN BRYANT

THE PATRIOT HYMN

OH, COUNTRY, fair and grand,
Our glorious Fatherland,
   Superb, star-crowned—
By Freedom's breezes fanned,
Firm in thy mountain band,
That guard on every hand
   Thy sacred ground!

Thy children come to-day
A wreath of love to lay
   Before thy feet.
In festival array,
With jocund hearts and gay,
Our homage pure we pay;
   With song we meet!

In War's hard Wilderness,
With bitter storm and stress,
   We've tarried long.
Now Peace thy sons shall bless!
Freedom and Righteousness
   Shall make them strong!

Strong in the cause of Right
To aid the weak with might
   Born of the Truth;

Strong as the hosts of Light
Arrayed against the Night,
To put all wrong to flight
  With zeal of Youth!

We are thy Sword and Shield!
To thee our all we yield
  At thy command.
But when War's wounds are healed,
In workshop and in field,
Our love is best revealed,
  Dear Native Land!
                    NATHAN HASKELL DOLE

LAND THAT WE LOVE

LAND that we love! Thou Future of the World!
Thou refuge of the noble heart oppressed!
Oh never be thy shining image hurled
From its high place in the adoring breast
Of him who worships thee with jealous love!
Keep thou thy starry forehead as the dove
All white, and to the eternal Dawn inclined!
Thou art not for thyself but for mankind,
And to despair of thee were to despair
Of man, of man's high destiny, of God!
Of thee should man despair, the journey trod
Upward, through unknown eons, stair on stair,
By this our race, with bleeding feet and slow,
Were but the pathway to a darker woe
Than yet was visioned by the heavy heart
Of prophet. To despair of thee! Ah no!
For thou thyself art Hope, Hope of the World thou art!
                    RICHARD WATSON GILDER

LAND OF THE FREE

AMERICA, O Power benign, great hearts revere your name,
You stretch your hand to every land, to weak and strong the same;
You claim no conquest of the sea, nor conquest of the field,
But conquest for the rights of man, that despots all shall yield.

Chorus:
America, fair land of mine, home of the just and true,
All hail to thee, land of the free, and the Red-White-and-Blue.

America, staunch, undismayed, your spirit is our might:
No splendor falls on feudal walls upon your mountain's height,
But shafts of Justice pierce your skies to light the way for all,
A world's great brotherhood of man, that cannot, must not fall.

America, in God we trust, we fear no tyrant's horde:
There's light that leads toward better deeds than conquest by the
    sword;
Yet our cause is just, if fight we must until the world be free
Of every menace, breed, or caste that strikes at Liberty.

America, home of the brave, our song in praise we bring—
Where Stars and Stripes the winds unfurl, 'tis there that tributes
    ring;
Our fathers gave their lives that we should live in Freedom's light—
Our lives we consecrate to thee, our guide the Might of Right.

ARTHUR NICHOLAS HOSKING

ONE COUNTRY

AFTER all,
One country, brethren! We must rise or fall
With the Supreme Republic. We must be
The makers of her immortality;
   Her freedom, fame,
   Her glory or her shame—
Liegemen to God and fathers of the free!

After all—
Hark! from the heights the clear, strong, clarion call
And the command imperious: "Stand forth,
Sons of the South and brothers of the North!
   Stand forth and be
   As one on soil and sea—
Your country's honor more than empire's worth!"

After all,
'Tis Freedom wears the loveliest coronal;
Her brow is to the morning; in the sod
She breathes the breath of patriots; every clod
   Answers her call
   And rises like a wall
Against the foes of liberty and God!

FRANK L. STANTON

OUR COUNTRY

ON PRIMAL rocks she wrote her name;
   Her towers were reared on holy graves;
The golden seed that bore her came
   Swift-winged with prayer o'er ocean waves.

The Forest bowed his solemn crest,
  And open flung his sylvan doors;
Meek Rivers led the appointed guest
  To clasp the wide-embracing shores;

Till, fold by fold, the broidered land
  To swell her virgin vestments grew,
While sages, strong in heart and hand,
  Her virtue's fiery girdle drew.

O Exile of the wrath of kings!
  O Pilgrim Ark of Liberty!
The refuge of divinest things,
  Their record must abide in thee!

First in the glories of thy front
  Let the crown-jewel, Truth, be found;
Thy right hand fling, with generous wont,
  Love's happy chain to farthest bound!

Let Justice, with the faultless scales,
  Hold fast the worship of thy sons;
Thy Commerce spread her shining sails
  Where no dark tide of rapine runs!

So link thy ways to those of God,
  So follow firm the heavenly laws,
That stars may greet thee, warrior-browed,
  And storm-sped angels hail thy cause!

O Lord, the measure of our prayers,
  Hope of the world in grief and wrong,
Be thine the tribute of the years,
  The gift of Faith, the crown of Song!
                JULIA WARD HOWE

THIS IS AMERICA

THIS is America, these quiet hills
So still and green beneath the summer sun,
Where not one clod by violence is upturned,
Nor one tree riven by a distant gun.

This is America, these wide, rich fields,
Golden with grain and hazy in the heat;
Only the farmer's hand shall mow them down,
Nor find one body lying in the wheat.

This is America, these sandy shores
Whence every day the fishers sail again,
Nor scan the skies for threat of sudden death
Fearing no enemy save wind and rain.

This is America—O happy land
Upon whose hills and plains God's peace is shed,
God keep thee still the same, a haven where,
Except in love, no alien foot shall tread.

                              KATHARINE JANEWAY CONGER

HARD ROWS TO HOE

A CHANT FOR AMERICANS

JAMESTOWN had its starving time;
Plymouth was a bitter clime;
Penn's stormed followers gave thanks
For shelters dug in river banks.

To the pioneer the soil
Gave the single gift of toil.
Riches from oneself must flow—
Our fathers had hard rows to hoe,
Hard rows to hoe!

What was easy in the lot
Of the stalwart Irish-Scot
Who passed the Alleghenies' spears
And dared the perilous frontiers?
What of comfort was there found
In The Dark and Bloody Ground?
To the Sierras it was so—
Our fathers had hard rows to hoe,
Hard rows to hoe!

Come, shall weakling harvests spring
From our fathers' furrowing?
Yonder the new conquest waits,
Yonder still the adverse fates
Challenge, and the hour is stored
With new hazard—and reward:
Harvests from oneself must grow—
Arouse! We have hard rows to hoe,
Hard rows to hoe!

                    DANIEL HENDERSON

I HEAR AMERICA SINGING

I HEAR America singing, the varied carols I hear,
Those of mechanics, each one singing his as it should be blithe and
    strong,
The carpenter singing his as he measures his plank or beam,
The mason singing his as he makes ready for work, or leaves off
    work,

The boatman singing what belongs to him in his boat, the deck-
   hand singing on the steamboat deck,
The shoemaker singing as he sits on his bench, the hatter singing
   as he stands,
The wood-cutter's song, the ploughboy's on his way in the morn-
   ing, or at noon intermission or at sundown,
The delicious singing of the mother, or of the young wife at work,
   or of the girl sewing or washing,
Each singing what belongs to him or her and to none else,
The day what belongs to the day—at night the party of young
   fellows, robust, friendly,
Singing with open mouths their strong melodious songs.

                                        WALT WHITMAN

THE BETTER WAY

Who serves his country best?
Not he who, for a brief and stormy space,
Leads forth her armies to the fierce affray.
Short is the time of turmoil and unrest,
Long years of peace succeed it and replace:
      There is a better way.

Who serves his country best?
Not he who guides her senates in debate,
And makes the laws which are her prop and stay;
Not he who wears the poet's purple vest
And sings her songs of love and grief and fate:
      There is a better way.

He serves his country best,
Who joins the tide that lifts her nobly on;
For speech has myriad tongues for every day,
And song but one; and law within the breast

Is stronger than the graven law on stone:
    This is a better way.

He serves his country best
Who lives pure life, and doeth righteous deed,
And walks straight paths, however others stray,
And leaves his sons as uttermost bequest
A stainless record which all men may read:
    This is the better way.

No drop but serves the slowly lifting tide,
No dew but has an errand to some flower,
No smallest star but sheds some helpful ray,
And man by man, each giving to all the rest,
Makes the firm bulwark of the country's power:
    There is no better way.

                              SUSAN COOLIDGE

INSCRIPTION ON THE STATUE OF LIBERTY

GIVE me your tired, your poor,
Your huddled masses yearning to breathe free,
The wretched refuse of your teeming shore,
Send these, the homeless, tempest-tossed, to me:
I lift my lamp beside the golden door.

                              EMMA LAZARUS

THE BARTHOLDI STATUE

THE land, that, from the rule of kings,
    In freeing us, itself made free,
Our Old World Sister, to us brings
    Her sculptured Dream of Liberty:

Unlike the shapes on Egypt's sands
   Uplifted by the toil-worn slave,
On Freedom's soil with freemen's hands
   We rear the symbol free hands gave.

O France, the beautiful! to thee
   Once more a debt of love we owe:
In peace beneath thy Colors Three,
   We hail a later Rochambeau!

Rise, stately Symbol! holding forth
   Thy light and hope to all who sit
In chains and darkness! Belt the earth
   With watch-fires from thy torch up-lit!

Reveal the primal mandate still
   Which Chaos heard and ceased to be,
Trace on mid-air th' Eternal Will
   In signs of fire: "Let man be free!"

Shine far, shine free, a guiding light
   To Reason's ways and Virtue's aim,
A lightning-flash the wretch to smite
   Who shields his license with thy name!

                JOHN GREENLEAF WHITTIER

AD PATRIAM

To DEITIES of gauds and gold,
   Land of our Fathers, do not bow!
But unto those beloved of old
   Bend thou the brow!

Austere they were of front and form;
    Rigid as iron in their aim;
Yet in them pulsed a blood as warm
    And pure as flame;—

Honor, whose foster-child is Truth;
    Unselfishness in place and plan;
Justice, with melting heart of ruth;
    And Faith in man.

Give these our worship; then no fears
    Of future foes need fright thy soul;
Triumphant thou shalt mount the years
    Toward thy high goal!
                CLINTON SCOLLARD

AMERICA

NOR force nor fraud shall sunder us! Oh ye
Who north or south, on east or western land,
Native to noble sounds, say truth for truth,
Freedom for freedom, love for love, and God
For God; oh ye who in eternal youth
Speak with a living and creative flood
This universal English, and do stand
Its breathing book; live worthy of that grand
Heroic utterance—parted, yet a whole,
Far, yet unsevered—children brave and free
Of the great Mother-tongue, and ye shall be
Lords of an empire wide as Shakespeare's soul,
Sublime as Milton's immemorial theme,
And rich as Chaucer's speech, and fair as Spenser's dream.
                SYDNEY DOBELL

From THE BUILDING OF THE SHIP

THOU, too, sail on, O Ship of State!
Sail on, O Union, strong and great!
Humanity with all its fears,
With all the hopes of future years,
Is hanging breathless on thy fate!
We know what Master laid thy keel,
What Workmen wrought thy ribs of steel,
Who made each mast, and sail, and rope,
What anvils rang, what hammers beat,
In what a forge and what a heat
Were shaped the anchors of thy hope.
Fear not each sudden sound and shock,
'Tis of the wave and not the rock;
'Tis but the flapping of the sail,
And not a rent made by the gale!
In spite of rock and tempest's roar,
In spite of false lights on the shore,
Sail on, nor fear to breast the sea!
Our hearts, our hopes, are all with thee,
Our hearts, our hopes, our prayers, our tears,
Our faith triumphant o'er our fears,
Are all with thee,—are all with thee!
                    HENRY WADSWORTH LONGFELLOW

THE FLAG

AN INCIDENT OF STRAIN'S EXPEDITION

I NEVER have got the bearings quite,
    Though I've followed the course for many a year,
If he was crazy, clean outright,
    Or only what you might say was "queer."

He was just a simple sailor man.
   I mind it as well as yesterday,
When we messed aboard of the old Cyane.
   Lord! how the time does slip away!
That was five and thirty year ago,
   And I never expect such times again,
For sailors wasn't afraid to stow
   Themselves on a Yankee vessel then.
He was only a sort of bosun's mate,
   But every inch of him taut and trim;
Stars and anchors and togs of state
   Tailors don't build for the like of him.
He flew a no-account sort of name,
   A reg'lar fo'castle "Jim" or "Jack,"
With a plain "McGinnis" abaft the same,
   Giner'ly reefed to simple "Mack."
Mack, we allowed, was sorter queer,—
   Ballast or compass wasn't right.
Till he licked four Juicers one day, a fear
   Prevailed that he hadn't larned to fight.
But I reckon the Captain knowed his man,
   When he put the flag in his hand the day
That we went ashore from the old Cyane,
   On a madman's cruise for Darien Bay.

Forty days in the wilderness
   We toiled and suffered and starved with Strain,
Losing the number of many a mess
   In the Devil's swamps of the Spanish Main.
All of us starved, and many died.
   One laid down, in his dull despair;
His stronger messmate went to his side—
   We left them both in the jungle there.
It was hard to part with shipmates so;
   But standing by would have done no good.
We heard them moaning all day, so slow

We dragged along through the weary wood.
McGinnis, he suffered the worst of all;
  Not that he ever piped his eye
Or wouldn't have answered to the call
  If they'd sounded it for "All hands to die."
I guess 't would have sounded for him before,
  But the grit inside of him kept him strong,
Till we met relief on the river shore;
  And we all broke down when it came along.

All but McGinnis. Gaunt and tall,
  Touching his hat, and standing square:
"Captain, the Flag."—And that was all;
  He just keeled over and foundered there.
"The Flag?" We thought he had lost his head—
  It mightn't be much to lose at best—
Till we came, by and by, to dig his bed,
  And we found it folded around his breast.
He laid so calm and smiling there,
  With the flag wrapped tight about his heart;
Maybe he saw his course all fair,
  Only—*we* couldn't read the chart.

JAMES JEFFREY ROCHE

THE AMERICAN FLAG

WHEN Freedom, from her mountain height,
  Unfurled her standard to the air,
She tore the azure robe of night,
  And set the stars of glory there!
She mingled with its gorgeous dyes
The milky baldric of the skies,
And striped its pure, celestial white
With streakings of the morning light;

Then, from his mansion in the sun,
She called her eagle-bearer down,
And gave into his mighty hand
The symbol of her chosen land!

Majestic monarch of the cloud!
   Who rear'st aloft thy regal form,
To hear the tempest trumping loud,
And see the lightning lances driven,
   When strive the warriors of the storm,
And rolls the thunder-drum of heaven,—
Child of the Sun! to thee 't is given
   To guard the banner of the free,
To hover in the sulphur smoke,
To ward away the battle-stroke,
And bid its blendings shine afar,
Like rainbows on the cloud of war,
   The harbingers of victory!

Flag of the brave! thy folds shall fly,
The sign of hope and triumph high!
When speaks the signal-trumpet tone,
And the long line comes gleaming on,
Ere yet the life-blood, warm and wet,
Has dimmed the glistening bayonet,
Each soldier's eye shall brightly turn
To where thy sky-born glories burn,
And, as his springing steps advance,
Catch war and vengeance from the glance.

And when the cannon-mouthings loud
Heave in wild wreaths the battle shroud,
And gory sabres rise and fall
Like shoots of flame on midnight's pall,

Then shall thy meteor glances glow,
  And cowering foes shall shrink beneath
Each gallant arm that strikes below
  That lovely messenger of death.

Flag of the seas! on ocean wave
Thy stars shall glitter o'er the brave;
When death, careering on the gale,
Sweeps darkly round the bellied sail,
And frighted waves rush wildly back
Before the broadside's reeling rack,
Each dying wanderer of the sea
Shall look at once to heaven and thee,
And smile to see thy splendors fly
In triumph o'er his closing eye.

Flag of the free heart's hope and home,
  By angel hands to valor given!
Thy stars have lit the welkin dome,
  And all thy hues were born in heaven.
Forever float that standard sheet!
  Where breathes the foe but falls before us,
With Freedom's soil beneath our feet,
  And Freedom's banner streaming o'er us!
                JOSEPH RODMAN DRAKE

THE FLAG GOES BY

     HATS off!
Along the street there comes
A blare of bugles, a ruffle of drums,
A flash of color beneath the sky:
     Hats off!
The flag is passing by!

Blue and crimson and white it shines,
Over the steel-tipped, ordered lines.
         Hats off!
The colors before us fly;
But more than the flag is passing by:

Sea-fights and land-fights, grim and great,
Fought to make and to save the State;
Weary marches and sinking ships;
Cheers of victory on dying lips;

Days of plenty and years of peace;
March of a strong land's swift increase;
Equal justice, right and law,
Stately honor and reverend awe;

Sign of a nation, great and strong
To ward her people from foreign wrong;
Pride and glory and honor,—all
Live in the colors to stand or fall.

         Hats off!
Along the street there comes
A blare of bugles, a ruffle of drums;
And loyal hearts are beating high:
         Hats off!
The flag is passing by!
                    HENRY HOLCOMB BENNETT

FREEDOM

ARE we, then, wholly fallen? Can it be
That thou, North wind, that from thy mountains bringest
Their spirit to our plains, and thou, blue sea,
Who on our rocks thy wreaths of freedom flingest,

As on an altar,—can it be that ye
Have wasted inspiration on dead ears,
Dulled with the too familiar clank of chains?
The people's heart is like a harp for years
Hung where some petrifying torrent rains
Its slow-incrusting spray: the stiffened chords
Faint and more faint make answer to the tears
That drip upon them: idle are all words:
Only a golden plectrum wakes the tone
Deep buried 'neath that ever-thickening stone.

We are not free: doth Freedom, then, consist
In musing with our faces toward the Past,
While petty cares, and crawling interests, twist
Their spider-threads about us, which at last
Grow strong as iron chains, to cramp and bind
In formal narrowness heart, soul, and mind?
Freedom is re-created year by year,
In hearts wide open on the Godward side,
In souls calm-cadenced as the whirling sphere,
In minds that sway the future like a tide.
No broadest creeds can hold her, and no codes;
She chooses men for her august abodes,
Building them fair and fronting to the dawn;
Yet, when we seek her, we but find a few
Light footprints, leading morn-ward through the dew:
Before the day had risen, she was gone.

And we must follow: swiftly runs she on,
And, if our steps should slacken in despair,
Half turns her face, half smiles through golden hair,
Forever yielding, never wholly won:
That is not love which pauses in the race
Two close-linked names on fleeting sand to trace;
Freedom gained yesterday is no more ours;
Men gather but dry seeds of last year's flowers;

Still there's a charm ungranted, still a grace,
Still rosy Hope, the free, the unattained,
Makes us Possession's languid hand let fall;
'Tis but a fragment of ourselves is gained,
The Future brings us more, but never all.

And, as the finder of some unknown realm,
Mounting a summit whence he thinks to see
On either side of him the imprisoning sea,
Beholds, above the clouds that overwhelm
The valley-land, peak after snowy peak
Stretch out of sight, each like a silver helm
Beneath its plume of smoke, sublime and bleak,
And what he thought an island finds to be
A continent to him first oped,—so we
Can from our height of Freedom look along
A boundless future, ours if we be strong;
Or if we shrink, better remount our ships
And, fleeing God's express design, trace back
The hero-freighted *Mayflower's* prophet-track
To Europe, entering her blood-red eclipse.

JAMES RUSSELL LOWELL

FOR YOU O DEMOCRACY

COME, I will make the continent indissoluble,
I will make the most splendid race the sun ever shone upon,
I will make divine magnetic lands,
           With the love of comrades,
           With the life-long love of comrades.

I will plant companionship thick as trees along the rivers of
    America, and along the shores of the great lakes, and all over
    the prairies,

I will make inseparable cities with their arms about each other's
   necks,
        By the love of comrades,
        By the manly love of comrades,

For you these from me, O Democracy, to serve you ma femme!
For you, for you I am trilling these songs.

WALT WHITMAN

PREAMBLE TO THE CONSTITUTION OF THE UNITED STATES

WE, THE PEOPLE of the United States, in order to form a more perfect union, establish justice, insure domestic tranquillity, provide
for the common defence, promote the general welfare, and secure
the blessings of liberty to ourselves and our posterity, do ordain
and establish this CONSTITUTION for the United States of America.

OATH OF ALLEGIANCE

I PLEDGE allegiance to the Flag of the United States of America and
to the Republic for which it stands—one Nation indivisible with
Liberty and Justice for all.

THE NATIONAL FLAG

EXTRACT FROM ADDRESS IN PLYMOUTH CHURCH, MAY, 1861

By
HENRY WARD BEECHER

FROM the earliest periods nations seem to have gone forth to war
under some banner. Sometimes it has been merely the pennon of a
leader, and was only a rallying signal. So, doubtless, began the
habit of carrying banners, to direct men in the confusion of con-

flict, that the leader might gather his followers around him when he himself was liable to be lost out of their sight.

Later in the history of nations the banner acquired other uses and peculiar significance from the parties, the orders, the houses, or governments, that adopted it. At length, as consolidated governments drank up into themselves all these lesser independent authorities, banners became significant chiefly of national authority. And thus in our day every people has its peculiar flag. There is no civilized nation without its banner.

A thoughtful mind, when it sees a nation's flag, sees not the flag, but the nation itself. And whatever may be its symbols, its insignia, he reads chiefly in the flag the government, the principles, the truths, the history, that belong to the nation that sets it forth. When the French tricolor rolls out to the wind, we see France. When the new-found Italian flag is unfurled, we see resurrected Italy. When the other three-colored Hungarian flag shall be lifted to the wind, we shall see in it the long buried, but never dead, principles of Hungarian liberty. When the united crosses of St. Andrew and St. George, on a fiery ground, set forth the banner of Old England, we see not the cloth merely; there rises up before the mind the idea of that great monarchy.

This nation has a banner, too, and . . . wherever it [has] streamed abroad men saw daybreak bursting on their eyes. For . . . the American flag has been a symbol of Liberty, and men rejoiced in it. Not another flag on the globe had such an errand, or went forth upon the sea carrying everywhere, the world around, such hope to the captive, and such glorious tidings. The stars upon it were to the pining nations like the bright morning stars of God, and the stripes upon it were beams of morning light. As at early dawn the stars shine forth even while it grows light, and then as the sun advances that light breaks into banks and streaming lines of color, the glowing red and intense white striving together, and ribbing the horizon with bars effulgent, so, on the American flag, stars and beams of many-colored light shine out together. And wherever this flag comes, and men behold it, they see in its sacred emblazonry no ramping lion, and no fierce eagle; no embattled castles, or insignia of imperial authority; they see the symbols of light. It is the banner of dawn. It means Liberty; and the galley-slave, the poor, oppressed conscript, the trodden-down creature of foreign despotism, sees in the American flag that very promise and prediction of God,—"The people which sat in darkness saw a great light; and to them which sat in the region and shadow of death light is sprung up."

Is this a mere fancy? On the 4th of July, 1776, the Declaration of American Independence was confirmed and promulgated. Already for more than a year the colonies had been at war with the mother country. But until this time there had been no American flag. The flag of the mother country covered us during all our colonial period; and each state that chose had a separate and significant state banner.

In 1777, within a few days of one year after the Declaration of Independence, and two years and more after the war began, upon the 14th of June, the Congress of the colonies, or the confederated states, assembled, and ordained this glorious national flag which now we hold and defend, and advanced it full high before God and all men as the flag of Liberty. It was no holiday flag, gorgeously emblazoned for gaiety or vanity. It was a solemn national signal. When that banner first unrolled to the sun, it was the symbol of all those holy truths and purposes which brought together the colonial American Congress.

Consider the men who devised and set forth this banner. The Rutledges, the Pinckneys, the Jays, the Franklins, the Hamiltons, the Jeffersons, the Adamses,—these men were all either officially connected with it or consulted concerning it. They were men that had taken their lives in their hands, and consecrated all their worldly possessions—for what? For the doctrines, and for the personal fact, of liberty,—for the right of *all* men to liberty. They had just given forth to the world a Declaration of Facts and Faiths out of which sprung the Constitution, and on which they now planted this new-devised flag of our Union.

If one, then, asks me the meaning of our flag, I say to him, It means just what Concord and Lexington meant, what Bunker Hill meant; it means the whole glorious Revolutionary War, which was, in short, the rising up of a valiant young people against an old tyranny, to establish the most momentous doctrine that the world had ever known, or has since known,—the right of men to their own selves and to their liberties.

In solemn conclave our fathers had issued to the world that glorious manifesto, the Declaration of Independence. A little later, that the fundamental principles of liberty might have the best organization, they gave to this land our imperishable Constitution. Our flag means, then, all that our fathers meant in the Revolutionary War; all that the Declaration of Independence meant; it means all that the Constitution of our people, organizing for justice, for liberty, and for happiness, meant. Our flag carries American ideas, American history and American feelings. Beginning with the colonies, and coming down to our time, in its sacred heraldry, in its glorious insignia, it has gathered and stored chiefly this supreme idea: *Divine right of liberty in man.* Every color means liberty; every thread means liberty; every form of star and beam or stripe of light means liberty; not lawlessness, not license; but organized, institutional liberty,—liberty through law, and laws for liberty!

This American flag was the safeguard of liberty. Not an atom of crown was allowed to go into its insignia. Not a symbol of authority in the ruler was permitted to go into it. It was an ordinance of liberty by the people for the people. *That* it meant, *that* it means, and, by the blessing of God, *that* it shall mean to the end of time!

From THE MEANING OF THE FLAG

By

WOODROW WILSON

How can any man presume to interpret the emblem of the United States, the emblem of what we would fain be among the family of nations, and find it incumbent upon us to be in the daily round of routine duty? This is Flag Day, but that only means that it is a day when we are to recall the things which we should do every day of our lives. There are no days of special patriotism. There are no days when we should be more patriotic than on other days. We celebrate the Fourth of July merely because the great enterprise of liberty was started on the Fourth of July in America, but the great enterprise of liberty was not begun in America. It is illustrated by the blood of thousands of martyrs who lived and died before the great experiment on this side of the water. The Fourth of July merely marks the day when we consecrated ourselves as a nation to this high thing which we pretend to serve. The benefit of a day like this is merely in turning away from the things that distract us, turning away from the things that touch us personally and absorb our interest in the hours of daily work. We remind ourselves of those things that are greater than we are, of those principles by which we believe our hearts to be elevated, of the more difficult things that we must undertake in these days of perplexity when a man's judgment is safest only when it follows the line of principle.

I am solemnized in the presence of such a day. I would not undertake to speak your thoughts. You must interpret them for me. But I do feel that back, not only of every public official, but of every man and woman of the United States, there marches that great host which has brought us to the present day; the host that has never forgotten the vision which it saw at the birth of the nation; the host which always responds to the dictates of humanity and of liberty; the host that will always constitute the strength and the great body of friends of every man who does his duty to the United States.

I am sorry that you do not wear a little flag of the Union every day instead of some days. I can only ask you, if you lose the physical emblem, to be sure that you wear it in your heart, and the heart of America shall interpret the heart of the world.

THE NOBLEST PUBLIC VIRTUE

By
Henry Clay

There is a sort of courage, which, I frankly confess it, I do not possess,—a boldness to which I dare not aspire, a valour which I cannot covet. I cannot lay myself down in the way of the welfare and happiness of my country. That, I cannot—I have not the courage to do. I cannot interpose the power with which I may be invested—a power conferred, not for my personal benefit, nor for my aggrandisement, but for my country's good—to check her onward march to greatness and glory. I have not courage enough. I am too cowardly for that. I would not, I dare not, in the exercise of such a threat, lie down, and place my body across the path that leads my country to prosperity and happiness. This is a sort of courage widely different from that which a man may display in his private conduct and personal relations. Personal or private courage is totally distinct from that higher and nobler courage which prompts the patriot to offer himself a voluntary sacrifice to his country's good.

Apprehensions of the imputation of the want of firmness sometimes impel us to perform rash and inconsiderate acts. It is the greatest courage to be able to bear the imputation of the want of courage. But pride, vanity, egotism, so unamiable and offensive in private life, are vices which partake of the character of crimes, in the conduct of public affairs. The unfortunate victim of these passions cannot see beyond the little, petty, contemptible circle of his own personal interests. All his thoughts are withdrawn from his country, and concentrated on his consistency, his firmness, himself! The high, the exalted, the sublime emotions of a patriotism which, soaring towards Heaven, rises far above all mean, low, or selfish things, and is absorbed by one soul-transporting thought of the good and the glory of one's country, are never felt in his impenetrable bosom. That patriotism which, catching its inspiration from the immortal God, and, leaving at an immeasurable distance below all lesser, grovelling, personal interests and feelings, animates and prompts to deeds of self-sacrifice, of valour, of devotion, and of death itself,—that is public virtue; that is the noblest, the sublimest of all public virtues!

From THE MAN WITHOUT A COUNTRY

By
EDWARD EVERETT HALE

As WE lay back in the stern sheets and the men gave way, he said to me: "Youngster, let that show you what it is to be without a family, without a home, and without a country. And if you are ever tempted to say a word or to do a thing that shall put a bar between you and your family, your home, and your country, pray God in his mercy to take you that instant home to his own heaven. Stick by your family, boy; forget you have a self, while you do everything for them. Think of your home, boy; write and send and talk about it. Let it be nearer and nearer to your thought the farther you have to travel from it; and rush back to it when you are free, as that poor black slave is doing now. And for your country, boy," and the words rattled in his throat, "and for that flag," and he pointed to the ship, "never dream a dream but of serving her as she bids you, though the service carry you through a thousand hells. No matter what happens to you, no matter who flatters you or who abuses you, never look at another flag, never let a night pass but you pray God to bless that flag. Remember, boy, that behind all these men you have to do with, behind officers, and Government, and people even, there is the Country Herself, your Country, and that you belong to Her as you belong to your own mother. Stand by Her, boy, as you would stand by your mother, if those devils there had got hold of her to-day!"

INDEPENDENCE DAY

By

JAMES GILLESPIE BLAINE

THE United States is the only country with a known birthday. All the rest begun, they know not when, and grew into power, they know not how. If there had been no Independence Day, England and America combined would not be so great as each actually is. There is no "Republican," no "Democrat," on the Fourth of July, —all are Americans. All feel that their country is greater than party.

From PREFACE TO 1855 EDITION OF "LEAVES OF GRASS"

By

WALT WHITMAN

THE Americans of all nations at any time upon the earth have probably the fullest poetical nature. The United States themselves are essentially the greatest poem. In the history of the earth hitherto the largest and most stirring appear tame and orderly to their ampler largeness and stir. Here at last is something in the doings of man that corresponds with the broadcast doings of the day and night. Here is not merely a nation but a teeming nation of nations. Here is action untied from strings necessarily blind to particulars and details magnificently moving in vast masses. Here is the hospitality which forever indicates heroes. . . . Here are the roughs and beards and space and ruggedness and nonchalance that the soul loves. Here the performance disdaining the trivial unapproached in the tremendous audacity of its crowds and groupings and the push of its perspective spreads with crampless and flowing breadth and showers its prolific and splendid extravagance. One sees it must indeed own the riches of the summer and winter, and need never be bankrupt while corn grows from the ground or the orchards drop apples or the bays contain fish or men beget children upon women.

Other states indicate themselves in their deputies . . . but the genius of the United States is not best or most in its executives or legislatures, nor in its ambassadors or authors or colleges or churches or parlors, nor even in its newspapers or inventors . . . but always most in the common people. Their manners speech dress friendships the freshness and candor of their physiognomy —the picturesque looseness of their carriage . . . their deathless attachment to freedom—their aversion to anything indecorous or soft or mean—the practical acknowledgment of the citizens of one state by the citizens of all other states—the fierceness of their roused resentment—their curiosity and welcome of novelty—their self-esteem and wonderful sympathy—their susceptibility to a slight—the air they have of persons who never knew how it felt to stand in the presence of superiors—the fluency of their speech —their delight in music, the sure symptom of manly tenderness and native elegance of soul . . . their good temper and open-handedness—the terrible significance of their elections—the President's taking off his hat to them not they to him—these too are unrhymed poetry. It awaits the gigantic and generous treatment worthy of it.

THE GREAT MELTING POT

By
ISRAEL ZANGWILL

"AMERICA is God's crucible, the Great Melting Pot, where all the races of Europe are reforming. Here you stand, goodfolk, think I, when I see them at Ellis Island, here you stand in your fifty groups with your fifty languages and histories and your fifty blood-hatreds and rivalries. But you won't long be like that, brothers, for these are the fires of God you've come to—these are the fires of God. A fig for your feuds and vendettas. Germans and Frenchmen, Irishmen and Englishmen, Jews and Russians, into the crucible with you all. God is making the American."

THE SPIRIT OF AMERICA

By
WOODROW WILSON

AMERICA lives in the heart of every man everywhere who wishes to find a region where he will be free to work out his destiny as he chooses.

From *Chicago Speech*

WHAT AMERICA EXPECTS OF ITS YOUTH

By
MRS. J. BORDEN HARRIMAN

AMERICA is not perfect. My generation knows that. But it is ours, and it has been for a century the dream of freedom of every European. We must keep it so. Its streets have never been paved with gold, and they never will be, but I should like to think that even for the democracies in the north, we should stand as a land of opportunity and enthusiasm and riches. By riches I mean not only raw materials, armies, navies, railroads, ships and cities, but a whole people full of good will towards the world, loyal to its own flag and beautiful continent, ready to work to educate its whole people.

The ancient republic of Greece, the modern kingdom of Greece, the Ancient empire of China, the modern and war torn republic of Asia, the United States of America, see what we have in common. *That* is something every American young man should study.

To prepare yourselves for the times you live in you must look over the whole world to find your allies in building a world of equality of opportunity for all classes and all races, for the greater part of mankind will be happiest in a democratic society. But do not hope to have your democracy in far places, or worth fighting for elsewhere, if in your own house, own schools, own factories and shops, in your own country and city, you do not find the slogans and spirit and the daily practice of helping each other and keeping your eyes open to know and guard not only your own advantage, but the common interests of mankind in justice and peace. Remember to rejoice and be happy over your blessings. Hold fast to your ideals. Lift up your eyes to the hills and realize that "Where there is no vision, the people perish."

INDEX OF AUTHORS

515

INDEX OF TITLES